FORGOTTEN RAILWAYS:

Chilterns and Cotswolds

THE FORGOTTEN RAILWAYS SERIES

Edited by J. Allan Patmore

North East England by K. Hoole
The East Midlands by P. Howard Anderson
Chilterns & Cotswolds by R. Davies and M. D. Grant

Other volumes are in the course of production

There is no remembrance of former things; neither shall there be any remembrance of things that are to come with those that shall come after. *Ecclesiastes I vii*

FORGOTTEN RAILWAYS:

Chilterns and Cotswolds

R. DAVIES and M. D. GRANT

DAVID & CHARLES
NEWTON ABBOT   LONDON
NORTH POMFRET (VT) VANCOUVER

ISBN 0 7153 6701 3

To Pamela

Set in 11 on 13 Baskerville
and printed in Great Britain
by Latimer Trend & Company Ltd Plymouth
for David & Charles (Holdings) Limited
South Devon House Newton Abbot Devon

Published in the United States of America
by David & Charles Inc
North Pomfret Vermont 05053 USA

Published in Canada
by Douglas David & Charles Limited
3645 McKechnie Drive West Vancouver BC

Contents

		page
List of Illustrations		7
Maps, Diagrams, and Drawings in Text		9
Introduction		11
1	London: Northern Heights and Green Belt	17
2	The Chiltern Foothills	42
3	The Vale of Aylesbury	77
4	The Ouse Basin	109
5	The Northampton Uplands	129
6	The Vale of Evesham	149
7	The Nene and Welland Valleys	162
8	The Great Central Railway	184
Gazetteer		208
Bibliography		240
Acknowledgements		248
Index		250

5

List of Illustrations

PLATES

        page

7374 at Finsbury Park (*British Rail*)   33
Edgware 1914 (*H. J. Patterson Rutherford*)   33
47355 near Tolpits (*J. R. Newman*)   34
1450 at Bourne End (*British Rail*)   34
1669 at Hemel Hempstead (*H. C. Casserley*)   51
46601 entering Leighton Buzzard (*H. C. Casserley*)   51
Ayot Bank (*Alan J. Willmott*)   52
Cheddington Station (*F. Goodwin*)   69
The Metropolitan at Verney 1936 (*H. C. Casserley*)   69
Mixed train at Brill (*London Transport Executive*)   70
Experimental railbus service at Buckingham (*Ian L. Wright*)   70
Henlow Station (*V. R. Anderson Collection*)   87
25319 near Sandy (*L. Hanson*)   87
Trains crossing at Kimbolton (*Ian L. Wright*)   88
First Train at Higham Ferrers (*Ian L. Wright Collection*)   88
Blisworth SMJR (*D. Thompson*)   105
Towcester 1924 (*V. R. Anderson Collection*)   105

page

Blakesley Hall Miniature Railway 1914 (*H. J. Patterson Rutherford*)   106

Kineton Station (*V. R. Webster Collection*)   106

Sarsden Halt and Signal box (*D. Thompson*)   123

Adderbury Station 1972 (*R. Davies*)   123

171 at Broom Junction 1949 (*H. C. Casserley*)   124

Goods at Evesham Midland Station c1960 (*Rev A. W. V. Mace*)   124

GWR Bearley branch train at Alcester c1901 (*M. D. Grant Collection*)   141

61006 *Blackbuck* at Oundle 1957 (*Ian L. Wright*)   141

Uppingham Terminus c1900 (*V. R. Anderson Collection*)   142

Uppingham Terminus 1960 (*P. H. Wells*)   142

Market Harborough LNWR station (*J. H. Brown Collection*)   159

Woodford & Hinton 1896 (*R. Davies Collection*)   159

46125 coasting into Brackley Central (*P. H. Wells*)   160

Up Master Cutler leaving Rugby (*Rev A. W. V. Mace*)   160

Maps, Diagrams and Drawings in Text

	page
Map of the Edgware, Highgate & London Railway and associated branches	19
Map of the Watford & Rickmansworth Railway and proposed Uxbridge Extension	31
Map of the Wycombe Railway, Stage 1	44
Map of the Hemel Hempstead branch, Midland Railway	47
Map of the St Albans branch, GNR	57
Map of the Hertford, Luton & Dunstable Railway	62
Map of the Dunstable branch, LNWR	74
Map of the Aylesbury Railway	79
Map of the Aylesbury & Buckingham Railway	83
Map of the Brill branch, Metropolitan Railway	92
Plan showing the original Brill Tramway connection, Quainton Road	92
Wood Siding, Brill branch (*Sketch by Fraser Cameron*)	93
Map of the Buckinghamshire Railway	99
Map of the Leicester & Hitchin Extension, Midland Railway	108
Map of the Bedford & Cambridge Railway	116

9

Map of Kettering to Huntingdon and Higham Ferrers *page*
  branches, Midland Railway   122
Map of the Stratford-upon-Avon & Midland Junction
  Railway   130
Map of the Banbury & Cheltenham Direct Railway   143
Map of Redditch to Ashchurch, Midland Railway   150
Map of the Alcester Railway   154
Map of the Northampton & Peterborough Railway   163
Map of the Rugby & Stamford Railway   170
Diagram of Clifton Mill Junction, Rugby   174
Map of the Uppingham branch, LNWR   178
Map of the Great Central Railway, Rugby to Quainton
  Road Section   185
Diagram of Woodford junctions 1899   201
Folding map of the railways in the area bounded by the
  Chilterns and Cotswolds   *Inside back cover*

Introduction

For many, it is impossible to view railway closures without some
degree of regret or sadness. Yet, at the same time, it is essential
to accept that change is necessary and that the solution adopted
for rural transport needs in the nineteenth century does not of
necessity suffice today. Whereas, prior to the construction of
branch lines there was very low mobility for rural dwellers, the
arrival of the railway heralded new opportunities for the
population to reach the expanding urban areas and supply
them with food and raw materials.

The area covered by this book is in this respect no exception
for there developed within it an extensive railway network.
Competition, however, first arose during the 1920s with the
widespread introduction of rural bus services with their greater
flexibility and cheaper operation and, since World War II, the
growth of car ownership and wider availability of goods vehicles
was bound drastically to reduce railway usage and cause many
secondary and branch routes to close.

The aim of this book has, therefore, been to attempt to
recapture the spirit of the railway era in this area before it is
too late. Lines which once served almost unknown villages and

quiet country townships deserve to be remembered before they fade too far into history, though lack of space necessitates a policy of deliberate selectivity. Not all closed lines in the area are therefore covered, while the accounts of those included attempt only to recall the more interesting and unusual events which occurred in the life of the lines.

As a first step it is necessary to define the area in geographical terms. Primarily it takes in most of the South Midlands, but definition presents some difficulties as its boundaries merge almost imperceptibly with surrounding areas. Unlike more readily distinguishable areas such as East Anglia or the West Country, this region cannot be so easily categorised, although it has common characteristics running through its constituent counties which bind it into a whole. For the purposes of this book, the region comprises the former County of Middlesex and the Counties of Hertfordshire, Buckinghamshire, Bedfordshire, Northamptonshire, Cambridgeshire (formerly Huntingdon and Peterborough), Leicestershire (formerly Rutland), Warwickshire, Hereford and Worcester (formerly Worcestershire) and Oxfordshire, and also takes in the fringes of some surrounding counties.

To discern the original purpose of railway construction it is not only necessary to consider the financial aspects of railway promotion but, sometimes more important, to relate the physical and economic geography of sub-areas to the various schemes. The region has, therefore, been split into sub-divisions based mainly upon the physical landscape. Some of these sub-divisions may seem a little contrived as it is not always easy to define a single geographical area. In cases where lines cross boundaries into other areas they have been included in the region to which they most logically belong.

In the south-eastern corner, the London basin, with its 'Northern Heights', provides an urban background from which to begin. To the north and west, the Green Belt gradually merges with the Chilterns and agricultural countryside of south and west Hertfordshire, which then gives way to the Vales of Oxford and Aylesbury. To the north-east of this is the Ouse

Basin, a continuation of the wide clay vale stretching in a south-west to north-east direction and eventually merging into the fens and plains of rural Lincolnshire. Again to the north, a further band of hills running from the Cotswolds on the south-west to the Northamptonshire Heights or Wolds on the north-east, forms the barrier between the South Midlands and the East and West Midlands. North-west of the Cotswold scarp, the Vale of Evesham comprises a minor part of the Midland plain. The resultant drainage pattern of the alternate ranges of hills and clay vales is towards the Rivers Severn and Thames, and The Wash, and the predominant south-west to north-east grain of the physical geography has had a significant effect upon the alignments selected by railway promoters.

Prior to the railway era, the area relied for its external links on the major through roads. The Great North Road (A1), the Holyhead Road (A5) and the West Coast Road (A6) brought some trade and prosperity during coaching days; the towns and villages on these roads have long histories which often go back well into the Middle Ages. In some cases, however, alternative reasons accounted for the importance of certain towns and their influence on surrounding communities. The City of Oxford, for instance, became established as a result of its University. Away from main routes, on the other hand, communications were extremely poor and contemporary accounts tell of the length and difficulty of rural journeys.

The invention of the steam locomotive, capable of rapid and safe movement of both passenger and freight, brought major changes. With its speed and reliability, it was the first satisfactory mode of transit which rapidly superseded all forms of horse-drawn transport whether by road or inland waterway.

The initial routes laid down were main lines with little relevance to the communities through which they passed, their objectives lying beyond the boundaries of the region. The London & Birmingham Railway, first to pierce the Chiltern barrier in 1837, formed the backbone of the railway network eventually constructed, and provided access to the London market for Midland industries. The next to be opened, in 1838, was the first stage of the Great Western Railway connecting London with the port of Bristol, but this line had only a very marginal influence on the region. Later main line constituents of the GWR, which had greater influence on the area, were the Birmingham & Oxford Railway, which originated as an attempt by the Grand Junction Railway to break the monopoly of the L & B, and the Oxford, Worcester & Wolverhampton Railway, which began life as a GWR satellite to expand its network into LNWR territory. To the east, the Great Northern opened-up in stages a trunk route in the early 1850s for Yorkshire and East Midlands coal traffic. This was to some extent supplemented by the Midland Railway London extension in 1868, the culmination of a policy of gradual expansion to shake off the dependence of this Derby-based railway on other companies for its access to London. Finally, the Great Central Railway, in a last flourish of competition, opened its extension to London in 1899 in alliance with the Metropolitan Railway. A subsequent liaison with the GWR to overcome Metropolitan obstruction led to the formation of the Great Western & Great Central Joint Committee in 1899 with a route which became part of the GWR Birmingham Direct line.

Within this framework of trunk lines, a web of secondary, cross-country and branch railways was created, serving their communities in many cases for a century or more. Great and small alike, however, have come under the demolition contractor's hammer, used so effectively to ensure that little remains of the lines bar rubble and weeds! As a consequence, someone seeking echoes of the traditional railway world will gain only little help from the few physical remains still in existence. Those of significance are listed in the gazetteer, an integral part of the book, which sets out the detailed information about each line that would otherwise intrude on the narrative.

The area possessed examples of almost all types of railway operation. Urban railways, trunk routes, useful stretches of cross-country line, branches of more than usual historical note, lines rooted in company politics, light railways privately owned and promoted, schemes which aimed to bring prosperity to particular areas, and traditional country branches, were all to be found within this area. The main exceptions were lines serving highly-industrialised areas such as those of the Black Country, Lancashire, South Wales or the North East, or the specialised summer peak railway operation required of lines with seaside holiday traffic.

In many ways the present land use and human geography of the region is little different from that of a century ago. The main towns have expanded with the growing population which has tended to congregate, as throughout the country, in urban areas, but the majority remains mostly rural agricultural land. The major difference has been the growth since the 1930s of new town developments to accommodate the overspill of population from Greater London and to absorb some of the south-eastward drift of population. In recent years, movement to overspill towns has been accentuated by the spread of people from London in search of cheaper housing and has resulted in greater demand for commuter travel on the main lines into London. The influence of the capital is thus heavy on a large part of the area, counter-balanced in the north-west by the West Midland conurbation.

The outward movement of population from London since the War has been of little or no assistance to branch railways, freight being best transported by road, and passenger traffic mainly of a commuting nature. Luton, once so famous for its straw plait industry, is now a thriving centre of motor manufacture, and has an important and busy commercial airport. Welwyn and Hemel Hempstead did little to assist their branch routes, while only the main line to Euston could be of help to Milton Keynes. Times have changed, and so have railway economics. Whereas the railway did so much to encourage early urban and industrial development, today its influence has waned into insignificance, apart from the key trunk lines, and the more intimate details of its history are in danger of being forgotten.

Yet in spite of their great interest, the railways of the South Midlands have been surprisingly neglected in the past by the railway historian and enthusiast alike and much as a result has been lost. Perhaps, however, some of the atmosphere of these former routes may still be recalled by a memory of Kimbolton Station in Leicestershire (formerly Huntingdonshire) on a warm June day in 1959. At the end of the platform, opposite a classic Midland wooden signalbox, stood an old green gas lamp which no doubt had lit the way of countless enginemen who had passed along that forgotten road. Wooden slatted fencing separated the platform from the rusty rails of the siding which served the cattle dock. Suddenly, the peace of the afternoon was broken by the sharp beat of the signalman's bell. Momentarily, all was activity in the box as levers were pulled off, moving rods and signal wires by the track, the signal at the end of the platform then indicating the imminent approach of a train. Then, a moment of peace as birds once again sang in the nearby fields and hedgerows. Slowly a porter walked down the platform and picked his way across the pointwork, casting an eye on the weeds which adorned the cattle dock but which were a disgrace to the station garden. Before he reached the steps, however, the train bustled into the station exchanging a handful of passengers. After the driver had received the staff, the train moved off and quickly rattled and clattered into the distance. A simple moment, once oft-repeated, but before the signal falls to danger, then and now, perhaps there is still time for railway and country lovers to discover a little more about the past highways and byways of the railway system in this neglected area of Britain's railway network.

CHAPTER 1

London: Northern Heights and Green Belt

Introduction

North London is difficult to define, but in the present context it comprises largely the former County of Middlesex, being bordered on the south by central London and on the north, east and west by Hertfordshire, Essex, and Buckinghamshire. North London ends rather abruptly at the Green Belt, deliberately designated to limit its growth and effectively inhibiting the continuously built-up area from sprawling considerably further northwards.

The railway was an important stimulant to London's development during the nineteenth century, providing for the first time convenient rail transport links from the rural environs to the central area, far superior to the road communications of the period. Later, however, improvements in road public passenger transport, with the evolution of trams and early petrol buses, and the expansion of the Underground system beyond the suburbs, stimulated new urban growth away from the immediate vicinity of main-line railway stations.

These developments are the background to the two railways included in this chapter. The former Great Northern Railway branches from Finsbury Park to Edgware, High Barnet, and Alexandra Palace were urban lines which initially contributed to the expansion of London into the fields, commons and woods of Middlesex during the middle of the last century. The London & North Western Railway branch from Watford to Rickmansworth, the other line included, is on the rural northern borders; although never of great significance, it is nevertheless an interesting contrast, owing its downfall for local journeys to the competitive bus services to Watford, and for London to the superior services provided by the Metropolitan Railway.

By a quirk of history the lines are related. At their inception, North London was insecure railway territory, with the promise of coups and counter coups and fierce rivalry between the Midland Railway and Great Northern Railway. As we shall see, our main hero, the Edgware, Highgate & London Railway, was in the midst and several schemes were mooted which would have led to the lines becoming connected. In the event, however, these schemes failed.

If on the one hand the Green Belt had not been designated, and on the other the electrification proposals for the former GNR Northern Heights branches had reached fruition, the railway might well have survived to play an important role in the community whereas today it lives on only as a memory of halcyon days before the War when steam reigned romantically over the Northern Heights.

Finsbury Park–Edgware; Alexandra Palace; Bushey Heath Extension

The Northern Heights, the high ground north of Central London, was once served by a branch of the GNR from Finsbury Park. This interesting line, with supplementary branches to Alexandra Palace and High Barnet, was an example of a railway promotion which paradoxically both succeeded and failed. A visit to either East Finchley or Finchley Central Underground stations during the rush hour demonstrates that part of the original route of this branch remains a thriving and important service to the community, operated by the London Transport Executive, while other sections are now no longer served by any railway facilities. If it had not been for World War II, however, and the post-war implementation of Abercrombie's Green Belt Policy, established under the Town and Country Planning Act,

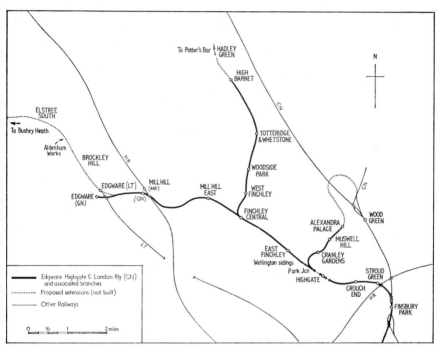

Map of the Edgware, Highgate & London Railway and associated branches

1947, the history of this notable group of branch services could have been very different and they would have formed, in their entirety, part of a complex system planned for the development of rail services in North London.

The branches owe their origins to the Edgware, Highgate & London Railway, which by an Act of Parliament dated 3 June 1862 was authorised to construct a line from Finsbury Park, then Seven Sisters Road Station, to Edgware. From the start the EH & L ran into financial and commercial difficulties, with the costly engineering work involved in a viaduct over the Dollis Valley, tunnelling problems at Highgate, and the competitive encroachment of the GNR and the Midland Railway London extension. To secure viability of its route, the EH & L supported a separate company, the Watford & Edgware Junction Railway, which was to connect the EH & L with the Watford & Rickmansworth Railway giving access to the LNWR, and an Act was passed in 1864. In the same year authorisation was achieved for its branch from Highgate to Muswell Hill.

Further rivalry was experienced from the North London, Highgate & Alexandra Park Railway whose Bill was successfully steered through Parliament in July 1865. Under its Act, the company was granted powers to construct a line from the North London Railway, close to Caledonian Road Station, to Highgate, where it was to have made connection with the EH & L and have running powers to Muswell Hill. Although this would have provided a more direct route into London than via Finsbury Park and King's Cross, the company faced the considerable force of GNR opposition and the proposals were never implemented.

A victory, if short lived, was achieved by the EH & L on 16 July 1866; in competition with proposals from the MR and the GNR, the latter of which intended to continue northwards from High Barnet via Hadley to rejoin the GNR main line at Potters Bar, the EH & L obtained an Act to construct its branch to High Barnet. Unfortunately, however, these remained only temporary successes for a company which bravely, but vainly, tried to remain free from the clutches of its main line competitors, and it was insufficient to prevent the GNR from absorbing both the EH & L and the Watford & Edgware Junction Railway on 15 July 1867. The GNR commenced the operation of services to Edgware on 22 August 1867, High Barnet on 1 April 1872 and Muswell Hill and Alexandra Palace on 24 May 1873. Powers for the Watford scheme were allowed to lapse.

The picture of railway development in this part of the Northern Heights is completed with a scheme proposed by the Muswell Hill Railway Company, another independent concern. In 1866, the company was authorised to connect the projected EH & L branch to Muswell Hill with that of the Great Eastern Railway's planned branch to Palace Gates (Wood Green), thereby serving the Alexandra Park and Palace, which was then under construction. The line as proposed would have been 1¾ miles in length, but only 38 chains and a substantial station, in the shadows of the massive Palace, were ever constructed. The Muswell Hill Railway Company, which later became the Muswell Hill & Palace Railway Company, remained independent until 1 September 1911 despite its fluctuating fortunes. On that date, it was formally absorbed by the GNR which had provided services from the outset.

When the Edgware Line was opened in August 1867, double track was laid as far as the west end of the west tunnel at Highgate, which later became Park Junction, and this was extended to East End, Finchley by 1 December 1867, and to Finchley and Hendon by 1 November 1869, in preparation for the extra services for the Barnet branch, which was constructed with double-track. On introduction of the Barnet services in 1872 the original Edgware 'main line' was reduced to branch status and remained single-track throughout, although provision had been made for doubling while constructing the Dollis viaduct and most of the bridges along its length.

After the opening of the High Barnet line, the Edgware branch received through trains to and from London after track modifications at Church End Station commissioned in 1896, undertaken because of public criticism of services, particularly from passengers using Mill Hill Station. This work provided an improved connection between the branch platform and the main line, enabling trains to travel through to Edgware without the considerable amount of shunting previously required.

During the early part of this century, the GNR made various attempts to promote its now considerable suburban network, and in the summer of 1906 undertook a piece of promotional work similar to that later adopted by the Metropolitan Railway's *Metroland* public relations and advertising promotion. Posters, with a map of suburban services to the Northern Heights—including the Edgware group of branches—endeavoured to entice people to move from the smoky, drab, and closely-packed streets of the inner suburbs to the nearby countryside. The advertising matter, aimed primarily at the increasingly prosperous middle classes, stressed the healthy aspects of the semi-rural life of the hinterland served by the railway, and gave much information useful to intending residents. At this time suburban development was beginning around the stations north of Highgate. At Finchley, settlement was affected by the railway's influence and the prosperous centre of Church End became firmly established. At Woodside Park, Totteridge and Barnet, substantial villa-type houses were erected, some of which remain in existence today; many have now been demolished and new flats built in their place, giving a higher density of land use. Most of the remainder have been converted into flats and command good rental value, being convenient for Underground commuters to Central London.

The rural character of the Edgware branch remained virtually unchanged until the London Electric Railway's Underground extension from Hendon Central to Edgware was opened on 18 August 1924. In 1921, Edgware parish had a population of only 1,516, but with the frequency of Underground services to central London, this began to expand rapidly, reaching 5,353 in 1931 and 17,253 by 1939. During the inter-war period housing construction in the Mill Hill area provided further passenger traffic, but most movement was only during peak periods, and the line retained a rustic nature and appearance more akin to a rural railway backwater.

In 1929, in an attempt to overcome the operating problems presented by the highly peaked nature of passenger traffic on the Edgware branch, the LNER experimented with a Sentinel-Cammell steam railcar, No 51912 *Rising Sun*, repeating a similar experiment which had been previously tried by the GNR in 1906. The variations in passenger loadings between peak and off-peak periods meant that the railcar had to be supplemented by extra coaches at busy times. The railcar, however, was not sufficiently powerful to haul the additional load unaided and it proved uneconomic to operate it solely in off-peak periods. A potential opportunity for the Edgware branch came during the years preceding World War II. The London Passenger Transport Board, created in 1933, had immediately begun planning the improvement of services in many parts of North London, and new life would have come to both the Edgware and Alexandra Palace branches under major proposals announced on 5 June 1935 by the Chancellor of the Exchequer, Neville Chamberlain. Electrification of services to the Northern Heights, previously considered seriously by the GNR in 1903 and the LNER in 1924 and again between 1929 and 1932, was to be included in the plan for improving London's transport, to be implemented between 1935 and 1940. Three Acts passed in 1936 and 1937 authorised works in preparation for the future electrification of all three branches. Track was to be doubled between Church End and Edgware and a link was planned between the branch and the Great Northern & City Railway at Drayton Park. The Charing Cross, Euston & Hampstead Railway, opened on 22 June 1907, was also to be extended from its terminus at Highgate (now Archway) to East Finchley. Church End station was to have been reconstructed with four platform faces for easier train movements, while Mill Hill East and Edgware Stations were to be enlarged.

Finally, the Bushey Heath Extension to Aldenham was authorised, necessitating a link between the LNER and LPTB at Edgware. History seemed to be repeating itself in view of the earlier Watford & Edgware Railway scheme, but this new proposal with Watford as the ultimate goal, appeared more likely to succeed. Work commenced at Edgware in October 1937, and continued over the next two years. The depot at Aldenham was completed prior to the outbreak of World War II, being used during the war as an aircraft factory. Much of the preparatory work along the route was also finished including drainage facilities, arches of a viaduct at Brockley Hill, where a station would have been built, and about 300yd of twin bore tunnel at Elstree Hill which could clearly be seen until concealed by motorway works in the early 1960s. The depot subsequently became the main bus body overhaul works for the London Transport Executive.

The outbreak of World War II spelt eventual death to the extension and many other electrification proposals. In early June 1940 the work was postponed, although much had already been completed. New tunnels between Archway and East Finchley were opened on 3 July 1939, together with an intermediate interchange station below Highgate LNER opened on 19 January 1941. Doubling and electrification of the Edgware branch, providing an alternative approach to the central area through Finchley, was also commissioned and steam train services were withdrawn between Church End and Edgware from 11 September 1939 to enable work to be completed. An alternative emergency bus service, on which through railway tickets were available, was introduced to replace the withdrawn facilities. Limited Underground services were provided to Mill Hill East, serving the nearby army barracks, on 18 May 1941, over a single line; passenger services were never reinstated throughout, and the premature closure of the branch beyond Mill Hill East went unheralded at a time of national emergency.

On 14 April 1940, Underground services were extended from East Finchley to High Barnet replacing the steam services which were cut back to East Finchley, to be finally withdrawn between East Finchley and King's Cross from 3 March 1941. The effect of this withdrawal was to close to passengers the short section between Park Junction and East Finchley. At Wellington Sidings, adjacent to Park Junction, car sheds were provided by conversion of the former LNER carriage sheds where the Royal train had previously been stabled. Between Finsbury Park and Alexandra Palace, substations, electric cables and conductor rails were laid and the tracks resignalled, and work was well advanced on the link between the GN & CR and the Edgware branches at Finsbury Park.

At the end of the War uncertainty hovered over the future of the uncompleted works, causing public debate which continued into the early 1950s. In June 1947, the LPTBs New Works (Review of 1935–40 Programme) Committee recommended that electrification to Alexandra Palace should be completed but not the Edgware electrification or Bushey Heath Extension. Two years later, the London Plan Working Party further urged as a high priority the completion of the 1935–40 New Works Programme, including electrification of the Alexandra Palace branch. In October 1950 LTE officially announced the suspension of the Bushey Heath proposals but for a further three years the Executive continued to re-examine the possibility of extensions. Compromise schemes were also discussed including for instance, in January 1952, a suggestion for operating a light diesel railcar service between Finchley and Edgware, a proposal eventually rejected on the grounds of high introductory cost and uneconomic operating expenses arising from a non-standard service. For a short while in the same year, consideration was again given to a limited extension of the Edgware branch as far as Brockley Hill and the Mill Hill East services to Mill Hill (The Hale). Both had their relative merits, but those of the Mill Hill extension rested primarily on improved interchange, at a possible combined station, with British Railways. The high cost of construction combined with the insufficient passenger potential of the Green Belt area where new housing projects were effectively stifled, killed both schemes, but the proposed electrification of the former Midland line was a further disadvantage of the Mill Hill Extension. Finally, in the Spring of 1953, the North-West Districts Light Railway Committee was formed calling for the completion of the abandoned tube workings from Edgware to Elstree Hill as part of a scheme to operate services from Finchley to Elstree as a light railway. All activity was of no avail and the final death of the schemes was announced officially in February 1954.

Meanwhile, an outburst of debate and public criticism surrounded the future of the steam push-and-pull services to Muswell Hill and Alexandra Palace. Questions were tabled periodically in Parliament, local authorities urged action on the LTE and BTC, and various public bodies and action committees became vociferous in their demands for improved services and electrification of the branch. On 10 November 1952, however, the London *Evening News* reported the removal of conductor rails between Finsbury Park and Alexandra Palace which, it was said, were required by British Railways for urgent renewal work on the Bow-Upminster line owing to the difficulty in obtaining new conductor rails at the time.

The War, and the austere years of economic reconstruction which followed, had exacted a severe toll on the Alexandra Palace rail facilities. Peak-hour services had been cut to a minimum and totally suspended from 29 October 1951 until 7 January 1952, because of acute national coal shortage. So much damage had now been done to the effectiveness of the line through inadequate and inconvenient services, poorly situated, dingy and unpainted stations, and gas-lit steam trains, that its future was seriously in doubt. Bus services had been gradually improved and, for many journeys into London, they provided a more direct, comfortable, convenient and frequent link to the nearby Northern Line at Highgate and Archway and various stations on the Piccadilly line.

Impending closure was announced late in 1953. In spite of public protest, the Transport Users' Consultative Committee for London finally approved these plans, being satisfied that adequate alternative bus services were to be provided, and passenger services ceased from 5 July 1954.

In complete contrast the romance of a journey on the Alexandra Palace line in happier days is caught by a letter to the author from a correspondent who was a schoolgirl in the early 1930s:

With two friends we made the journey nearly every Saturday morning to Alexandra Palace for the children's skating session. We lived at Finchley and went by tram to Highgate, where we took return tickets to the Palace on the old railway. Although we enjoyed the skating, I am sure that if we would but have admitted it, the train journey was every bit as exciting. We often seemed to be about the only passengers, but I suppose the line was widely used in business hours and in the evenings when there were glorious concerts and other attractions at the Palace. The carriages were far from clean, the door handles particularly being grimed with dirt from the engine, and although this did not annoy us, it must have been a constant annoyance to the daily travellers.

So the dream had almost ended. Gone were the trains of the North London Railway which had first worked from Broad Street to High Barnet on 18 January 1875, and Alexandra Palace on 1 May 1875, later to be operated until October 1940 by the LMSR; gone also were the cross-London trains which had run until the summer of 1907, having first commenced in March 1868 when some GNR and LC & DR trains ran between Victoria and New Barnet, a few of the GNR trains going in later years to High Barnet. From 1 June 1878, some GNR trains also ran to Woolwich but from 1 August 1880 these were replaced by trains of the South Eastern Railway some of which ran to Alexandra Palace. These trains were withdrawn from 1 May 1907 and the LC & DR services from 1 October 1907. Finally, gone too were the GNR services, including those on the Alexandra Palace branch which had suffered throughout its history from the varying fortunes of the 'People's Palace' at whose foot it terminated.

One vestige of the old days of steam remained as a reminder of a past era. Mixing rather strangely with the tube gauge LT stock between Highgate, East Finchley, High Barnet and Mill Hill East, steam-hauled freight trains were still run by BR. The staple freight traffic through the greater part of the life of the branches was in coal, building materials, notably bricks and cement, and a fairly substantial milk traffic in the early days. A major freight user in addition was the North Middlesex Gas Company, which opened a works at Mill Hill in 1862, receiving most of its coal by rail through reception sidings just to the west of Mill Hill East Station. It was a rapidly-increasing source of revenue for the branches as more and more coal was needed with the expansion of the plant. In 1900, the works carbonised only 8,000 tons of coal, but by 1950, at the peak of its importance as a coal-gas plant, the railway was carrying to Mill Hill most of the 77,000 tons of coal used. The plant, however, ceased production of coal gas in November 1961 (having used as much as 59,500 tons of coal during 1960) and in consequence coal traffic dwindled very rapidly. The reduction of coal usage at the gasworks came also at a time of increasing road competition for carriage of goods. With the modernisation schemes of the late 1950s, BR was also looking for more economical methods of freight despatch, choosing freight distribution centres and local road delivery.

The first freight facilities to cease were on the Alexandra Palace branch, Muswell Hill closing completely from 14 June 1956 and Cranley Gardens from 18 May 1957. Closure of services to Mill Hill East and High Barnet was from 1 October 1962, and the goods yards at East Finchley, Finchley Central, Woodside Park, Totteridge and High Barnet were converted into car parks for the Underground. Goods facilities at Mill Hill (The Hale) and Edgware survived officially until February and June 1964 respectively. At Mill Hill (The Hale), the cutting through which the line had passed beneath the Midland Railway was filled in to enable the M1 extension to cross the line without need for a bridge. A short distance to the east of the coal yard at The Hale, part of the track alignment, where it had passed under the A1/A41, was also used as the bed for a slip road from the motorway.

In the early years, Sturrock and Stirling 0-4-2Ts provided motive power for passenger train workings over the Northern Heights branches. Later, Stirling and Ivatt 0-4-4Ts dominated. In 1899, Ivatt 4-4-2Ts began to share the work, while North London Railway 4-4-0T locomotives were also common. As trains became heavier, there was a need for a more substantial locomotive design, especially to cope with the stiff climb to Highgate from Finsbury Park. Gradients generally were not easy, the climb up Highgate bank being the most difficult with grades varying between 1 in 75 and 1 in 50 before the summit was reached at Park Junction. To meet this need, some

American-built 2–6–0 tender locomotives were tried for a short while at the turn of the century, but as no turntable facilities were available this was a temporary measure until a more powerful tank locomotive could be supplied. In the Autumn of 1903 Ivatt, conscious of the need for higher-powered loco-motives, experimented with giant 0–8–2Ts, but these were too cumbersome and they were soon transferred to coal hauling in the East Midlands. Their best features, however, were incor-porated into his Class N1 0–6–2T design, the first of which appeared four years later in 1907 to replace the 4–4–2Ts.

The N1, improved by Gresley, proved popular and successful until gradually replaced in the mid-1920s by Gresley's own Class N2 0–6–2T which provided the basic steam motive power until almost the final withdrawal of the branch services. Freight trains, which had been handled until electrification by a variety of GNR tender engines, were then hauled by these tank loco-motives regularly until late 1960, when the first BTH Type 1 Bo-Bo diesels appeared on the Edgware and Barnet freights, and by March 1961 all steam traction had ceased apart from diesel failure replacements. Main line steam locomotives had from time to time penetrated into this suburban territory but because of turning difficulties these occasions were comparatively rare.

On 6 October 1970 the final chapter of history was recorded on the closed sections of the former EH & L. The transfer work-ings of LT Northern City stock for maintenance and major overhaul purposes from Drayton Park to Highgate Sidings and Acton Works were withdrawn because of the structural weakness of certain bridges between Park Junction and Finsbury Park No 7 box in addition to the flyover bridge at Finsbury Park. From that date, these services were re-routed via Finsbury Park, York Road, Farringdon, Barbican (reverse), Farringdon, Baker Street, Finchley Road and finally to Neasden. The track, having now become superfluous, was soon lifted and the Fins-bury Park to Park Junction section joined the previously closed Alexandra Palace and Mill Hill East to Edgware portions as no more than a mere stretch of forgotten trackbed.

There is much to be thankful for in that the remainder of the route, from Park Junction to East Finchley, High Barnet and Mill Hill East, remained for LTE services. As a result, a good deal of the pleasing, if simple, architecture of GNR rural station design has been preserved and incorporated into the Northern Line stations north of East Finchley. In spite of East Finchley and Highgate having been almost totally rebuilt, the remainder of the stations are predominantly unaltered and a little imagination will soon recapture something of what GNR station facilities must have been like over the whole line. Even the former GNR signal boxes still stand by the lineside at East Finchley and Woodside Park, while many of the GNR brick road overbridges which spanned the line provide evidence of former days by the soot stains, built up by the passage of a wide variety of steam motive power.

Exploration of the entire route of the former GNR branches from Finsbury Park still provides a flavour of the once proud realm of steam. Examples of stations, which until the 1920s could be found in delightfully situated country settings with goods yards and platforms splashed during the Summer by the rich colour of glorious hollyhocks, still exist, on the one hand in a state of dereliction smashed almost to ruin and overgrown by choking weeds, while on the other almost perfectly preserved in operational stations served by LTE. Such contrast hardly seems possible particularly when the curling wisps of steam and smoke from busy shunting locomotives can still be recalled so easily as though they were at work only yesterday.

In spite of the destruction of a large part of the former route, schemes have been prepared to preserve the best of what still remains. The London Borough of Haringey hopes eventually to use part of the former trackbed from Highgate Woods, close to Park Junction, to Alexandra Palace as a parkland walk and the London Borough of Barnet has similar plans between a point a little beyond Mill Hill East Station and Page Street, Mill Hill. But whatever the future holds for the lines, now completely lifted, the slopes of this part of North London will never again reverberate to the deep throb of steam locomotives

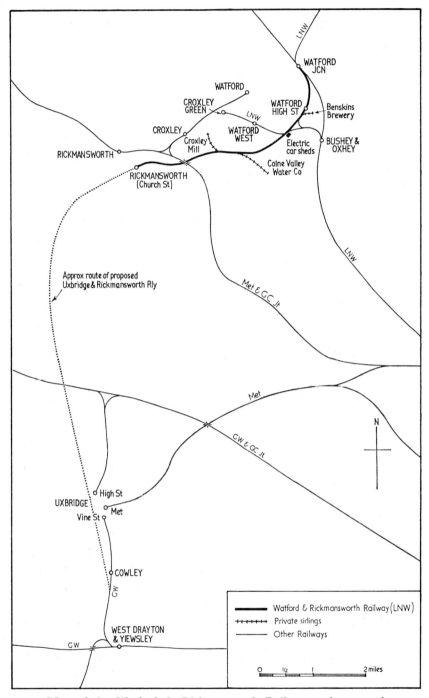

Map of the Watford & Rickmansworth Railway and proposed
Uxbridge Extension

as they laboriously scale the Highgate bank of the Northern Heights.

Watford–Rickmansworth: The Unfinished Symphony

You could stumble across the line quite by chance where in the open land of Croxley Moor close to the canal, the path suddenly came upon it. Immediately in front were objects of intrigue to a young and fertile imagination—an old gate, a rusty sign and a pair of little used rails which stretched into the distance on both sides of the crossing before being lost among trees. It was a railway! Where did it go and what purpose did it serve? Close by stood a disused terminus in Church Street, Rickmansworth, with its little coal yard nearby, complete with wagons which never seemed to move; and the junction at Watford High Street where a branch curved away past the electric car sheds. You never saw a train! It was always deserted, mysterious and unfathomable, a railway which went nowhere!

Today, it all makes sense. The three images were one, and the line linked Watford with Rickmansworth, two market towns whose fortunes were considerably affected by the influence of the railway which first reached the area in 1837. It was on 20 July that year that the first stage of Robert Stephenson's London & Birmingham Railway was opened between Euston and Boxmoor. The London & Birmingham originally served a small station at Watford, situated just north of the bridge carrying the St Albans Road over the railway, before sweeping southwards across high embankments and viaducts in a wide arc to the east of the town, through Bushey and beyond. Watford's next railway, the branch to St Albans opened by the LNWR on 5 May 1858, gave Watford its present station site and status of a railway junction. The Rickmansworth branch, which curved away sharply to the west from the main line, the alignment at present used by the Euston to Watford suburban electric trains, followed four years later.

The Watford & Rickmansworth Railway was an unfulfilled dream of Robert Grosvenor, the third and youngest son of the

Page 33 (above) The 17.40 to Alexandra Palace leaving Finsbury
Park on 7 July 1950; (below) Edgware GNR in May 1914, showing
Terminal facilities and engine bay

Page 34 (*above*) Ex-LMS 0–6–0T 47355 in rustic surroundings near Tolpits on a branch freight from Watford, 30 July 1962; (*below*) 14XX Class 0–4–2T 1450 on local motor-train service at Bourne End, 4 July 1958

Marquis of Westminster. Grosvenor was MP for Middlesex from 1847 to 1857 before being created Baron Ebury with a splendid country residence at Moor Park, where he prepared plans for the Rickmansworth branch and other railway projects. This building is now in the care of the local authority who lease it to the Moor Park Golf Club, but it is open to the public at certain times or by arrangement. Lord Ebury obtained authorisation for the W & RR in July 1860 and immediately submitted a further Bill, passed less than a year later, to construct an extension from Rickmansworth to Uxbridge. The route was intended to allow trains to pass from the GWR Uxbridge branch opened in 1856, via the new railway, to reach the LNWR at Watford. Evidence suggests, however, that Ebury eventually hoped to complete a wider scheme by providing a cross-country route from Uxbridge to Hertford, possibly making connections with the Midland, Great Northern, and Great Eastern Railways. Although the line would have been of some value to passengers, particularly for those from the west wanting to reach the Midlands and the North, its great value could have been as a freight route to transfer goods from one company to another around the northern fringes of the Metropolis.

The complete line from Uxbridge to Watford, as it would seem that Lord Ebury had planned it to be, was welcomed by the townsfolk of Uxbridge and Rickmansworth for its potential improvements to communications and mobility. It also promised to bring further economic development and prosperity to the area, providing services additional to those already offered by the Grand Junction Canal, along which small industrial factories and warehouses had become established. In 1861 for instance, Rickmansworth with a population of 4,873, had five paper mills, two breweries, a silk-spinning mill and a tannery, and the railway brought potential for further expansion and greater employment prospects. The reverse in fact occurred with Watford growing in importance at a far greater pace. People from villages surrounding Rickmansworth, who had previously shopped at its market, soon discovered that they could reach the larger Watford market by the railway, and as a result the importance of Rickmansworth as a market town declined.

Construction began after a simple ceremony near Moor Park and contemporary records report that the day, Thursday 22 November 1860 was warm and clear, one of those rare perfect days of autumn prior to the onslaught of winter. It was a considerable contrast to the cold and windy day in early March 1952 when passenger facilities were withdrawn.

The construction and operation of the line were accompanied by financial difficulties, a problem which continuously dogged the progress of Lord Ebury's various railway projects. The W & RR had an authorised capital of £40,000 but because of insufficient funds, extra cash had to be raised and a further Act, the Watford & Rickmansworth Railway (Sale) Act, was passed in 1863 to authorise the issue of further shares to a value of £30,000. The railway remained in private ownership until purchased by the LNWR in 1881 for £65,000 after the private company had become bankrupt.

Concurrently the Uxbridge extension project was suffering similar problems, although one of the major causes of its financial embarrassment was capital wasted through costly legislation to obtain minor route deviations and time extensions. The W & RR was completed and opened without public ceremony on 1 October 1862, and a weekdays only service of five trains each way per day was provided. The branch was four and a half miles in length and originally single throughout, with an intermediate station conveniently situated at the southern end of Watford High Street.

It was operated from the outset by the LNWR under an agreement dated 16 June 1862. According to this contract, the LNWR paid the Watford & Rickmansworth Railway 'a sum equal to 50% of the actual amount of the gross earnings from tolls, rates, and damages received by the LNWR in respect of traffic of all kinds, as well as local and through traffic passing over the railway of the Watford & Rickmansworth Company, or any part thereof, but subject to deduction therefrom of

£100 p.a.' This agreement was serviced until the railway was absorbed by the LNWR.

Lord Ebury's unfinished symphony resulted largely from a shortage of capital which brought to nought, as in many similar unsuccessful railway promotions of the period, a disproportionate amount of time, effort and money which was expended on the project over a period of 40 years. The final score of legislation for the ill-fated Uxbridge extension and its branch to Scott's Bridge Mill was eleven Acts of Parliament promoted by three separate companies, all of which came to nothing.

Following absorption of the branch by the LNWR, little substantial change occurred until the radical effects of that company's electrification proposals of the early twentieth century. A scheme for electrifying the suburban services between Euston and Watford was first mooted in 1907, but it was not until November 1911, after the LNWR had taken over the management of the North London Railway, that firm plans were announced. The scheme, as it affected the W & RR, provided for a new branch between Watford and Croxley Green, opened for steam passenger operation on 15 June and freight on 1 October 1912, leaving the W & RR at Croxley Green Junction. The track of the W & RR between this junction and Watford Junction was to be doubled to allow for the extra trains. Perhaps more significant, however, was the new suburban line from Euston which was to diverge from the main line at Bushey and Oxhey Station and in a wide sweep cross the Colne Valley to make a junction with the W & RR about 250yd south-west of High Street Station. This was opened for steam operation on 10 February 1913. In addition, a new section of double track, forming a triangle junction, from Colne Junction to the W & RR at Croxley Green Junction allowed through running of trains from Croxley Green to Euston. This was also opened on 10 February 1913, while an electric car stabling shed, with its sidings making connection with the W & RR at Croxley Green Junction, and a new island platform at High Street Station were also to be constructed.

Electric operation commenced over the W & RR on 16 April

1917 with trains of the London Electric Railway running through from Queen's Park to Watford on weekdays only until a daily service was introduced in July 1919. These services were supplemented by LNWR trains from Broad Street during peak periods. Steam trains from Euston were finally withdrawn in 1922 on completion of electrification works at Euston, and on 10 July that year, LNWR electric services ran daily between Watford and Euston, and also to Broad Street during weekday peak periods. With the electrification of the Croxley Green branch on 30 October 1922 the only steam services remaining over the W & RR, apart from freight workings, were those on the original branch services to Rickmansworth.

Lord Ebury, who died in 1893, would no doubt have been flattered by the extra use made of the eastern part of his original W & RR scheme. The new electric facilities brought considerable expansion to passenger traffic and the future of this section of Lord Ebury's railway was made secure far beyond his wildest hopes.

All that remained was for the electrification of his branch to Church Street, Rickmansworth. This was completed cheaply by using existing sub-stations from Croxley Green Junction and was opened for traffic between Watford and Rickmansworth on 26 September 1927. Services had become vested in the London Midland & Scottish Railway in 1923 and, when new LMSR rolling stock was delivered at the end of the 1920s, nine cars of the original joint LNWR/LER electric tube stock were retained to work the Croxley and Rickmansworth services. The joint stock on the Rickmansworth branch acquired the nickname *watercress trains* because of the use often made of their luggage space. Situated in the delightful Chess Valley, Rickmansworth was well-known for its watercress and the trains were used to transport it quickly to market at Watford and elsewhere. This stock was finally withdrawn in 1939, when emergency war timetables were introduced, and the service was taken over by spare main line size electric stock.

The branch was selected for early axing by British Railways, and in 1951 closure notices were published. In spite of local

public criticism, the branch finally closed to passengers from
3 March 1952 and as the *West Herts Post* reported at the time
it was:

> . . . a sad end to a valiant enterprise, for the railway is a link
> with old Rickmansworth and the days of gracious living, when
> Lord and Lady Ebury lived at Moor Park Mansion.

Although the branch remained open throughout for freight,
the decision to withdraw passenger services was hardly surprising for it had never been greatly used and its facilities were
often second best: only on Saturday afternoons if the local
Watford Football Club was playing at home were the trains
crowded, although the line was sadly missed by local people,
many of whom still knew it affectionately as *Lord Ebury's Line*.

Closure was precipitated by three main causes. First,
Metropolitan and Great Central Railway services at Rickmansworth during the latter years of the nineteenth century took the
few passengers that had previously used the branch to reach
London via Watford. Secondly, competition from bus services
between Watford and Rickmansworth further eroded the daily
traffic and finally, increased car ownership after World War II
took away most of the remaining passengers.

Of the three, bus competition had the most significant effect
and is worthy of some amplification as it grew extremely rapidly
in the 1920s. Apart from early horse bus and fly services, the
first motor bus operated between the two towns was in 1921,
by the Rickmansworth & District Omnibus Company. This
company went quickly into liquidation but the service was
taken over by the National Omnibus & Transport Company
operating in the area on behalf of the London General Omnibus Company. The National company numbered this service,
which ran through to Amersham and Chesham, N6, and soon
introduced two further routes between the towns, the N16
(introduced 1923) and the N24 (introduced 1922). In 1924,
the route N1 was extended from Croxley Green to Rickmansworth providing an extra through Watford bus service, together
with a new route N22 between Watford market place and

Harefield via Rickmansworth. In 1923, a private operator, Frederick Lewis, also began operating between the towns. Bus facilities therefore built up very quickly and by the mid-1920s road competition between Watford and Rickmansworth in terms of frequency was already very strong.

Freight traffic was of the normal general nature, with coal, building materials and milk, forming a considerable proportion of the total goods carried by the railway. The line had, however, some specialised private siding freight traffic. Under an agreement dated 2 May 1887, the LNWR provided siding facilities for Benskin & Co to serve its brewery in Watford High Street near the W & RR station. New agreements were negotiated with the LNWR in 1914 and 1917 which remained in force until 1 January 1960. Connections were removed in 1961 although the sidings had been little used for some years previously.

Only a short distance further west, the Watford electricity generating plant was opened in 1899 and coal was brought in from Staffordshire, Nottinghamshire and Derbyshire through a private siding on the northern side of the original W & RR section of the triangle, between Croxley Green Junction and High Street Junction. Prior to nationalisation in 1947, all coal was brought by rail but during the 1950s road haulage reduced the tonnage although even in 1965 some 20,000 tons of coal were carried to the plant by rail compared with only 3,500 tons by road. Rail delivery ceased at the end of 1967 and the siding was lifted shortly afterwards.

Private sidings were also laid in 1899 to the Croxley Mills of John Dickinson & Co Ltd, first opened in 1830, to bring coal from the Midlands and china clay from Cornwall. These have since been transferred to road transport but at the time of writing the company still has a contract with BR to carry oil to the mills, and these workings remain the only services using the original W & RR west of Croxley Green Junction.

The line also served the Eastbury Pumping Station of the Colne Valley Water Company by transferring goods from a siding to the Water Company's own 2ft 0in gauge private railway. This was opened during the 1930s to enable large quantities of salt and coal to be delivered direct to the pumping station, but the connection was dismantled in 1967.

Freight facilities were withdrawn between Croxley Mill Siding and Rickmansworth Church Street from 2 January 1967 and so approximately a third of Lord Ebury's original route remains in daily use, an honourable epitaph to the unsuccessful exploits of a luckless railway promoter.

Those exploring the remains of the former branch will still find a good deal of interest. Sadly the platform and buildings which once comprised Rickmansworth Church Street Station, which for many years remained in private ownership, within a short distance from Rickmansworth's impressive Parish Church and the Grand Union Canal along which the proposed Uxbridge extension would largely have followed, now no longer exist. Use of the line as far as Croxley Mill Siding has also meant that much of the alignment has been preserved, with narrow brick bridges spanning the line at various points. At Watford, little structural change has occurred to the High Street Station since the LNWRs electrification work early this century, while Watford Junction Station has more than a little architectural evidence of its LNWR origin. Perhaps in years hence future generations may still be able to discover something of the influence of the North Western that served so well old 'Ricky' and the memory of its noble railway hero!

CHAPTER 2

The Chiltern Foothills

Introduction

The beechwoods of the Chilterns are always delightful, having some of the finest unspoilt woodlands within easy reach of London. A prominent band of chalk hills, the Chilterns run in an approximate south-west to north-east direction and, with Reading and the Thames Valley at their western end, they comprise much of southern Buckinghamshire and Oxfordshire until blending in with the gentler land of Hertfordshire to the east.

The very nature of the terrain has tended to preclude development of good communications apart from major north to south routes which were chosen by the main line railways for their trunk lines. As a result there were few branch lines, which perhaps helped the area to retain much of its natural rural beauty. In this chapter only a single truly 'Chiltern' railway has been selected, that running from Bourne End to High Wycombe, formerly part of the Wycombe Railway. Instead, lines in the undulating, rich agricultural lands of Hertfordshire have been included from the adjoining but complementary area which for the present purpose is called the Chiltern Foothills. The former GNR branches from Hatfield to St Albans, and to Luton and Dunstable met the LNWR lines from Leighton Buzzard to Dunstable, and Watford to St Albans and formed the watershed in this area between these two great companies. Somewhat later the Midland valiantly forged its way along that watershed, forced to do so mainly by the intransigent attitude of the GNR over the question of running powers between Hitchin and King's Cross. It was this relative newcomer, seeking an independent main line to London, which was to operate the little branch from Harpenden to Hemel Hempstead.

Bourne End–High Wycombe

The former Wycombe Railway, an independent company until absorbed by the GWR in 1867, was built up from various branches which it constructed radiating from High Wycombe. The section from High Wycombe to Bourne End formed part of the oldest portion, authorised by Act of Parliament on 27 July 1846. The single-track line was laid to broad gauge although converted to standard gauge in 1870, two years after the company's Aylesbury branch. It was operated from the outset by the GWR after it was opened between High Wycombe and Maidenhead via Bourne End on 1 August 1854. The remaining arms of the Wycombe Railway were completed by 1864, with the opening of branches to Thame on 1 August 1862, Aylesbury from Princes Risborough on 1 October 1863, and finally to Oxford from Thame on 24 October 1864. Bourne End to High Wycombe was therefore just part of what was to become a quite substantial railway system contributing to the development of a large part of southern Buckinghamshire.

For many years the line remained the principal route to London for the residents of the High Wycombe and Princes Risborough areas. When the Great Western & Great Central joint line was opened in 1906, however, it then became $6\frac{1}{4}$ miles further to London via Bourne End and Maidenhead, and the

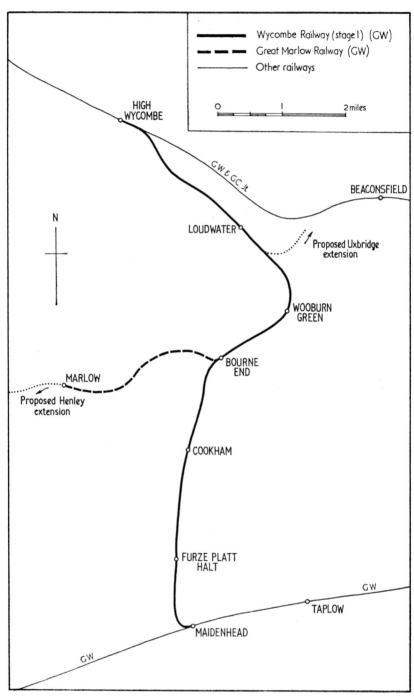

Map of the Wycombe Railway, Stage 1

London traffic quickly transferred to the new direct lines to Marylebone and Paddington.

Some compensation for loss of passengers was made on the section between Bourne End and Maidenhead by development of traffic on the Marlow branch, opened with the support of the GWR by the Great Marlow Railway in 1873. The area served by this branch became a fashionable part of the Thames Valley for wealthy middle-class commuters, which is one factor for the continuing retention of this service, affectionately known as the 'Marlow Donkey'. On the other hand, the Bourne End to High Wycombe section grew of less importance, although it retained some through London trains for many years and sufficient traffic to weather the immediate post-Beeching closure programme.

An interesting scheme which might have provided an extra leg to the ambitious Wycombe Railway's system was the proposed Uxbridge extension. This developed only as far as a Bill drawn up in 1864 seeking authority for a line diverging just south of Loudwater station via Beaconsfield, Chalfont St Peter and Denham to a junction with the GWR Uxbridge branch near its terminal station. Soon after absorbing the Wycombe Railway the GWR abandoned the proposal as it was unlikely to have financially justified construction. A further proposal which could have affected traffic levels over this line was the Marlow & Henley Railway promoted by the GWR in 1898 to link the Marlow and Henley branches, but never authorised.

The branch from High Wycombe to Maidenhead was opened only after considerable financial problems. A year after having obtained its Act, the board of the Wycombe Railway agreed sale of the land to the GWR for £20,000 but were prevented from carrying out the agreement by an Act intended to avoid the premature sale of railway companies. This Act forbade sale of any line where its company had spent less than half its capital on construction works and construction of the line had hardly begun at this stage.

The GWR was, however, considerably involved and Brunel,

the famous railway engineer, was retained as engineer for the company. Little progress was made until the early 1850s, and although the branch was due to open by May 1853 it was delayed by financial crisis and bankruptcy of its contractor. These crises were successfully weathered and the line opened a year and a quarter later.

The small station at Bourne End, now terminal for the Maidenhead and Marlow services, has altered little since the days of the GWR and, although cramped, still preserves the air of grandeur which surrounded the typical GWR rural junction station. The line from Bourne End first crossed a level crossing and then proceeded to follow closely the west side of the valley of the River Wye which rises near West Wycombe and which in the past must have been a beautifully wooded vale. With the growth of industry in the area the valley became host to a number of small paper mills, as a result losing some of its rural charm, and the line had several connections to mills along its route. The branch must also have considerably assisted development of the furniture industry of High Wycombe by providing a greatly improved means of sending finished products to the London market. Both Wooburn Green and Loudwater Stations were simple, unpretentious structures, originally nestling in the lee of the hills and must have quietly served their communities almost as part of the village scene.

Before dieselisation, the line was a good place to see the attractive GWR Class 14XX 0-4-2 tank engines, while examples of the larger Class 61XX 2-6-2 tank locomotives were also often in evidence. On Sunday, 29 July 1956, however, a noteworthy visitor to the line was ex-LBSCR Class H2 locomotive No 32425 *Trevose Head* which hauled an excursion from the Southern Region of BR to Marlow over the line via High Wycombe, returning by way of Bourne End and Maidenhead!

Hemel Hempstead–Harpenden: The Not-So-Forgotten Railway!

The Midland, like the Great Central, might be considered by
some as an interloper to London, for it reached the capital some
years after the other two great railway companies serving the
north of England had already become well established. In spite
of the Midland's great years of prosperity around the turn of
the century, St Pancras, with its towering overall roof and ornate

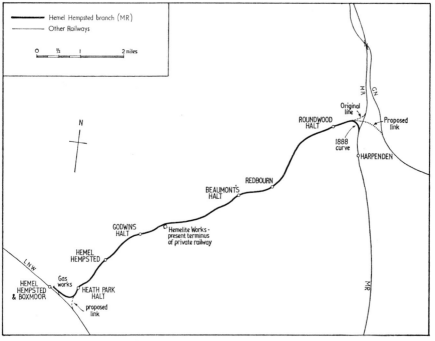

Map of the Hemel Hempstead branch, Midland Railway

Victorian Gothic hotel, somehow failed to achieve quite the
atmosphere, grandeur, or chaotic bustle of Euston or King's
Cross.

Logically, Euston would have appeared the most likely
London terminus from which to travel to Hemel Hempstead.

Instead the town was served by a Midland branch giving a service into St. Pancras, although Boxmoor on the LNWR main line was no great distance. The LNWR was forced to serve the town by a single-deck horse-bus, connecting with trains at Boxmoor, as opposition from landowners, particularly the Boxmoor Trust, precluded any likelihood of an eastwards spur. In the event a connection was laid during the construction of the branch but no passenger services were ever provided. Like so many towns, spellings have changed over the years. It was not until the late 1950s that BR finally recognised the 'a' in Hempstead when the LNW station received new signs.

The grand days of steam passenger services on the Midland branch ended shortly after World War II and, with bomb damage and devastation all around, a nostalgic journey from St Pancras to Harpenden and Hemel Hempstead would have been a very different one from that today. The first part, through grey and dreary suburbs, caused the locomotive to toil through smoke-filled tunnels past the grimy sheds at Kentish Town and Cricklewood, both full of a splendid variety of steam locomotives. Apart from St Albans, the surroundings then became comparatively rural until reaching Harpenden, a pleasant Hertfordshire town which was the eastern junction for Hemel Hempstead. A change to the branch train, sometimes known locally as 'Puffing Annie of the Nicky Railway', was necessary. At one time, there was a small bay platform for the branch trains, but this was later abandoned and trains picked up and set down at the main line platforms.

The background history of the branch has some interest. The L & B reached the area as early as 1837 when, on 20 July that year, it opened its line from Euston to a temporary terminus at Boxmoor to the west of Hemel Hempstead. It was, however, some years before any serious moves towards construction of the Harpenden branch took place. In 1863, the Hemel Hempstead Railway Company successfully obtained an Act to link Boxmoor with Hemel Hempstead, but this proposal failed to make much progress. It seems that although a line was laid down as a result of this Act, which ran from the LNWR goods yard across Boxmoor to the vicinity of Cotterells, where a depot was later established, relations between the LNWR and the Hemel Hempstead Railway Company were so poor that no connection was made to LNWR metals, nor was any use made of the line. A further Act was obtained in 1866 allowing a portion of the line to be abandoned but it is thought that rails were never removed. Approaches were made at this time to both the Midland and GNR and the possibilities were considered of making connection at Harpenden with the recently-opened Hatfield to Luton and Dunstable branch of the GNR, and of extending the line westwards from Hemel Hempstead to Chesham. The Chesham extension scheme was promoted by the Hemel Hempstead & London & North Western Railway Company, usually referred to as the Bucks & Herts Union Railway, but was later abandoned.

The Harpenden to Hemel Hempstead portion was undertaken in a revised form, fitting in with the southern extension of the Midland. Construction began in 1866 from Heath Park towards Harpenden, although the line was not completed until 1877. It was laid with single track, but provision was made throughout for possible conversion to double track.

Powers were obtained in a further Act in 1872 to re-open the Cotterells to Boxmoor section of the branch and this permitted development of some freight traffic. It appears that a turntable link was provided in the LNWR goods yard at this time enabling trucks for Cotterells to be transferred to the branch. In July 1877, the Midland obtained Parliamentary authority to work the line and began to operate services between Luton, Redbourn and Hemel Hempstead on 16 July 1877.

How far the Midland locomotives worked goods trains is not clear, but accounts suggest that in the 1880s there was friction between the Midland and the LNWR over territorial rights. One such account appeared as follows:

On one occasion a Midland Company's engine which penetrated into the London & North Western yard at Boxmoor was
forcibly restrained from leaving by the removal of rails in front
of it owing to a dispute between the two companies as to the
right use of the yard by the Midland Company . . .

The Hemel Hempstead Railway Company was finally
absorbed by the Midland in 1886. Passenger trains never made
the complete journey, terminating at Hemel Hempstead, and
it is likely that by the early 1890s, all freight for Cotterells' depot
and the Boxmoor Gasworks came via Harpenden rather than
from the LNWR.

The line originally had a north facing junction with the
Midland as the economic links were towards Luton rather than
London and in particular were concerned with the straw hat
industry, Hemel Hempstead being an important source of the
straw plait raw material from reed beds in the vicinity of the
town. Nevertheless, this north-facing junction was replaced in
July 1888 by one facing south which had a deep cutting and
sharp curve which still meets the main line at Harpenden
Junction, some distance north of the main line station.

The difficult gradients and route chosen by the promoters
made the branch far from routine to operate, with a murderous
incline of 1 in 37 near the Harpenden end which sometimes
proved impossible for an overloaded engine, and loads were in
consequence strictly limited. The light nature of the construction of the line also meant that only relatively small locomotives
were permitted to work over the branch, aggravating the
difficulties.

The busiest days of the branch were at the turn of the
twentieth century and it was during the summer of 1905 that
the Midland introduced a rail-motor push-and-pull service;
subsequently an ex-Pullman car and 4–4–0T were introduced
on this service on 2 April 1906. Trains were extended on 9
August 1905 from Hemel Hempstead to Heath Park Halt,
which made it one of the few branch lines to have passenger
trains terminate at a halt. The train was stabled overnight at
St Albans and operated on a roster which took it first to Luton

Page 51 (*above*) MR Johnson 0–6–0T 1669 at Hemel Hempstead on branch train from Harpenden, 19 October 1929. The site of this station is now a small housing development; (*below*) Webb 2–4–2T 46601 drifting past the former MPD at Leighton Buzzard on a branch train from Dunstable North, 11 May 1949

Page 52 Class N7 0–6–2Ts 69631 and 69698 storm out of Ayot,
bound for Welwyn Garden City, on 2 May 1959

and back to Harpenden before commencement of the branch services for the day. Additional halts were also opened at Beaumont's, Godwin's and, in 1927, Roundwood.

In 1923, the line was absorbed by the LMSR which introduced an alternative bus route in 1929 and reduced branch passenger train services to rush hours only, enabling one locomotive to work the branch all day. In 1931, with a view to combating the problems of rural branch line operation, the branch was selected by the LMSR for an experiment with a road-rail bus built by the Karrier Motor Company of Huddersfield; this could travel on road or railway lines by lifting and lowering the road wheels as necessary, and was designed with rural branch lines in mind. The experiment was stifled, however, by the creation of the London Passenger Transport Board in 1933 which absorbed the LMSR bus undertakings in this area and shelved the experiment just as it was proving itself.

The War came and went and somehow services on the branch, although in all respects a shadow of those which had operated in the early years of the century, survived until being withdrawn officially from 16 June 1947. Throughout its life the branch remained a useful freight link and in 1944 development of it as an orbital freight line linking Watford with Chelmsford was proposed in Abercrombie's Greater London Plan. New connections were to be constructed at both ends, with a junction facing Euston at Hemel Hempstead and a bridge over the Midland allowing a connection to be made with the GNR, permitting trains to reach Hertford and the GER via the GNR as originally intended. This scheme, like most of the orbital freight route proposals, failed to progress further than this initial planning stage as it would have required major reconstruction of the branch because of the severe gradients.

The line remained virtually intact until work began on building Hemel Hempstead new town. One of the reasons for selecting either Hemel Hempstead or Redbourn as the site for the new town was that double-track rail connection could be provided at little extra cost. In particular, the industrial estate was sited to allow connection for private sidings, but the nature of the industries taking industrial space obviated the necessity. As part of the work the track bed from Heath Park to Hemel Hempstead was needed and the alignment, including an impressive viaduct over the main street, was demolished in 1960.

A physical junction was finally opened between the former LNWR goods yard and the Harpenden branch on 31 August 1959 allowing direct delivery of coal from the Euston main line to Boxmoor Gasworks. The junction had only been operative for a couple of weeks before production of coal gas ceased at the works and the line fell into disuse, although the track was not removed again until 1972.

British Railways continued to provide freight facilities from the Harpenden end over part of the branch until July 1964. A large proportion of the branch, from Claydale's sidings to Harpenden Junction, survived demolition and was sold to the Hemel Hempstead Lightweight Concrete Co, for movement of raw materials.

Sale of the branch as far as Claydale's has saved some of the lineside facilities from extinction, although little remains of the former station buildings along the route. Indeed, the only evidence now remaining of the stations on the line are the overgrown platforms which were once Redbourn Station and Roundwood Halt! Otherwise, basic structures such as bridges, cuttings and embankments over this operational stretch are much as they were in Midland days. Not surprisingly, many traces of the alignment in the Hemel Hempstead area have disappeared and no doubt will continue to do so as in-filling development proceeds around the New Town, although it is likely to be many years before all traces of the route have gone; part of the trackbed to the east of the town has been re-opened as a tree-lined public right of way.

Locomotives employed on the branch were always diminutive. In its early years, the trains were worked by 2-4-0s purchased from the Somerset & Dorset Railway and allotted Midland Nos 1397-9. At the beginning of the rail-motor services, an outside cylinder 4-4-0 tank was acquired after which the line became generally operated by 0-4-4T and 0-6-0T engines. In the latter years of passenger operation, the usual engine was a Fowler Class 3 2–6–2T from St Albans shed, employed on a 'one engine in steam' basis. When heavier goods traffic warranted, Midland Class 3F or 4F 0–6–0 tender locomotives were sometimes employed and between 1947 and 1954, Class 3F 0–6–0 No 43245 was regularly seen on the line. This was replaced briefly by Class 4F No 43888 until Ivatt 2–6–0 No 43119 was transferred to St Albans in 1955. This remained the regular locomotive until closure of the local shed, after which motive power was supplied from Cricklewood. BR provided a Type 2 diesel until 1968, when the line was sold to the Hemelite Company who then purchased two ex-BR Class 04 diesel shunter locomotives numbered D2203/7 for the private workings. A Clayton Type 1, formerly BR No D8568 has also recently been purchased to reduce the number of workings that have to be made over the branch, and will help to keep alive some of the memories of the past glory of this little travelled rural backwater.

The Railways of Hatfield
'Sero Sed Serio—Late, but in Earnest'

Hatfield was once a centre of railway activity quite unrelated to its size, and it is somewhat surprising that it attracted so much attention from the railway builders. The town has a long and distinguished historical background being situated strategically abreast the former Great North Road and is the well-known family seat of the Marquis of Salisbury, a member of the Cecil family (whose family crest above might well be related to the branch railways of the town!). It is, therefore, a place worthy of visit in its own right, the House having been the childhood home of Queen Elizabeth I and containing many interesting relics concerning her. To those with railway interests, it is a convenient centre from which to explore the remains of three former branches of the GNR.

Two of these predominantly rural branches served areas to the west of the East Coast main line. The third, the former Hertford branch, falls outside the scope of this book, although it is almost impossible to separate it from the Luton and Dunstable branch of which it was intended to be part.

Hatfield today has comparatively little industry, and the surrounding locality is one of mainly undulating countryside, being in a transitional area between the Chiltern Hills and the flatter agricultural lands of east Hertfordshire. The St Albans and Dunstable branches, while unspectacular, were known and loved locally for the pretty countryside through which they passed as they served the towns and villages along their way, which still makes a journey by foot over their route a delightful experience on a summer's day!

Hatfield–St Albans Abbey

The cathedral of St Alban commands the skyline as it looks out over Old Verulamium, once a Roman garrison town on Watling Street. Tucked away inconspicuously in the valley of the River Ver, at the foot of the hill on which the cathedral stands, is St Albans Abbey station. This was to become the terminus of two branches from Hatfield and Watford and preceded the Midland main line station by ten years. Little unfortunately remains of this terminus as the original buildings have been demolished and Watford trains now terminate at a rather exposed single-track platform.

In the same way as the LNWR and GNR provided a cross-country rail link between Hatfield and Leighton Buzzard via Dunstable and Luton, the two companies provided a similar link between Watford and Hatfield via St Albans. Indeed, all four lines are related as the branches were closely woven in schemes which could have linked them all, including also the Hemel Hempstead to Harpenden branch, as proposals were laid down to annex the territory and serve the local communities of this part of west Hertfordshire.

Passengers for London from St Albans before either branch railway was constructed travelled for some years by coach from St Albans to Hatfield and thence via the GNR to King's Cross. The status quo was threatened when on 4 August 1853 the LNWR successfully gained powers to construct its Watford branch, thus threatening to capture the St Albans traffic from the GNR. Seven years previously the L & B had unsuccessfully proposed a loop line between Watford and Leighton Buzzard, passing via St Albans and Redbourn to Dunstable, where it was to join the Leighton Buzzard to Dunstable branch.

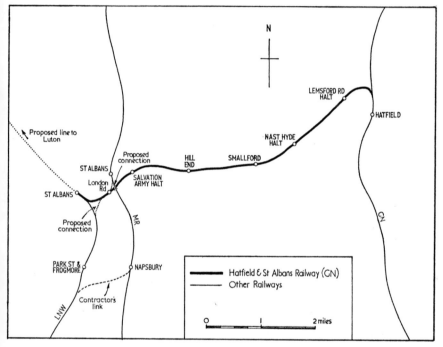

Map of the St Albans branch, GNR

Parliamentary authority was obtained by the LNWR in 1847 for a similar scheme except that the route was to take a more easterly direction after Redbourn, enabling the line to pass through Luton and Dunstable in completing the loop. The GNR, obviously seeing a territorial threat, proposed at the same time a branch from Hertford through Hatfield to St Albans with running powers over the LNWR to Luton, having had its proposals for a direct link between Hatfield and Luton rejected in the previous year.

In the event the loopline scheme failed to mature and only the Leighton Buzzard to Dunstable and Watford to St Albans sections were built under separate Acts, paving the way for the two GNR branches to be constructed later. It took almost five years before the LNWR finally opened its single-track branch to St Albans on 5 May 1858, linking the town by rail for the first time. Three years later the GNR, worried at its loss of St Albans traffic to the LNWR, decided to support a branch to St Albans and on 30 June 1862 authority was obtained by the Hatfield & St Albans Railway, largely supported by the GNR, to construct a line. It appears that all was not plain sailing for the promoters, as records of land purchased from St Albans School indicate considerable financial weakness. The necessary capital was nevertheless raised and the line duly completed and opened on 16 October 1865. A rival scheme, the Hertford & St Albans Railway, of which Lord Ebury was the main promoter, failed to prevent completion of the branch, which was eventually absorbed by the GNR on 1 November 1883.

The branch curved away from the main line just north of Hatfield Station and yard. The station itself was a place of some interest with a waiting room, used in the past by the nobility and special guests visiting Hatfield House, at the southern end of the up slow line. This was converted in recent years to a railway signal training school. Unfortunately, this has all been swept away and the reconstructed station has minimal frills. On the western side of the station and main lines, a busy group of goods sidings provided reception and marshalling facilities for the considerable volumes of freight emanating from the three branches and goods stations in the vicinity on the main line. The Luton and Dunstable branch, in particular, brought a good deal of goods traffic to and from Hatfield Yard, and there was sufficient traffic to maintain full employment of a tank locomotive shunting throughout the day. In the 1920s, to which it is interesting to look back as these were still thriving days for the railway at Hatfield, there was an 0–6–0 saddle tank allocated to the shed for this purpose, and which did little else apart from the odd journeys on refuse trains to Fiddle Bridge Sidings.

The motive power depot was on the extreme western edge of the station area and was originally a two-road shed. At the northern end of its yard was a small turntable, just capable of accommodating one of the GNR 0–6–0 goods locomotives shedded there. Life at the shed, though difficult, was much the same as elsewhere, and an allocation usually of about 35 locomotives and a staff of 150, made it a depot of some local importance. Sadly, a visitor to the present Hatfield Station would hardly be aware that anything more than a couple of sidings ever existed on the west side of the running lines and as a consequence tangible memories of much of Hatfield's railway life have been lost forever.

Climbing through a shallow cutting, the St Albans branch curved well over 90° from a south-facing junction with the main line to proceed in a south-westerly direction for the greater part of its route. At approximately the first mile, the trains called at Lemsford Road Halt, opened during World War II mainly for workers at the nearby De Havilland aircraft plant. The station was staffed by a porter from Hatfield, but no tickets were issued, fares being collected at destination stations. A short distance further, still on gradually rising grades, was Fiddle Bridge Sidings where there was a small coal depot and facilities for a daily refuse train from Hatfield and goods for De Havilland's. The area surrounding the route of the line is now built up as far as about this point, the Hatfield new town and grounds of the Polytechnic absorbing much of the previous rural nature of the vicinity. At around the $1\frac{1}{2}$ mile point the line was crossed by the A1 Barnet By-pass, which took from the original route, now the A1000, the status of the Great North Road. The bridge was optimistically constructed to accommodate double track should it have been required, and the soot stain from some years of steam working can still be plainly seen. At last the countryside was reached at the level crossing at Nast Hyde Halt, opened in 1910 to serve new residential areas but also, according to local folklore, opened at the instigation of Mr Oliver Bury, who owned a house nearby and used the line to reach King's Cross.

At once the branch changes its character and, passing close to the source of the River Colne, the surroundings immediately become softer and more pastoral as the line crossed meadows to Smallford originally appropriately named Springfield. The station buildings here are still virtually intact being owned, like St Albans (London Road) station, by a firm of scrap metal merchants which uses the buildings for offices. Today the vicinity of the station is far from soft, with mounds of scrap metal littered about, the waste of our modern sophisticated, motorised society!

Since the 1930s, the area north of the branch as it progressed towards St Albans has become progressively built up by factory estates linked to the branch by private sidings. The line then approached the outer perimeter of the city, reaching Hill End station and yard at the four mile post. Deliveries of coal and stores to Hill End Hospital were effected by means of a siding into the grounds, which provided useful goods traffic to the branch. There was also a public goods siding at Fleetville.

On the southern outskirts of the city a private business of orchid growing became established by Messrs Sander and Sons, the hothouses being linked by a siding for the despatch of orchids to market. For many years, the GNR provided three special vans for this purpose but they were later also used for carriage of straw hats from Luton to London. In addition, a sleeper-built platform halt was provided at this point for the use of Sander's staff, and was later used also by personnel at the Salvation Army's Campfield Printing Works. From the siding, Salvation Army periodicals were sent in large quantities for distribution throughout the world and as well as the coal and general freight formed an important traffic on the branch which, together with the scrap metal train workings, were one of the final freight facilities to be withdrawn.

The branch then passed beneath the majestic arch of the Midland Railway main line. The original railway plans at this point became a little confused, several schemes being mooted for linking the Midland to the LNWR and GNR. One scheme was for a connection from the Midland main line to the GNR at a level junction at London Road station, with a triangle junction to the LNWR just north of Park Street station. This was never built, but a second scheme was constructed running from Napsbury station on the Midland to a point just south of Park Street station; this was laid by the contractors for the supply of materials and despatch of earth via the LNWR during construction of the main line. It would seem that something more permanent could have been intended, as the line was sturdily built and the bridge at Park Street was demolished only comparatively recently. In the last few years there have been many requests locally for this link to be properly reinstated, giving a direct rail passenger service and interchange between the main line stations at St Albans and Watford and permitting closure of St Albans Abbey station. This, however, would now be impossible on grounds of cost, although much of the earthworks to the west of the A5 (148038) still exist.

After London Road station, the line gradually curved in a north-westerly direction to a junction with the LNWR, over which the GNR had running powers to the LNWR station. Usual practice was for GNR trains to terminate in the bay on the eastern edge of the single station platform. To the west of the station the extensive sidings of St Albans gasworks fanned out and both the LNWR and GNR brought coal to the plant. The general position of St Albans Abbey station shows clearly the original objective of northward extension, but perhaps it was best that the line terminated here, for had it continued many of the Roman remains of Verulamium could well have been lost and construction of the Hemel Hempstead to Harpenden branch would hardly have been justified.

The Hatfield to St Albans branch was an early casualty of British Railways, closing throughout to passengers from 1 October 1951. Freight traffic, however, lingered into the 1960s, with Hill End and London Road sidings closing in October 1964. Fleetville and Salvation Army sidings closed also in

December that year, but a contract with a scrap dealer at Smallford meant trains to this station until January 1969.

The branch was worked under 'one engine in steam' and, in the 1920s, was the home of the attractive Class C12 4–4–2T locomotives which were the mainstay of the branch at this

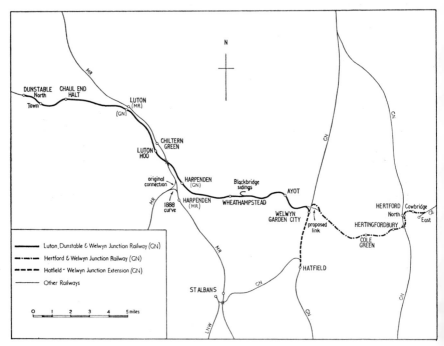

Map of the Hertford, Luton & Dunstable Railway

time, carrying out from Hatfield all passenger and freight workings apart from the final passenger train of the day, on which any locomotive which Hatfield had available would make the out and home journey. On a cold night in winter, this might have been an unpleasant journey if one of the tender engines was used, for there were no turntable facilities at St Albans. A log of one of the final passenger train workings over the branch which closed officially from 1 October 1951 is detailed below:

BR—Eastern Region
Friday, 28 September 1951
Train No 2316, 17.08 Hatfield to St Albans Abbey
Locomotive No. 69644 Class N7/1 0–6–2T
Shed—Hatfield (34C)
Weather—fine

| Distance | | Stations and sidings | | Times | |
M	Ch			Booked	Actual
0	00	HATFIELD	dep	17.08	17.10
1	00	Lemsford Road Halt	arr	17.12	17.12¼
			dep	17.15	17.16½
1	20	Fiddle Bridge Siding		—	—
2	03	Nast Hyde Halt	arr	—	17.19
			dep	17.18	17.19½
2	68	Smallford	arr	—	17.21½
			dep	17.21	17.22
4	15	Hill End	arr	—	17.25
			dep	17.26	17.25½
4	61	Fleetville Siding		—	—
5	17	Sanders & Salvation Army	arr	—	17.28
		Works Siding	dep	—	17.28½
5	54	St Albans (London Road)	arr	17.31	17.30
			dep	17.32	17.31
6	34	ST ALBANS ABBEY	arr	17.35	17.33

Timed by J. Press

Hatfield–Luton and Dunstable

In some respects, it is remarkable that Hatfield's two other branches to Dunstable and Hertford should have ever reached the town, for intentions were to incorporate them as part of a cross-country route linking the LNWR, GNR and GER. Owing mainly to opposition from the GNR, the bridge over its main line at Welwyn Junction was never permitted, in spite of some of the earthworks having been carried out. The promoters of the two branches were forced to look to Hatfield as their objective, which they did by running separate tracks parallel to the main line from Welwyn to Hatfield, a distance of almost three miles.

The schemes were separately conceived, promoted by local interests, but with some of the promoters common to both companies. The Hertford branch, incorporated by an Act of 3 July 1854 as the Hertford & Welwyn Junction Railway, and the Dunstable branch, authorised on 16 July 1855 as the Luton, Dunstable & Welwyn Junction Railway, were amalgamated into the Hertford, Luton & Dunstable Railway on 28 June 1858.

The proposal to link Hatfield with Luton went back into the 1840s when in 1846 the embryonic GNR unsuccessfully proposed a branch to Luton, largely to stave off competition from the L & B. In 1848, Dunstable was linked to the main line by the LNWR, but there the line stopped. In the early years of the 1850s, the Lutonians, concerned at having missed their earlier opportunity of a railway extension from the LNWR, unsuccessfully petitioned the GNR to provide a link. In due course, however, local interests, which included the M P for Hertford and various landowners, promoted the Luton, Dunstable & Welwyn Junction Railway Co which was to run from Dunstable, where connection was to be made to the LNWR, through Luton to Welwyn, with a triangular junction to the main line. A bridge was also to cross the GNR to permit trains from the Luton and Dunstable branch to make a through connection with the Hertford branch and Eastern Counties Railway beyond.

The Luton, Dunstable & Welwyn Junction, finding its financial resources over extended, first approached the LNWR to take over the line, but could procure no more than a limited offer to work the section from Dunstable to Luton. As a result, the Company looked to the Hertford & Welwyn Junction as a means of pooling resources and raising further capital, and in spite of opposition the amalgamation was duly completed. The Hertford Branch was opened on 1 March 1858, and the section between Dunstable and Luton on 5 April (goods) and 3 May 1858 (passengers) but the Dunstable branch was not opened throughout until 1 September 1860. From these humble if politically complex beginnings, the two branches therefore set out to serve their local communities faithfully for 93 years in the case of the Hertford branch, and the Dunstable branch for almost 105 years.

The Luton and Dunstable route curved away sharply west-wards from the main line at Welwyn, near the site of the original Welwyn Junction Station which was built to serve the two branches. This station was soon abandoned and trains from both branches ran into Hatfield, but in 1920 the site was selected for a halt served additionally by local trains from Hatfield, which ran to Ayot to turn before returning to Hatfield. The present Welwyn Garden City Station replaced this halt in 1926. The line passed through the residential outskirts of Welwyn on the climb to Ayot, renowned for the burdens that the bank put on locomotives hauling heavy freight trains over the branch. At its steepest, the ascent was 1 in 56, and banking engines were provided for the string of early morning freights bound from Hatfield for Luton and Dunstable. On some occasions, trains attempted to climb unassisted and stalling on the greasy rails on wet or frosty mornings brought much criticism from local residents awakened by noisy attempts to restart!

At Ayot there was a crossing point and until September 1949 a station also, but this was destroyed by fire on 26 July 1948 and not replaced by a permanent structure. The construction of the A1 (M) removed most traces of this former station site. The branch, which since leaving the main line had somewhat tortuously curved into the neighbouring countryside, now entered some of the finest rural areas of Hertfordshire. To the north of the line were the nearby villages of Ayot St Peter and Ayot St Lawrence, the latter famous as the home of George Bernard Shaw, and to the south Brocket Hall, where Lords Palmerston and Melbourne died. Reaching the valley of the River Lea, along which the line passed as far as Luton, it was flanked by meadows and copses of some beauty before passing Wheathampstead.

Soon after leaving Wheathampstead Station, the branch crossed the river and proceeded on the west bank to the eastern outskirts of Harpenden, once the site of horse racing on the Downs, which brought some traffic to the station. Today, one would hardly know of the former existence of a railway station here for the line and its station, with passing loop, have been absorbed in a small housing development, to the sadness of those who once rode on the footplate over the branch. The line, now travelling in a north-westerly direction, then passed beneath the former Midland main line with its impressive embankment, entering Bedfordshire at this point. Suddenly, the next station was reached, nestling quietly in the folds of undulating wooded countryside, the single platform of Luton Hoo, lying close to the former stately home of the Marquis of Bute who owned a good deal of the land on which Luton was subsequently built. The branch then paralleled the Midland main line for some distance, with the eastern fringes of the Luton Hoo Estate to the west.

On reaching the edges of Luton, the branch passed the factory of Vauxhall Motors, now the symbol of Luton's new industrial prosperity, before reaching Luton (Bute Street) Station, situated almost next to the Midland main line station. Bute Street was originally a simple single-platform station but in 1863, as traffic was already growing rapidly, an island platform and refreshment room were added making the station a fairly impressive one for what was basically a single-track branch.

Luton, however, formed the eastern end of what was almost a 'different' railway. For some distance to the west of Bute Street the line was double track and had far less picturesque countryside as it skirted the northern foot of the low Chiltern scarp. Luton was also the destination and starting point of numerous freight train workings and the western approaches to Bute Street were commanded by the façade of the GNR bonded warehouse, built about 1906 to handle increasing goods traffic. The line then ran approximately parallel to the Icknield Way, laid down many centuries previously along the safe foot of the Chiltern hills. Next to both road and railway, in addition to residential development, industry of an essentially light nature has grown up since the early twentieth century and a number of private sidings added considerable extra freight traffic to that plying to and fro between Dunstable and Hatfield.

The suburbs of Luton and Leagrave now merge with neighbouring Dunstable, a town of Roman and earlier origin which grew up at the intersection of the Icknield Way and Watling Street at the neck of a natural corridor through the Chilterns. Dunstable was, therefore, an obvious early target for the railway promoters. It is a little surprising that Luton, which had a far less impressive start than Dunstable and was served later by the railway, should have grown to become the town of far greater importance, due in no small part to the direct influence of the Midland Railway. It is also difficult to understand why several halts were not provided between Bute Street and Dunstable after the residential areas sprang up in the 1930s, for this might have bolstered flagging passenger traffics in spite of the good parallel bus services, although there was a private halt at Chaul End during World War I.

Rounding a wide curve, the train reached Dunstable Town, formerly named Church Street, situated fairly conveniently to the town centre. Church Street was a very unpretentious structure with wooden platforms, although the station building had previously been destroyed by fire and rebuilt in 1871. The line finally skirted the northern edges of Dunstable, passing the printing works of Waterlow & Sons and London Road Goods Depot. Under the Act authorising the Luton, Dunstable & Welwyn Junction Railway, the branch ended at this point but a bridge over Watling Street (A5) gave the GNR access to the LNWR Dunstable North station, into which it had running powers. Similarly, the LNWR possessed running powers over the GNR to Bute Street, and from 1881 the Anglo-Scottish rivals amicably ran on weekdays a joint service between the two towns. Indeed, it is interesting that the whole area did not become the scene of fierce inter-company rivalry in the early days of railway construction, for the territory was ripe for conflict. It must have appeared to have been too insignificant for the giant LNWR and GNR to become seriously concerned in squabbling over the area, but it need not have been so, for to some extent the great rivalry between the LNWR and the GWR in north Buckinghamshire and Warwickshire was for lesser rewards. Amicable agreement to share the excellent potential seemed to have worked well, even after the arrival of the Midland, although it was understandably the GNR which gained most from the situation.

Apart from the general freight traffic of coal, sand and lime, quarried materials, and raw materials and finished articles from the many factories along the Luton end of the line, some comment on the straw plait trade is interesting, for this was Luton's staple industry before the development of its modern light industries. In 1898, *The Railway Magazine* reported that the GNR kept eighteen drays and the LNWR three drays at Luton to deliver general goods, empty straw hat boxes, and plait, and to collect the full boxes at night. In addition it reported:

> During the evening a sight will present itself the like of which it will be difficult to find in any town similar in size to Luton. This is the work of carting to the stations all the boxes which have been packed with hats during the day. The principal thoroughfare of the town is George Street . . . the sight is well worth seeing, the railway companies drays rumbling heavily along, stopping here and there to have their loads increased . . . muscular draymen heaving boxes on to their drays with a dexterity that is surprising; in short, to see George Street at 6 p.m. during the season with its railway drays loading up is a sight which can never be forgotten.

Goods vans were consigned not only to the City and London Docks but also to many parts of Britain, most going via the GNR to Hatfield for marshalling to destinations beyond. This traffic began to decline at a time when engineering in the town was in its embryonic stages, eventually culminating in the rise of the motor industry. Vauxhall's, in particular, brought a new industrial prosperity to Luton, and in later years a considerable amount of goods traffic travelling via both Hatfield and Leighton Buzzard. On 3 January 1966, this traffic was diverted to the Midland main line at Luton by means of a new junction, allowing the Luton to Blackbridge Sidings section to be closed from early 1966, and this connection is still in daily use for cement and oil train workings to private sidings at Dunstable.

Page 69 (*above*) Early view of Cheddington station, looking north, with an Aylesbury branch train on the left, and showing the single 'up third' relief line used by the southbound LNW freights on the right; (*below*) Metropolitan 4-4-4T 107 about to leave Verney Junction with a train for Baker Street, 9 May 1936. Buckinghamshire Railway services of the LNWR used the tracks on the left

Page 70 (above) Metropolitan Class A 4–4–0T 41 prepares to depart from Brill on a mixed train to Quainton Road; (below) diesel railcar at Buckingham on 9 March 1957 bound for Banbury (Merton Street), a contrast to the steam service from Bletchley

Another interesting source of freight revenue arose from refuse trains working from Ashburton Grove to Blackbridge Sidings near Wheathampstead. Until the end of steam these were usually hauled by Class N7s from Hatfield, where the locomotives were changed. After dieselisation, trains were generally operated by BTH Type 1 diesels, although there were several experiments with other classes. These services were withdrawn with effect from 24 May 1971.

Motive power over the branch has been of considerable variety, ranging from tank engines to many types of tender locomotive. Sturrock 0–4–2 well tanks provided power in the early years, and various Stirling tanks also ran over the branch at the end of the nineteenth century, along with 2–4–0 locomotives. More powerful tanks came to the branch during the early years of the twentieth century with the introduction of H. A. Ivatt's Class N1 0–6–2T locomotives which, together with his Class C12 4–4–2Ts, gradually replaced the Sturrock and Stirling tanks. During the 1920s, Gresley's Class N2 0–6–2Ts replaced the C12s, which were mainly relegated to the St Albans branch trains, later being joined by a small number of Class N7 tanks new from the GER. Both of these classes were mainly responsible for the passenger train workings until the cessation of steam.

Hatfield goods locomotives also played a significant role in the haulage of passenger trains; during the 1920s, Hatfield possessed a sizeable stud of 0–6–0 tender locomotives of Class J1, J3 and J4, and these could be seen regularly on Luton and Dunstable trains. In recent years, diesel multiple units provided some of the passenger services supplemented by passenger and goods trains hauled by D8XXX and D55XX Class locomotives.

It was a pity that the GNR route from Hatfield to Luton and Dunstable including through trains from King's Cross was never given the recognition that it deserved, for the line was always overshadowed by its great competitor the Midland, whereas for many the service provided was a useful facility. With the LNWR, it provided a valuable cross-country connection which it is lamentable to have lost.

HATFIELD LOCOMOTIVES—1924

GNR No	LNER No	BR No (if any)	Class	Wheel arrangement	Branches worked
1	3001	—	J1	0–6–0	Luton
2	3002	—	J1	0–6–0	Luton
3	3003	65002	J1	0–6–0	Luton
11	3011	—	J1	0–6–0	Luton
49	3049	—	D2	4–4–0	Luton
101	3101	—	J4	0–6–0	Luton
190	3190	69430	N1	0–6–2T	Luton (Occasional)
384	3384	—	J3	0–6–0	Luton
684	3684	—	J57	0–6–0ST	Hatfield Shunter only
717	3717	—	J3	0–6–0	Luton
745	3745	—	J4	0–6–0	Luton
770	3770	—	G1	0–4–4T	Luton/St Albans (Occasional)
1073	4073	—	D3	4–4–0	Luton
1078	4078	—	D3	4–4–0	Luton
1100	4100	—	J3	0–6–0	Luton
1169	4169	—	J3	0–6–0	Luton
1377	4377	62177	D2	4–4–0	Luton (Occasional)
1534	4534	67385	C12	4–4–2T	St Albans
1537	4537	67387	C12	4–4–2T	St Albans
1541	4541	67391	C12	4–4–2T	St Albans
1548	4548	67398	C12	4–4–2T	St Albans
1550	4550	—	C12	4–4–2T	St Albans
1758	4758	69537	N2	0–6–2T	Luton
1759	4759	69538	N2	0–6–2T	Luton
1760	4760	69539	N2	0–6–2T	Luton
1761	4761	69540	N2	0–6–2T	Luton
1762	4762	69541	N2	0–6–2T	Luton
1763	4763	69542	N2	0–6–2T	Luton
1766	4766	69545	N2	0–6–2T	Luton

1767	4767	69546	N2	0–6–2T	Luton
1770	4770	69549	N2	0–6–2T	Luton
GER No					
993E	7993	69615	N7	0–6–2T	Luton
994E	7994	69616	N7	0–6–2T	Luton
995E	7995	69617	N7	0–6–2T	Luton

Notes:

   (i) The final train of the day to St Albans was usually hauled by any locomotive in steam in Hatfield yard, providing a variety of motive power.

  (ii) The three GER Class N7 0–6–2Ts were new locomotives straight from Stratford works, to replace Class N2 0–6–2Ts returning to Doncaster for modification.

 (iii) The table ignores the fact that locomotives ran also to Hertford and London.

Leighton Buzzard–Dunstable

This line, on the fringes of both the Vale of Aylesbury and the Chiltern Foothills, completed the cross-country route afforded by the GNR branch from Hatfield though in practice the potential for through working was never realised. Like the GNR branch, the line (built as a branch from the LNWR main line) had considerable local importance, mainly for traffic comprising finished goods, raw materials and locally quarried stone to and from the industrial areas around Dunstable.

The branch was generally a very ordinary double-track line almost seven miles in length. Its main feature was the steep gradients at both ends, which made it a place of interest to watch labouring goods trains, especially on the 1 in 40 climb to the Chilterns to reach Dunstable North Station.

The branch curved away rather inconspicuously to the southeast from Leighton Buzzard station with a sharp falling gradient and could well have been missed by those unaware of its presence, being tucked away behind goods sidings and earthworks. It then travelled in an almost straight line, with very easy gradients across the gentle valley of the River Ouzel before again reaching the foot of the incline to Dunstable near Sewell.

The chief purpose of the branch was to link the old coaching town of Dunstable with the main line, although Stephenson undoubtedly intended to make Luton his ultimate objective.

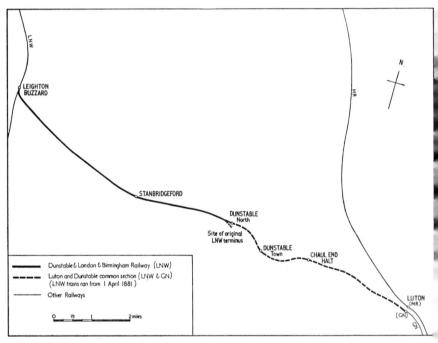

Map of the Dunstable branch, LNWR

It is well known, however, how his delegation received a humiliating rebuff from the Lutonians, resulting in shelving of the extension plans. Both parties suffered as a result, Luton not receiving a rail connection until 1858; the LNWR never really gained a foothold in Luton, which they might otherwise have obtained, even after negotiating running powers over the GNR.

Parliamentary authority for construction of the branch was given in 1845 when the Dunstable & London & Birmingham

Railway Act was passed on 30 June. It was therefore a very early scheme, and was originally part of the L & B's unsuccessful loop line project planned to link Leighton Buzzard with Dunstable across the wedge of relatively flat, rather uninteresting countryside, pockmarked by quarry and sand workings at the foot of the Chiltern Hills. The Dunstable branch was also seen as a means of allowing the LNWR to tap the traffic of south Bedfordshire, but because of the earthworks required during construction, particularly the embankment and cutting through the scarp at Sewell, the branch was not opened until 29 May 1848 for goods and 1 June 1848 for passengers.

An intermediate station was provided at Stanbridgeford which served the villages of Stanbridge, Totternhoe and Tilsworth, and the original station building is still in existence today as a private residence. Passenger traffic over the branch in the latter years was not very great, except on market days, and when Luton Town Football Club was playing at home, which sometimes brought football excursions bound for Luton and some interesting locomotive workings to the branch on through trains.

The LNWR owned the station at Dunstable North, situated adjacent to Watling Street at the top of the long climb from Stanbridgeford. Watling Street was originally to be crossed by level-crossing but authority would only be granted to the connection to the GNR if a bridge were provided. The matter was eventually resolved by a deviation from the original line of route to the west of the former Dunstable North station, crossing Watling Street by bridge under which the road passed in a shallow dip. As a result of this a new station was required, and the original LNWR terminus situated in what became the goods yard was closed. At the time of writing remains of the platforms and the station approach can still be explored, and the original alignment of the LNWR line into the goods yard remains apparent.

The Hertford, Luton & Dunstable Line was opened as we have seen from Luton to Dunstable in 1858, and worked from the outset by the LNWR until GNR trains were introduced from Hatfield on 1 September 1860. The LNWR, however, worked no more through trains from Leighton Buzzard to Luton until 1 April 1881. These were not finally withdrawn until closure of the branch and became known by the nickname 'The Skimpot' after a local farm passed by the trains!

The branch had no Sunday services because of a restrictive covenant with the landowner over whose land the predominant part of the branch ran. For many years the LNWR provided a weekdays-only service of seven trains each way, some of which ran through to Luton.

The line was operated for a long period by Webb 0–6–2 and 2–4–2 tank locomotives, replaced in the early 1950s by H. G. Ivatt's 2–6–2Ts which handled the passenger trains almost entirely until the end of steam. The final train, which ran on 30 June 1962, was in fact hauled by one of these locomotives No 41222, and the push-and-pull train was called 'The Last Dasher' after the nickname for which these trains were known. The nature of the branch required far more powerful locomotives for freight traffic, and ex-LNWR 0–8–0s, sometimes in tandem, provided an invigorating sight on the 1 in 40 incline between Stanbridgeford and Dunstable North. In recent years, Stanier Class 8F 2–8–0s and occasional Class 5 4–6–0 locomotives made appearances over the branch, penetrating as far as Bute Street, providing an interesting mix of LMR and ER locomotives between Dunstable and Luton. Until closed from 5 November 1962, there was a small brick two-road shed at Leighton Buzzard to house the locomotives working on the branch. Occasionally, ex-GNR 0–6–2T locomotives were known to work through to Leighton Buzzard on goods trains.

CHAPTER 3

The Vale of Aylesbury

Introduction

The Vale of Aylesbury has much to offer the student not only of railways, but of geography and local history and indeed, the countryman and those seeking the peace of England's rural byways. Geographically, the area forms part of a wide clay vale stretching northwards from the foot of the Chiltern Hills and is pleasantly undulating prosperous countryside. At its western end is the historic City of Oxford, while its eastern borders merge with the stark industrial areas of Bedfordshire, in marked contrast to the pastoral landscapes of the Vale.

The presence of the Chilterns along the southern edge of the area produces an interesting pattern of communications, with natural gaps in the line of hills providing funnels for north-to-south road and rail routes. These gaps are commanded by the towns of Dunstable, Tring, Wendover, Princes Risborough, Stokenchurch and Wallingford and of these, only Stokenchurch was not on a main or branch line route. Within the Vale itself secondary east-to-west lines of communication became established and several railway projects were promoted to meet this need.

77

The town of Aylesbury is the focal point of the area, and its early status as a railway junction gave it superiority over its neighbour, the former county town of Buckingham. The Aylesbury Railway, a short direct branch from the London & Birmingham Railway at Cheddington, was first to serve the town. The Aylesbury & Buckingham Railway also had a terminus here, while the projected southern arm of the Buckinghamshire Railway, although never completed, was intended to pass through the town on its way to join the L & B at Tring. Of the lines included in this chapter, only the Wotton Tramway, which joined the A & B at Quainton Road, was not originally intended to reach Aylesbury.

Aylesbury has been a market centre for many centuries. It now plays a dominant role in the economic life of the region and can owe this heritage in some part to the early development of the railways which served it. Needless to say, the town is a good base from which to set out in search of clues to the railways of a bygone era.

The Aylesbury Railway

The Aylesbury Railway was a seven mile long, single track branch from Cheddington, junction with the L & B, to Aylesbury. The rationale for the branch goes back to the 1820s when George Stephenson surveyed a railway route between London and Birmingham via Uxbridge, the Wendover Gap, Aylesbury and Coventry, following a similar route to Aylesbury to that later chosen by the Metropolitan Railway. The proposal met unyielding opposition from landowners in the Chilterns and consequently Robert Stephenson's L & B adopted an alignment to the east of Aylesbury.

A scheme was accordingly proposed in November 1835 to link the town by then the county town of Buckinghamshire, with the main line, and it was Sir Harry Verney, a prominent local landowner, who helped the railway company to obtain its Act on 19 May 1836. Construction work was initially postponed because of a proposal to open a line to Cheltenham via Aylesbury, but this failed, and work on the branch commenced

in May 1838 under the direction of Robert Stephenson. The
line, operated from the outset by locomotives and stock of the
L & B, was opened to the public on 10 June 1839 and the day
was declared a public holiday in Aylesbury. At Cheddington,
the line made a north facing junction with the L & B and

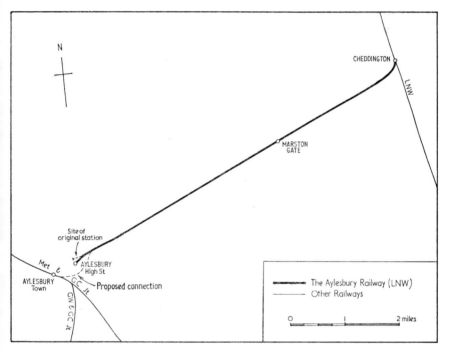

Map of the Aylesbury Railway

curved away at almost right-angles from it, proceeding with
very easy gradients in a virtually straight alignment to Aylesbury. It had only one intermediate station Marston Gate which,
like Stanbridgeford, was situated in a relatively flat, exposed
location and is now used as a private residence.

The railway remained the only link serving the large area of
virgin territory between the GWR and the L & B until the
Buckinghamshire Railway was partially opened eleven years

later, and it was the only line to reach Aylesbury prior to the extension of the Wycombe Railway in 1863.

The company's early financial history was unstable, but somehow the line was constructed and the company managed to survive. In 1844, the London, Worcester & South Staffordshire Railway Company planned to absorb the greater part of the line, and a year later a further company, the Aylesbury & Thame Junction Railway, proposed an extension of the branch to Thame along the foot of the Chilterns, but both plans came to nothing. The L & B opposed the A & TJR by initially supporting a further scheme, the Cambridge & Oxford Railway. The L & B did not approve of the C & OR as it would have run through its territory, and the L & B already wished to link the University towns. After the Thame extension had been abandoned, it withdrew support to the C & OR. The L & B finally absorbed the Aylesbury branch under powers obtained on 16 July 1846.

The LNWR, as the L & B now became, retained its initial monopoly of services to Aylesbury until the GWR and the A & B reached the town. The new spirit of competition however forced the LNWR to take positive action to improve services over the branch, but in spite of this, traffic remained relatively stable until the arrival of the Metropolitan Railway in 1892. With the imminent threat from the more direct route to the capital, the LNWR immediately began improving its facilities at Aylesbury, but the changes were too little and too late, and the best days of the branch quietly passed into history. A great improvement was made, when on 16 June 1889 the LNWR opened a new station with a frontage onto the High Street, replacing the less conveniently sited original station described in Whishaw's *Railways of Great Britain & Ireland* (*1842*) shortly after it was opened as:

> . . . one of the best arranged stations for a short line of railway that we have anywhere met with.

On 1 January 1894 the joint Metropolitan and GWR station was opened and immediately assumed greater imporance, particularly after through GCR main line trains became available. The LNWR could no longer compete for the London traffic and a decline set in, although passenger services on the branch lingered until withdrawn with effect from 2 February 1953. The final passenger train was hauled by ex-LNWR Webb 2–4–2 tank No 46601.

Aylesbury is served, as was Buckingham, by an arm of the Grand Junction Canal, which indicated that even in the early years there was some freight potential in the town. Aylesbury was therefore provided with a small goods yard, adjacent to the station, with siding connection to the gasworks which generated a substantial traffic in coal. Agricultural products and livestock were also carried and in particular there was a heavy flow of milk traffic. A small locomotive shed was situated in the yard.

With BR's freight concentration policy of the early 1960s the remaining freight traffic, which sometimes brought Stanier Class 5 4–6–0 and 8F 2–8–0s in addition to ex-LNWR 0–8–0s, Ivatt Class 2 2–6–2Ts and BR Class 4 2–6–4Ts to the branch, once a haunt of the delightful Webb tanks, was withdrawn and the line eventually closed from 2 December 1963.

The Metropolitan Railway North of Aylesbury

The crowded commuter trains which ply to and from Baker Street station during the daily London peak hours seem a far cry from those trains which used to run to the rural outposts once commanded by the Metropolitan Railway. Today, the 'Metropolitan's' influence extends only as far as Amersham in the Chiltern foothills and it is interesting to remember that trains of the Metropolitan Railway once ran to Aylesbury and the countryside beyond.

Apart from the transition from steam to diesel multiple units on BR trains from Marylebone and Princes Risborough, little has changed south of Aylesbury. Since 1966 Aylesbury has been the terminus for all trains, except occasional freight workings using the remaining single track of the former Great Central alignment through Quainton Road to Calvert.

The section of line between Aylesbury and the former Quainton Road Station is thirty years older than the Great Central, having originally been the route of the Aylesbury & Buckingham Railway, which diverged at Quainton Road to make a junction with the LNWR at Claydon. It is with the A & B and the Wotton Tramway, which ran from Quainton Road to Brill that the Metropolitan Railway once attempted to further its status from pioneer underground railway to becoming an important main line company.

The Aylesbury & Buckingham Railway

The Aylesbury & Buckingham Railway was incorporated by an Act of Parliament on 6 August 1860 to construct a railway from Claydon, on the Buckinghamshire Railway, to Aylesbury. The A & B's seemingly tenuous link with the Buckinghamshire Railway project was in fact far more significant, as the original scheme of that company had been to extend southwards via Aylesbury to Tring to connect with the LNWR as part of an ambitious project to open up the County for the first time. Powers had been obtained for the route from Claydon to Aylesbury in the Act authorising the Buckinghamshire Railway, considered more fully in the next section, but because of opposition from the LNWR the option was never exercised and was allowed to lapse. This left an important section of the north-to-south line of communications incomplete between Claydon and Aylesbury across the Vale.

Pressure from local interests to complete the line was great and in 1850 a group of memorialists, which included Acton Tindal, a well-known Clerk of the Peace in Aylesbury, and Sir Harry Verney and Frederick Calvert, who were both large landowners in North Buckinghamshire, petitioned the LNWR, only to receive further rebuffs from Euston. Demand was such that it was only a matter of time and money before the need for the rail link across the Vale was satisfied. Eventually, the initiative came from the local landowners, who were headed by

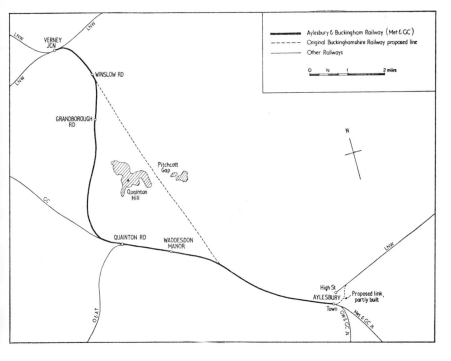

Map of the Aylesbury & Buckingham Railway

the Marquis of Chandos (later to become the third and final
Duke of Buckingham and Chandos in 1861) who was chairman
of the LNWR from 1853 to 1861, and Sir Harry Verney, MP
for Buckingham, both of whom had previously been driving
forces behind the Buckinghamshire Railway. The Duke of
Buckingham was appointed chairman and Sir Harry Verney
the vice chairman of the new concern.

The original proposals of the Buckinghamshire Railway had
been for a direct route between Claydon and Aylesbury through
the Pitchcott Gap, east of Quainton Hill. Under the Duke of
Buckingham's influence, however, the route chosen by the A &
B was more circuitous, deviating to the west of Quainton Hill,
bringing the railway closer to the Duke's estates at Wotton.
The line then approached Aylesbury from the north west and

it was proposed that by circling the southern part of the town, a junction could be effected with the Aylesbury Railway.

Parliamentary assent to the connection was received but in the meantime LNWR policy had altered and, as no satisfactory working agreement could be reached, the link with the Aylesbury Railway though started was never completed. Instead, the A & B looked to the proposed extension of the Wycombe Railway, operated by the GWR, as a potential new ally. Its approach to the GWR for an operating agreement was readily accepted by Paddington, which was only too happy to obtain a foothold in LNWR territory.

The Wycombe Railway reached Aylesbury 24 years after the LNWR branch from Cheddington and its single-track route was opened on 1 October 1863. It was originally laid as broad gauge, but after the agreement was reached to operate the A & B, provision was made in 1868 to convert it to standard gauge to be compatible with the A & B. Conversion began on 14 October 1868 and was completed to enable services on the branch to be reinstated from 23 October: this was the first GWR line to be so treated. As work on narrowing the gauge was not started until after the opening of the A & B, rolling stock for the new line had to be brought to Aylesbury via Oxford and Verney Junction.

The A & B, also single track, was finally opened on 23 September 1868 having taken eight years to build. It was operated from the outset by the GWR under the working agreement and intermediate stations were provided at Winslow Road, Grandborough Road and Quainton Road. An additional station between Aylesbury and Quainton Road was opened by the Metropolitan on 1 January 1897 and named Waddesdon Manor, now reduced to a mound of earth. The northern terminus at Claydon, junction with the LNWR, was named Verney Junction after Sir Harry, on whose land it was built.

In 1874, the GWR had the chance to absorb the A & B which throughout the first six years of its history had been operated by its own staff, except for footplate crews who were

GWR employees. The opportunity was missed by the GWR and the local company remained in private ownership until later approached and absorbed by the Metropolitan Railway on 1 July 1891, vesting powers having been obtained by an Act of 25 July 1890.

Metropolitan services north of Aylesbury were largely the result of the speculative influence of the remarkable Sir Edward Watkin who, towards the end of the nineteenth century, besides being chairman of the Metropolitan, held similar posts with the Manchester, Sheffield & Lincolnshire Railway and the South Eastern Railway. It is widely credited that he envisaged a through route between Lancashire and the Continent using the Metropolitan as a convenient cross-London connection between the other two systems, linking nicely with the Channel Tunnel project, then also under consideration. The acquisition of the A & B by the Metropolitan was probably motivated by this scheme.

It is not really surprising to discover the Metropolitan Railway extending its line from Chalfont Road (Chalfont & Latimer) to Aylesbury, with the result that the former main line between Chalfont Road and Chesham now became a branch of the Aylesbury line. The new Aylesbury section was opened on 1 September 1892 and a temporary station was provided at Brook Street until a junction could be installed by the GWR to enable Metropolitan trains to work into the main station.

Aylesbury station of the GWR and A & B has always been a joint station. When the Wycombe Railway extension from Princes Risborough was being surveyed, the GWR had intended to open its own station in Aylesbury closer to the town centre. However, this would have prevented the A & B from either completing a junction with the Aylesbury Railway or extending southwards along the Missenden valley as had been previously mooted by the Company. The A & B subsequently objected to the GWR proposals and an agreement was reached to open the joint station, ideal for the operating arrangement later agreed between the two companies. When the Metropolitan absorbed the A & B, it negotiated new agreements with the GWR and modified the joint station to accommodate the extra services: the present station was opened on 1 January 1894.

Soon after taking over the A & B, the Metropolitan commenced doubling the track in preparation for through services from the City to Verney Junction, in the heart of Buckinghamshire, 50½ miles from the Metropolitan's Baker Street headquarters. By the close of the nineteenth century, therefore, the A & B was set to enter a new phase of prosperity and expansion under the management of the Metropolitan Railway. However, a further development was in the offing which was to stem the Metropolitan's gallant advance. A new north–south main line was to be forged by the Manchester, Sheffield & Lincolnshire Railway (which became the Great Central Railway in 1897) directly through the centre of Buckinghamshire and the Vale of Aylesbury, successfully bringing a trunk route to the area on alignment previously envisaged by the London & Birmingham Railway seventy years earlier. The extension, which joined the Metropolitan about a quarter of a mile north of the newly reconstructed Quainton Road station, was opened to passenger traffic in March 1899, having been available for coal trains some months earlier. As a more direct route northwards via Calvert it soon overshadowed the section of the former A & B from Quainton Road to Verney Junction and the Great Central stifled any further northward expansion of the Metropolitan Railway.

The Great Central's intrusion into Metropolitan territory south of Quainton Road brought friction and conflict between the officials of the two companies. In his book *Great Central*, Vol II, George Dow relates the remarkable incident at Quainton Road which occurred on 25 July 1898 when Mr J. Bell, then general manager of the Metropolitan Railway, tried unsuccessfully to stop the GCR from exercising its running rights over the Metropolitan between Aylesbury and London. The result of the incident was that the GCR looked to the GWR for assistance in much the same way as the A & B had done under its earlier disagreement with the LNWR and, by a joint Act of Parliament of 1 August 1899, the GWR and GCR promoted a

Page 87 (*above*) Henlow station before the line was singled, with architecture of the style of the Leicester & Hitchin Extension; (*below*) LNWR 4–4–0 25319 drifts down from the flyover into Sandy with a train from Bletchley to Cambridge in 1936

Page 88 (*above*) GER 0–6–0 65450 with the 17.25 Kettering to Cambridge waits for an Ivatt Class 2 at Kimbolton on 11 June 1959; (*below*) MR 0–4–4T 2022 and 0–6–0T 212 with the first train at Higham Ferrers on 1 May 1894. Beyond the bridge lay the goods yard and the intended course to Raunds

line from Grendon Underwood, a mile or so north of Quainton Road Station, to Ashendon and Princes Risborough, giving the GCR access to either Marylebone or Paddington Stations. A large proportion of the Great Central traffic was subsequently directed by the alternative route over the joint lines and Aylesbury lost the potential opportunity of a more intensive main line service to London.

From 2 April 1906, all Metropolitan services north of Harrow South Junction to Verney Junction, including the Brill Branch, came under the auspices of the Metropolitan & Great Central Joint Committee, set up under an Act of 1905 to manage the joint lines of the two companies. A similar joint committee was established between the GWR and GCR. Apart from the grouping in 1923, when the GCR became vested in the LNER, little organisational change to the management of services north of Aylesbury occurred until 1933 when the Metropolitan Railway was absorbed as part of the London Passenger Transport Board. The former A & B remained jointly operated until as an economy measure the Board withdrew passenger services between Aylesbury and Verney Junction from 6 July 1936.

Despite generally light passenger loadings, the former A & B maintained a special character of its own, and its considerable goods workings continued even after initial closure to passengers in 1936. The two World Wars brought an increase in freight traffic as the line from Verney Junction into London was a valuable alternative to other main lines to the capital. Considerable volumes of goods passed through the transfer sidings at Verney Junction during and after World War II and Quainton Road was also an important freight distribution yard. In 1939, the line between Quainton Road and Verney Junction was singled and freight services were totally withdrawn over this section from 8 September 1947. A connecting spur, brought into use on 14 September 1940, was provided between the LNWR and GCR lines at Calvert, which enabled freight traffic from the Oxford to Bletchley line to work south over the GCR and allowed much of the traffic previously passing over the Verney Junction to Quainton Road line to be diverted to the Calvert route. Quainton Road station was closed to passengers finally from 4 March 1963 and goods from 4 July 1966. All regular passenger services north of Aylesbury were withdrawn from 5 September 1966.

Returning briefly to the early years of the twentieth century, an interesting Pullman train service was introduced by the Metropolitan on 1 June 1910 with the object of competing with the improved services for first class passengers offered by the GCR. The Metropolitan operated two Pullman cars for the purpose, *Mayflower* and *Galatea*, and used them on alternate weeks between Verney Junction, Chesham and the City. After the closure of the Verney section, the Pullman cars were retained for the Aylesbury and Chesham services until finally withdrawn in early October 1939 and sold.

The first passenger services on the A & B under the operating agreement with the GWR used former Oxford, Worcester & Wolverhampton Railway coaching stock acquired from the West Midland Railway when it was absorbed by the GWR. Local GWR services north of Aylesbury continued until 31 March 1894 when these facilities were suddenly withdrawn, and as the Metropolitan had no suitable light-weight loco-motives and rolling stock, services were run briefly with stock loaned from the LNWR. In due course, the track was re-laid and in the late 1890s the Metropolitan began local and through services with new stock.

GWR motive power between Aylesbury and Verney Junc-tion was provided initially by two light 0-4-2 saddle tank engines of the 1040 Class supplied new to the line, later replaced by side tank engines. After the LNWR interlude, early local Metropolitan services were worked by two 'D' Class 2-4-0T locomotives Nos 71 and 72, built by Sharp Stewart & Co in 1895, and these were later transferred for a brief spell on the Brill branch. Prior to World War I, through passenger and freight traffic north of Aylesbury was handled mainly by 0-4-4 'E' and 0-6-2 'F' Class tanks, but during 1915 the first of the 'G' Class 0-6-4 tanks became available to haul the heavier trains arising from wartime conditions. The 'main line' spirit of the Metropolitan Railway lingered well into the twentieth century and, as trains became heavier, the Company sought new and larger tank designs which culminated in the final phase of its locomotive development in the 1920s. This final fling saw the advent of the large 'H' Class 4-4-4 tank locomotives, followed shortly afterwards by a batch of six 'K' Class 2-6-4 locomotives, built in 1925 by Armstrong, Whitworth & Co, to a design by R. E. L. Maunsell. Both the latter classes put in good work north of Aylesbury, the 'K' Class being particularly useful on freight workings between Verney Junction and Finchley Road.

After closure, the track was eventually lifted but the northern section of the line between Verney Junction and Winslow Road, including the former Metropolitan transfer sidings at Verney Junction, was retained until the early 1960s for storage of rolling stock. Many veteran railway vehicles subsequently spent their final years here, rotting on tracks which had never carried very heavy levels of traffic, but which had played an interesting role in the expansion of the Metropolitan Railway Company.

The Brill Branch

To all but its regular users, the Brill Branch of the Metropolitan Railway was something of an enigma. Observing its situation in a sparsely populated part of rural Buckinghamshire, anyone unaware of its colourful history might well have asked about its original purpose. The nearest it came to serving a population of any size was at its western terminus, situated at the foot of Brill Hill, upon which stands the picturesque village of Brill, noted in the past for the nearby spa at Dorton.

A closer analysis reveals the story of a line which promised greater things but never quite achieved them. The Brill branch was another imaginative project of the third and last Duke of Buckingham and Chandos, and was built primarily to serve his estates at Wotton, after the completion of the A & B in 1868. Construction work started, using estate workers, on 8 September 1870 and, being almost entirely laid on the Duke's land, required no Act of Parliament.

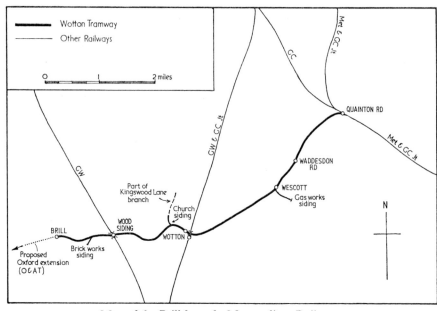

Map of the Brill branch, Metropolitan Railway

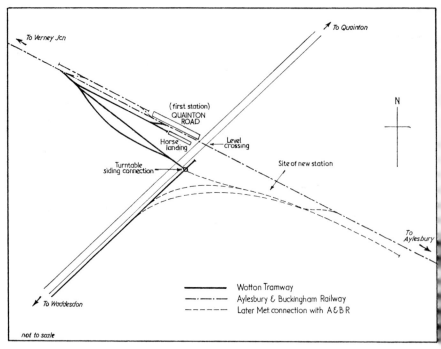

Plan showing the original Brill Tramway connection, Quainton Road

The 6½ mile line, built to standard gauge and laid on longitudinal sleepers, was opened to Wotton on 1 April 1871 and the extension to a brickworks near Brill was completed by November that year, although evidence suggests that certain sections of the line had been opened before that date. The final three-quarter-mile section to the terminus at Brill was opened during the Summer of 1872.

The original purpose of the tramway-type light railway was to carry agricultural produce and minerals to and from the Duke's estates, but because of local public demand, in particular from the residents of Brill, a passenger service was commenced in January 1872, utilising a borrowed carriage and a four-wheeled Aveling & Porter geared locomotive. The railway was under construction during a period of great interest in light agricultural railways in the UK and the line's early history was recorded in several documents published at the time.

WOTTON TRAMWAY (1871 - 1935)
TRAIN AT WOOD SIDING.

Woodland peace is momentarily broken; Metropolitan A Class 4-4-0T pauses at Wood Siding before continuing the final leg of its journey to Brill

The railway was first known as the Wotton Tramway, but was later called the Oxford & Aylesbury Tramroad, after the company formed to carry out an abortive attempt to reach Oxford. After having been taken over by the Metropolitan Railway the line became known simply as the Brill Branch. At Quainton Road Station, the tramway originally met the A & B at right-angles and no direct junction was provided, although a connection was made by means of a small turntable at the end of the tramway which enabled trucks to be turned through 90° and propelled into a short siding which joined the A & B to the north of the original station.

The first A & B station at Quainton consisted of a single platform to the north-west of the present site close to a level crossing which carried the road across the railway at this point. This crossing was later replaced by the Metropolitan Railway who provided the present overbridge after resiting the station and doubling the A & B in 1896. The Metropolitan also provided a bay platform for the tramway and installed a junction with the A & B facing towards Aylesbury. The bridge over the A & B line was opened and the level crossing closed in 1899.

For just over the first mile, the tramway followed closely to the south side of a lane to Waddesdon Road Station, after which the line crossed fields to Westcott, where there was a short spur to serve a small private gasworks built to supply Waddesdon Manor. At Wotton, the original objective of the tramway, the line was later crossed by the Great Central Railway's Metropolitan avoiding line, constructed as a joint venture with the Great Western, referred to previously. This section of the GCR was opened to passenger traffic in 1906 and together with the GWR Ashendon to Aynho line, which became part of the Birmingham direct line opened four years later, abstracted a considerable amount of traffic from the tramway.

A longer spur from the tramway was a branch of about $1\frac{1}{2}$ miles to a coal wharf at Moate Farm on Kingswood Lane which was also in use by November 1871. This branch made connection with the tramway at Church Siding, which for many years was an advertised station on the railway. Here was also a large wooden water tower which marked the site of a well sunk to replenish water for the locomotives. Little appears to have been recorded of the history of the Kingswood branch, but it seems that it never carried passengers and remained horse-worked to the end. Trucks consigned to the wharf were shunted into Church Siding by the locomotive of a passing train and laboriously hauled the remaining distance by man and beast. Local stories also blame the poor siting of the wharf, which was situated on low ground prone to flooding, on the toss of the hat of the dogmatic duke in an argument with an adviser. Where the hat fell, so the story goes, the wharf was built! Traffic ceased in 1910 and rails were lifted in 1915, leaving only a short section of about a quarter of a mile in length known as Church Siding, which remained until closure.

The final intermediate station on the line was situated in the woods near Brill at a point where the GWR main line to Aynho later passed beneath. The little platform, and the short siding for collecting local farm produce, was tucked away amongst the trees and was known appropriately as Wood Siding. The station was a popular alighting point in the summer months for local picknickers going to the woods, and by all accounts it was a delightfully quiet spot. A short distance further towards Brill were sidings into a small brick and tile works, which provided the tramway with some valuable freight traffic throughout the year. Later, the premises were converted into a factory for a company manufacturing hayloaders and use of the sidings for its products continued until closure of the branch. Today, the buildings are still in use as a sawmill for the local forestry industry.

Brill station, the isolated terminus of the tramway, was reached after negotiating a sharp reverse bend. A diminutive wooden two-road engine-shed, somewhat akin to a large garden tool-shed, was built at the eastern end of the site, while a substantial goods shed stood adjacent to the station platform. Between the two, in later years, stood the remains of the original tramway-type car which was used as a plate-layer's hut until closure of the branch. Photographs of the station and of the whole branch during the early 1930s record the beautiful antiquity of the line, which became a haven for those who wished to escape from the rigours of urban life, as little seemed to have changed on the branch over the previous thirty years of Metropolitan rule!

A further interesting aspect of the early operation of the tramway was the duke's insistence on a printed book of *Rules & Regulations for the Conduct of the Traffic, and for the Guidance of the Officers and Men engaged on the Wotton Tramway* and a table of fines for those found guilty of breaking them! All this would seem quite unnecessary for a railway which operated with no fixed signals and one engine in steam, except when viewed in the light of its promoter having formerly been chairman of the giant LNWR. Obviously the high standards of a full-scale railway were demanded by the duke when these documents were published in January and March 1873 respectively over the signature of the manager, a Mr R. A. Jones.

The line had been operating for less than eleven years in its simple tramway form when an extension from Brill to Oxford was suggested which, had it been constructed, might have done much to transform the prosperity of this part of Buckingham-shire. The railway as planned would have provided a useful west-to-east line of communication across the Vale of Aylesbury linking the towns of Aylesbury and Oxford. Once again, the proposal was supported by the same landed interests who had been behind the Buckinghamshire and Aylesbury & Buckingham Railway projects.

On 20 August 1883, an Act of Parliament incorporated the Oxford, Aylesbury & Metropolitan Junction Railway Company, with the Duke of Buckingham and Sir Harry Verney as directors, with powers to construct a railway from premises in the High Street, St Clements, Oxford to Quainton Road, and running powers over the A & B to Aylesbury. The line was to have been completely reconstructed under the OA & MJR plan as the Oxford branch of Watkin's new trunk route, and electric traction was also briefly considered.

Cash was scarce, however, and during the five years allowed by the Act for completion of the line, little work had been carried out. As a result a further Act, allowing for a less ambitious project, was passed on 7 August 1888. It provided for the alteration of the name to the Oxford & Aylesbury Tramroad Company and substituted the construction of a tramroad extension for the railway project, which was to be abandoned. Another Act, providing a two-year extension of the O & AT powers, was passed in 1892 and a final Bill of 1894, which never became law, proposed a deviation from the original course of the extension. The nearest achieved to any progress was at the end of September 1894 when the O & AT, having taken over operation of the line from October 1894, commenced relaying the track with heavier rails and transverse sleepers, re-opening the line during December, although the line was again completely relaid by the Metropolitan Railway in 1910. The lack of available finance and in 1889 the death of the duke, who had played such a leading role in the development of the railways of the Vale of Aylesbury, were contributory causes of the failure of the extension scheme. After the duke's death, the line became vested in his nephew, Earl Temple, in whom it remained until closure.

No further significant changes took place until 1 December 1899 when the Metropolitan Railway took over the lease of the tramway, with an option to purchase the line outright. This option, as with the O & AT's earlier opportunity to buy the railway, was never exercised and, on closure of the Brill Branch after traffic on 30 November 1935, ownership reverted to the freeholders, with whom it rests today. As with the Verney Junction section, the branch came under the control of the Metropolitan & Great Central Joint Committee in 1906 and its operation was transferred to the London Passenger Transport Board in 1933.

The first motive power to work the tramway was two Aveling & Porter geared locomotives, one of which is preserved by London Transport along with Metropolitan Railway 'A' Class tank No 23, which also worked for some years on the line. Two new Bagnall 0–4–0 saddle tanks were soon purchased; the first, named *Buckingham*, arrived in 1876, followed a year later by the other named *Wotton*. The reason for purchase of these locomotives remains a mystery, unless they had some connection with the proposed Oxford extension, since the traffic was easily handled by the geared locomotives, which remained in service until 1894. With the takeover by the O & AT, two Manning Wardle & Co 0–6–0 saddle tanks were bought. No 1 *Huddersfield* built in 1876, was second-hand, and was subsequently renamed *Wotton No 1*, but No 2 *Brill* was newly built. In 1899, *Wotton* was replaced by a third Manning Wardle named *Wotton No 2*. As the Metropolitan Railway influence became felt, various Metropolitan tank designs were tried on the branch, but eventually several already aged Beyer Peacock 'A' Class 4–4–0 tank locomotives were selected to spend years of semi-retirement providing the basic motive power for the tramway until its closure. Nos 23 and 41 were the two usually seen on the line, and No 41 hauled the final train.

Many older inhabitants of the area still gratefully recall the service given by the tramway and wonder whether, had the Oxford extension proceeded, developments in the locality might have been different. Although closure of a branch which possessed so much rural charm and beauty is sad, it is good to know that a preservation society is restoring Quainton Road station. Perhaps some charm may yet return to remind future generations of exploits of the Metropolitan north of Aylesbury!

The Buckinghamshire Railway—A Faithful Servant

> So now to all the Shareholders,
> Wishing them good reserves,
> Likewise their Noble Chairman,
> For he great praise deserves
> And to all concern'd upon the line,
> Who moved the clay and rocks—
> I am your humble servant still—
> CHARLES WHITEHALL, Gawcott, Bucks.
> 1849

The simple words of this rhyme by a local Buckinghamshire poet introduces a railway which well served the north of the

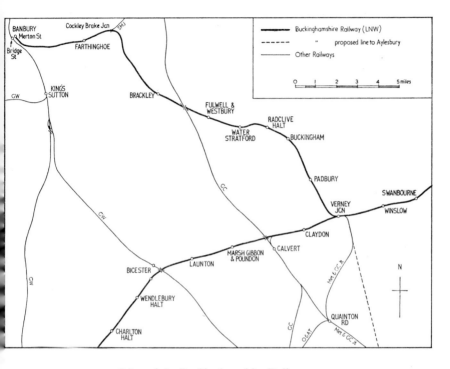

Map of the Buckinghamshire Railway

county of Buckinghamshire and the Vale for well over a hundred
years. Assuming the name of the Buckinghamshire Railway it
had an interesting derivation. During the war fought inter-
mittently between the London & Birmingham and Great
Western Railways over which should control the intermediate
areas between their enlarging spheres of interest, the first railway
mania, which reached its heights in 1845, brought competing
rail route proposals to this insecure railway territory. One such
line was the Buckinghamshire Railway, whose purpose it was
to link the large tracts of countryside and the small but prosperous townships of the county hitherto without railway communication.

The Buckinghamshire Railway as first envisaged was never

99

completed, and it remained primarily a local line serving the border localities where Buckinghamshire meets Northamptonshire and Oxfordshire. When still in its embryonic stages, however, it became a pawn in the tactical warfare between the two great companies over the territorial and gauge questions. A glance at a map of Buckinghamshire in 1845 immediately shows the predicament as far as the area was concerned, for it lay directly between the disputed domains of the L & B and GWR.

The L & B opened its line from Euston to Tring on 16 October 1837, extending along the eastern side of the county to a temporary terminus at Denbigh Hall, just over two miles north of the village of Bletchley in April, and to Birmingham in September 1838 respectively. In June that year the GWR opened the first stage of Brunel's 118½ mile broad gauge line from Paddington to Bristol, skirting the southern edge of the county, further opening a branch from Didcot to Oxford on 12 June 1844. In the same year, it began scheming the Oxford & Rugby Railway, posing the first serious territorial threat to the L & B. At this time yet another project supported by the GWR, the Oxford, Worcester & Wolverhampton Railway, was being planned which would again take the broad gauge deep into the heart of the Midlands. By 1845, therefore, the county had become almost encircled but, apart from the Aylesbury Railway it had no railway facilities, and offered itself as virgin territory to the two major railway companies. The L & B, supported by the Midland, saw the GWR schemes as a menacing two-pronged intrusion by the competing company, and immediately sprang into counter-attack by supporting the London, Worcester & South Staffordshire Railway.

Excellent accounts appear elsewhere of the ensuing fight between the companies over the gauge and territorial problem! First, the Board of Trade appointed a group of five well-known figures from the commercial and railway worlds to consider competing schemes such as these; then, in June 1845, Captain Mark Huish of the Grand Junction Railway pledged his company's support to the GWR schemes with a view to forcing the L & B into amalgamation with his own company, eventually achieved with formation of the LNWR in 1846; finally it resulted in the Gauge Commission, whose recommendations came out largely against the broad gauge, and the Gauge Act which followed in August 1846. The problem was resolved with the formation of the LNWR, and the successful passage of the Oxford & Rugby, and Oxford, Worcester & Wolverhampton Railway Acts through Parliament. The L & B subsequently withdrew its London, Worcester & South Staffordshire Railway and the OW & WR went ahead, becoming the West Midland Railway before being absorbed by the GWR in 1863. The O & RR, however, reached no further than Fenny Compton, where it was eventually to make connection with a further company, the Birmingham & Oxford Junction Railway, giving the GWR its route to Birmingham.

The brief outline of the gauge and territorial war in this area is a necessary preamble to the skirmish that led up to the Buckinghamshire Railway. The B & OJR was originally fostered by the Grand Junction Railway during its conflict with the L & B. When the LNWR was formed, the Birmingham & Oxford Junction Railway nevertheless proceeded in spite of withdrawal of the GJR's support, looking rather to the GWR as an ally. The L & B had already seen the challenge, and with help from the Midland who introduced its supporting Warwickshire & London Railway scheme, proposed a system of loop lines which were intended to defeat the new intrusion and, once and for all, annex the Buckinghamshire territory into its empire.

During the Committee stages of the Bills in the Commons, the GWR was unsuccessful in opposing the Buckinghamshire Bill, but the House of Lords were more sympathetic and preferred the GWR's arguments. As a result, the Birmingham & Oxford Junction Railway obtained its Act in full at the expense of the loop line scheme which was only partially sanctioned. The remains of the proposed loop lines became the Buckingham & Brackley Junction Railway and the Oxford & Bletchley Junction Railway.

Progress was achieved by the initiative of the Duke of Buckingham and Sir Harry Verney, who conceived the Buckinghamshire project as an excellent opportunity to serve the wide areas of their county still without railway communication. The railway was to take the form of a cross, the southern arm as first proposed being a line from Harrow to Aylesbury. This was soon abandoned as it required two substantial tunnels and resources were limited, and the proposal was reduced to only the centre portion from Claydon (later Verney Junction) to Brackley (Buckingham & Brackley Junction Railway). Sanction was also obtained for the east-to-west arms of the cross from Bletchley to Oxford (Oxford & Bletchley Junction Railway).

By an Act of 1847, the two routes from Bletchley to Oxford and Brackley via Claydon were amalgamated into the Buckinghamshire Railway Company which successfully obtained in the same year a 9½ mile extension from Brackley to Banbury. At the same time, plans for the southern arm were revived and powers were obtained for a line from Claydon to Aylesbury which was planned as an extension to the Aylesbury Railway. LNWR opposition however led to the abandonment of the scheme only later fulfilled by the Aylesbury & Buckingham Railway.

Construction began in July 1847 but delays occurred through financial difficulties in late 1847 and in 1849, and as a result the section from Claydon to Banbury remained only single track instead of the double intended. The line from Bletchley to Banbury was completed on 30 March 1850 and opened to passengers amidst enthusiastic celebrations on 1 May that year, and to freight several weeks later. The Oxford line was opened to Islip on 1 October 1850, extended to a temporary station at Oxford Road on 2 December 1850, and opened throughout on 20 May 1851. Throughout the work the Buckinghamshire Railway had been supported by the LNWR, who worked the line from the outset, leasing the whole railway for 999 years from 1 July 1851 before finally absorbing it in 1879.

Little more need be said about the east-to-west line as this grew in importance, and although losing its passenger facilities from 1 January 1968, it remains today a relatively well-used freight route. The 1955 Railway Modernisation Plan proposed improvement of cross-country facilities between Oxford and Cambridge. The aim was to provide a link between the major main line railways outside the congested Greater London area, thereby allowing freight traffic to be transferred between railway regions and easing the burden on London marshalling yards. The story of changed policy is well known and need not be related here, but the Bletchley flyover remains a monument to the fruitless plan. Had the scheme not been partially put into force, however, it is conceivable that the former Buckinghamshire Railway in its entirety might well be closed today.

The single-line section from Verney Junction to Banbury however had no such strategic advantages and although attempts were made to save it, closure was inevitable. The major objective of the railway was Buckingham. This small market town has a long and historic past but because it was missed by the main line railways it failed to attract early development and tended to decline in relation to Aylesbury.

Before the railway, transport facilities to the town were not good, although William Potts records a coach service which in 1773 ran from the Red Lion Inn, Banbury, every Monday, Wednesday and Friday via Buckingham and Winslow to Holborn, returning on the alternate days. A branch of the Grand Union Canal also reached Buckingham in 1801 but even after the canal and the opening of the railway little development occurred.

The busiest part of the line was the $5\frac{1}{2}$ mile section from Merton Street to Cockley Brake, where there was a junction with the Stratford-upon-Avon & Midland Junction Railway. The relationship with the SMJ began with the Northampton & Banbury Railway, promoted in July 1847 to provide a connection to South Wales for the transport of ore from the Northamptonshire ironstone workings. No progress was made for many years but eventually the Northampton & Banbury Junction Railway, as the company had now become, managed to proceed with its scheme and the section from Towcester to

Cockley Brake Junction was opened throughout on 1 June 1872. The N & BJR was amalgamated into the SMJ from 1 July 1910. The LNWR and SMJ jointly served Farthinghoe and Merton Street until absorbed into the LMSR on 1 January 1923. Former SMJ passenger services were withdrawn from 2 July 1951.

Passenger traffic over the whole line was comparatively light, although the LNWR operated various specials and excursions over the years to encourage greater use. Passenger levels reached their peak just before World War I, after which they declined more-or-less continually as competition from the bus and growing car ownership began to increase. World War II brought a shortlived improvement but with new BR management the line was obviously under review. A threat to its future became imminent in 1952 when BR reduced services to three trains each way per day, having withdrawn Towcester trains in the previous year. In spite of this, the line survived and was selected for an experiment as part of the 1955 Railway Modernisation Plan using lightweight single-unit diesel railcars. These units were introduced during the summer of 1956, the line being the first to be converted. Strangely, the units ran only from Banbury to Buckingham, where connection was made with the traditional steam push-pull service. New halts at Radclive and Water Stratford were opened between Fulwell & Westbury and Buckingham and a third on the edge of Buckingham was suggested but not provided.

The results of the experiment were significant, attracting a reported traffic increase of over 400 per cent. The services became well used on market days and Saturdays when the units, M79900 and M79901, ran together. In spite of the reduced costs and extra revenue from increased traffic, the improvement proved insufficient to save the service between Buckingham and Merton Street, which closed from 2 January 1961. The remaining passenger facilities between Buckingham, Verney Junction and Bletchley lingered until 7 September 1964 using the diesel units transferred from the Banbury section.

Freight comprised a considerable proportion of agricultural

Page 105 (*above*) In LMS days MR 0–6–0 3695 waits at Blisworth SMJR station. In the yard a horse-drawn cart is being loaded, while the LNWR station can be glimpsed behind the signal; (*below*) Towcester station in 1924, looking towards Greens Norton Junction. The group on the island platform appears to be measuring heights, possibly for a new footbridge

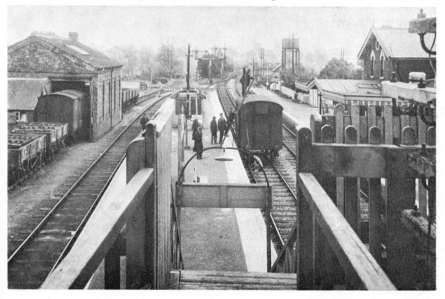

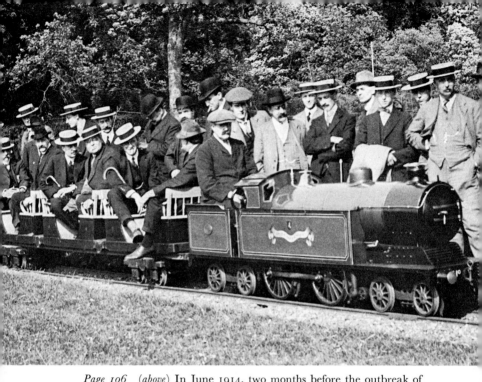

Page 106 (above) In June 1914, two months before the outbreak of the Kaiser's War, a Railway Club party takes a ride on the Blakesley Hall Miniature Railway; (below) SMJR 2–4–0T 5 waits at Kineton with two GCR coaches on a Stratford-upon-Avon to Marylebone service, about 1910

products with milk and cattle traffic forming a significant part. There was a cattle market next to Merton Street station and regular cattle train workings from Northampton via the SMJ were a feature of the line. These continued via Bletchley after closure of the SMJ. Iron ore trains from Wroxton were also transferred from the GWR at Banbury. Coal and building materials were carried in addition, while Buckingham yard was provided with oil storage facilities as early as the 1920s. As the smaller goods yards at stations along the line were closed during the early 1960s, freight delivery to the area was concentrated at Buckingham, until facilities there were finally withdrawn from 5 December 1966, after which all local deliveries were made by road from Bletchley.

The line was not only a faithful servant to the local population, but also to the gentry and aristocracy of the area. Stowe, the former home of the Duke of Buckingham, attracted a number of visitors to Buckingham and many arrived by the railway. The third and final Duke of Buckingham was given a civic welcome at the station in 1881 when he returned from service in India. Festivities again accompanied the arrival of the Duke after his marriage in 1885 and, following his death in 1889, a special train was operated to Quainton Road from Buckingham for mourners at the funeral at Wotton. For several years, the house was then let to the Comte de Paris and on occasions various dignitaries used the line to reach Stowe; a special train was operated on the death of the Comte in 1894. The Prince of Wales visited Stowe in 1898, but on 13 May 1950 the line received even more eminent Royal visitors. Mr H. Whitney, then stationmaster at Brackley, recalls the day he was honoured to entertain the late King George VI, Queen Elizabeth and other members of the Royal Family, on their way to nearby Silverstone. A final visit was made by the present Queen and the Duke of Edinburgh on 4 April 1966, sometime after the regular passenger train service had been withdrawn, and the Royal Train was stabled overnight at Padbury.

Financial difficulties at Stowe, which were ever-present during the early years of the nineteenth century, lingered until the house was finally sold in 1921, to become the famous Stowe Public School in 1923. This brought new traffic to the line and special trains were run at the beginning and end of terms to carry boys to and from the school. In the early 1960s new industry was established in Buckingham and the surrounding areas, but the railway unfortunately failed to attract additional patronage.

From 1 January 1968, the Buckinghamshire Railway finally lost its last passenger services, although in the spirit of its early history it did not fall without a fight. Perhaps the Vale might have been better served if trains had run direct from Banbury via Buckingham to Aylesbury and beyond, eliminating the change required at Verney Junction, but this can now only be conjecture. Although the promoters may have failed to unite the county by this railway, it will long be remembered as the line which first brought mobility to rural north Buckinghamshire and faithfully continued to do so for 116 years.

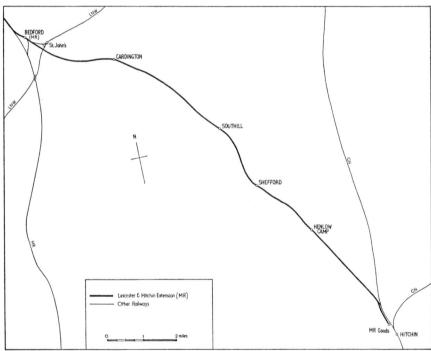

Map of the Leicester & Hitchin Extension, Midland Railway

CHAPTER 4

The Ouse Basin

Introduction

In the era of railway building, some areas seemed unusually destined by their very location for route promotion and if one project was unsuccessful, another would take its place within a few years. The Ouse Basin was one such area. The original proposals for all the lines considered in this chapter came to naught but the project was brought to fulfilment by other hands.

During the Railway Mania of the 1840s one of the schemes to be advanced to a public avid to purchase railway shares was the South Midland. Ultimately this was to form part of a trunk line from Leicester to London, a precursor of the later Leicester & Hitchin Extension, with the addition of a subsidiary branch to Huntingdon. It merged with a similar rival scheme but owing to the post-Mania slump it was never constructed.

When its successor, the Leicester & Hitchin, was promoted, the Great Northern replied with a proposed branch from Sandy to Bedford. It intended to follow much the same route as the line eventually built and would have terminated at the LNWR station in Bedford. Ultimately this project also was withdrawn and it later fell to the Bedford & Cambridge Railway to translate idea into reality.

Bedford to Hitchin

Having a quick pint in the *Leicester Railway* at Hitchin must have been no different from a drink in any other pub. True the name was odd, for any connection between Hitchin and Leicester would seem obscure, but then pubs often have strange names. Yet Hitchin was once connected with Leicester and, what is more, by a main line. But through trains only ran for a comparatively short time and were replaced by an obvious misfit, a branch line service. To understand this momentary glory, an appreciation of the early history of the Midland Railway is necessary.

In 1844 the three railways which centred on Derby amalgamated to form the Midland Railway. Having no route of its own to London, the Midland had to feed such traffic on to the London & Birmingham Railway from Rugby. The consequent delays to Midland traffic south of Rugby inspired the promotion of two schemes for alternative routes to London, which ultimately merged into a line from Leicester to Hitchin. Although the Act for this was passed, the Midland, who had adopted the joint scheme, suffered financial difficulties in the post-Mania slump and the project was abandoned.

By 1852 economic conditions had improved and local inhabitants began to press for a revival of the scheme. A deputation, an eminent member of which was William Whitbread, met the Midland board at Derby in that year. Whitbread, a prominent Bedfordshire landowner, left the board in no doubt that if it did not support the project, he would look elsewhere for assistance. Afraid that the line would be built by another company, the Midland introduced a Bill for the Leicester & Hitchin Extension, planned to join the Great Northern Railway main line at Hitchin and to make use of it to reach King's Cross. The decision to seek parliamentary powers was not only a defensive move, but was also influenced by the discovery of iron ore in Northamptonshire, a valuable traffic for the line, and by the congestion on the old London & Birmingham route between Rugby and Euston. The Great Northern at first opposed the line, proposing the construction of a branch from Sandy to Bedford, but agreement by arbitration was reached. In return for withdrawal of opposition, the Midland would provide a reasonable connecting service at Hitchin.

The Act for the new line was passed in 1853 and construction began with Thomas Brassey as the principal contractor, although Warden Tunnel was built by a local man, John Knowles of Shefford. The work was undertaken during the Crimean War, a period when the cost of labour and materials rose sharply. In order to economise, the engineers, Charles Liddell and John Crossley, had to keep the earthworks to a minimum; the consequent gradients with maxima of 1 in 120 have bedevilled the route ever since. The formal opening to passengers took place on 7 May 1857, a day treated as a public holiday in Bedford, where trains initially had to use the London & North Western station. Plans were originally made for a joint station, south of the Ouse, but these did not materialise and the Midland opened its own station on Freemen's Common, north of the Ouse, in 1859. All the stations were similarly built of local materials, outlined in red, with ornamental diamond-paned windows, a style unique to the Leicester & Hitchin.

Midland trains at first terminated at Hitchin but passenger services were extended to King's Cross in 1858. Initially there were four passenger trains a day each way on weekdays, with freight services commencing about six months later. Yet ultimately Hitchin was to prove as unsatisfactory as Rugby had been. Matters reached a head in the exhibition year of 1862, when the Great Northern summarily evicted the Midland from the overcrowded sidings at King's Cross. Forced to take a stand, the Midland determined to shake off the yoke of dependence on other companies to reach London. The extension from Bedford to St Pancras was the result and its opening in 1868 reduced the section to Hitchin to the status of a rural branch. Bereft of its *raison d'être*, the erstwhile trunk line faced a long period of gradual decline. Having been built as part of a trunk route, intermediate traffic had not been a primary consideration and so the section was ill-prepared to face its new role.

But face it, it did. Passenger facilities were reduced to a shuttle between Bedford and Hitchin, serving the intermediate communities, but some heavy freight services continued to use the line. Coal from the Midland for the Great Northern goods yard at Luton, for example, was forced to travel via Hitchin and Hatfield, as there was no connection between the two systems there until 1966. However, the decline in use prompted the Midland to reduce the branch to single track in 1911, except between Shefford and Southill. This ran into opposition from a farmers' organisation who tried to persuade the Great Northern to run trains over it, increasing its use and preventing singling.

The influence of the Whitbread family could be seen in this section of the line. Southill station had a private waiting room for the family and in Southill Park nearby stands a stone obelisk with the inscription, 'To William Henry Whitbread for his zeal and energy in promoting railways through the County of Bedford, 1864. Erected by Public Subscription.' Rumours abounded that the Whitbreads prohibited Sunday trains, but these were run when the route was a main line and also for a short period just before World War II, to enable conscripts to return home from RAF camps at Cardington and Henlow. Similarly the story that the Warden tunnel was forced on the Midland by Whitbread is untrue. The relief of the area makes a tunnel necessary and in any case this would be incompatible with William Whitbread's support of the Leicester & Hitchin, a support which extended to allowing a picnic to be held in his park for the passengers of an excursion train on the opening day.

The Whitbreads did have some connection with Warden Tunnel, as it was specifically exempted from the agreement made in 1905 between Samuel Whitbread and the Midland Railway. On payment of £1 a year, the Whitbread gamekeepers were permitted to enter the company's property between Shefford and Bedford to trap and protect game and birds' nests, but on no account were they to walk through the tunnel. Not that anybody would want to, as it had a reputation for bad smoke and fumes among the footplatemen, who were usually prepared with a wet handkerchief to cover mouth and nostrils. One driver of a freight train is said to have jumped off the footplate in the tunnel and run ahead into the open air. On another occasion a fireman climbed down to the bottom step of the tender to try and avoid the smoke. His temporary absence gave the driver a momentary shock!

Some developments did take place after the transformation, however, as recorded in the *Midland Railway Weekly Notices*. On 3 June 1890 new boxes were opened at Southill, Shefford and Henlow and block telegraph working was established between Southill and the Midland Goods Yard, Hitchin. Similarly block telegraph working between LNW Junction, Ouse Bridge and Bedford Junction was inaugurated on 25 January 1892 'and the practice of backing trains and engines on the wrong line between these points will be discontinued'. Finally Plowman's Siding, between Henlow and Shefford, was opened on 19 December 1893, controlled by home and distant signals and a shunt signal for exit from the siding. Here household refuse from London was dumped and the emptied wagons were hauled by horses across the road to a brickyard to be loaded and returned.

The growth of RAF camps at Cardington and Henlow afforded the line valuable passenger and goods traffic. Indeed, during World War I a halt, Cardington Workmen's Platform, was in use beside the overbridge carrying the Bedford to Hitchin road. In later years the camp was served by a number of sidings and it was from here that the line made its final retreat in 1969, having existed in its last years for the sole purpose of serving the base. World War II saw the extension of one of the platforms at Henlow, especially to cater for troop specials. When the line was singled, the track was obviously left in place on the down side, where the station offices were situated. When the time came for the platform extension, the down platform was unsuitable, as it would have fouled the connection to the goods yard. So the track was slewed over to the up platform, which presented no difficulties but resulted in the absurd situation of the offices being on the wrong platform.

The specials from Henlow to King's Cross brought a touch of variety to the motive power using the line. The Eastern Region provided the locomotives for this service, usually a Class J15 0–6–0 from Hitchin shed. These trains ran to King's Cross on Friday evenings and Saturday mornings and returned on Sunday nights, stopping at certain intermediate stations on the Great Northern line. Comprised of Gresley Quad-Art coaches, these trains had to run out empty to Shefford to reverse, as there were no run-round facilities at Henlow, and then return to pick up their passengers there. Goods traffic was exchanged with the camp's internal railway and the diesel locomotives *Ebb* and *Flo* were kept busy shuttling around within its confines.

Of course, Henlow station originally existed to serve Henlow village, a considerable distance away and the change of name to Henlow Camp was inspired by the coming of the RAF. No trace remains of the line at Henlow, where a small commercial development has been built on the former course of the railway.

Since the St Pancras route bore away at the south end of Bedford station, a new platform had to be built to serve these trains. This was built west of the existing platforms for use by trains to the north. The other face of the former northbound platform was adapted for St Pancras-bound trains and the two new platforms thus provided were connected to the main station buildings by a walkway, built across the former track-bed. The original through platforms therefore became bays and the Hitchin trains departed from the south set. The station still remains in virtually its original condition, although the copper for heating the footwarmers has been removed from the lamp-room, and the steps once used to help the old and infirm enter the Hitchin trains from the low platforms have also disappeared. Most of the sidings on either side of the Ouse, which employed three shunting locomotives, have now been lifted. During these shunting operations, the locomotives had to come out onto the

Ouse bridge and consequently work was interrupted by the passage of trains. Connections were made with the LNWR line, whose tracks were crossed on the level. The flat crossing was originally designed as an economy measure but in later years its upkeep became expensive.

At the other end of the line, trains ran into the ex-Great Northern station at Hitchin, although there was a separate goods yard for the Midland, together with a small locomotive depot complete with turntable. Entry to the GNR was controlled by a somersault signal to the end, and trains were accepted by the GNR Cambridge Junction box. Since there were no bay platforms at Hitchin, Midland trains had to cross all the running lines to the London platform, deposit their passengers and reverse out the same way into a siding. When ready to leave for Bedford, they would then run into the north-bound platform, load and then depart. This manoeuvre had to be fitted in between the passage of trains on the busy GNR main line.

Shefford station buildings were an exception to the general run of architecture, as they were originally of wood and stood on a high level, astride the end of the viaduct which carried the line across the main street. In British Railways days they were demolished and replaced by a prefabricated concrete structure at road level, while the platforms were replaced by timber that had come from the old Carpenders Park station. The goods yard was on the other side of the road, and although small it handled quite a substantial amount of agricultural traffic. After the line was closed, the formation was suggested as a by-pass road for the town but the idea was not prosecuted.

In later years the line was frequented by some of the experimental railbuses that British Railways purchased. In 1958 three Park Royal railbuses M79970–2 were introduced, preceding by five weeks the introduction of a more frequent service. The 'Greenhouses', as they were called, rode very roughly and suffered quite frequent mechanical failures. Consequently they were replaced by two-car diesel multiple-units. When these were transferred, steam-hauled push-and-pull trains returned and it was with these that the line closed to passengers. During this Indian summer the tank engines would take the two coaches of the train to the shed and under the coaling plant, when they refuelled at Bedford. The last passenger train left Hitchin at 19.00 on Saturday 30 December 1961 and little groups stood in the cold night air at the intermediate stations to watch the last train, as it drew away with a farewell shriek on the whistle.

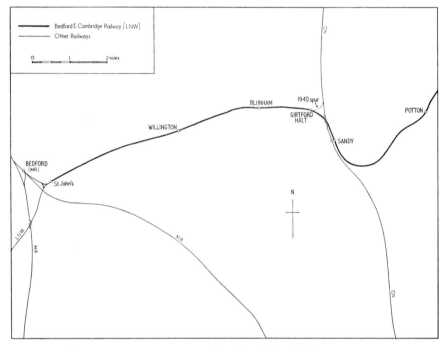

Map of the Bedford & Cambridge Railway

Shortly afterwards the line achieved temporary glory, when scenes for *Those Magnificent Men in Their Flying Machines* were shot near Warden tunnel, using ex-Highland Railway locomotive No 103 and a set of coaches, disguised as a train of the Nord Railway of France. Goods services lingered on but were eventually withdrawn in 1969, and now little remains. Even the *Leicester Railway* has changed its name. But in the hamlet of Ireland the influence of the railway still lingers. Local legend says Brassey's navvies, engaged on building the line, were not close to any pub. So they transformed the front room of a cottage into a bar and the result is today's *Black Horse*.

Bedford to Sandy

In the 1950s a traveller with an idle hour to spare might have walked down the platform at Wantage Road station in Berkshire to see what the locomotive was that stood under a shelter by the footbridge. *Shannon* looked unexciting and appeared to have spent a tranquil existence on the Wantage Tramway. Yet it had shunted at Crewe, had acted as a contractor's locomotive and originally started life on the Sandy & Potton Railway, the brainchild of an extraordinary Victorian, Captain William Peel, VC. Third son of Sir Robert Peel, he saw naval service in many parts of the world and died in Cawnpore in 1858 without seeing his railway in operation.

In 1852 he had purchased the land for the railway, which formed a part of his programme for improvements to his estate, about 1,400 acres lying between Sandy and Potton, and he brought this hitherto worthless land under cultivation. As the railway ran through land owned by the Captain, it needed no Act of Parliament and opened to passengers in November 1857. To judge from reports, the ceremonial opening of this $3\frac{1}{2}$ mile line in June 1857 was quite an event. Starting from a junction with the Great Northern Railway on the Biggleswade side of Sandy, it curved away on a direct course for Potton, where a banquet was held to celebrate its opening. The 500 guests dined in the Market Place, being entertained by the Bedford Militia Band and artistes who 'gave a variety of glees and songs in superior style'.

Apart from *Shannon*, which was 'built expressly for the purpose' and was named after the ship the Captain had commanded in India, the rolling stock comprised another tank engine, a brake van, two wagons and one trolley. The signalling system was rather primitive; it consisted of a red flag, which was waved when a passenger wished to entrain. Although the line fulfilled its purpose of carrying heavy flows of agricultural produce, an extension towards Cambridge was greatly desired.

Instead of extending itself, however, the Sandy & Potton was purchased by the Bedford & Cambridge Railway, a line authorised in 1860, and *Shannon* was put to work hauling contractor's trains over its former stronghold. To save money, the Bedford & Cambridge intended to use most of the Sandy & Potton formation, which it had to adapt for use as a through route. As its name indicated, the Bedford & Cambridge started from a junction with the London & North Western at its Bedford station and ran through to the Great Eastern station at Cambridge. It seems to have been a railway that caused mixed feelings. On the one hand *The Bedfordshire Times* said the line could not 'fail to exercise a material influence on the prosperity and progress of the entire district' and events would 'turn out . . . [very] advantageous to all the parties concerned'. By contrast *Herapath's Railway Journal* failed 'to see any good in it' to the London & North Western, the company to whom the line was leased, a move made necessary because of the local promoters' difficulty in raising the required capital. Both journals did, however, agree that the line was not so much useful in itself but as part of a through route between east and west.

The line was worked by the LNWR from its opening in 1862 and was finally absorbed in 1865. To cater for growing traffic, the section from Sandy to Cambridge was doubled in 1871 but, because of the expense of widening the river bridges between Sandy and Bedford, this section remained single track, although the introduction of the electric train staff system on the single line in 1888 did alleviate congestion.

As the promoters had foreseen, local traffic on the railway was of an agricultural nature. Hitherto Bedford had been served by the River Ouse from King's Lynn but the arrival of the Bedford & Cambridge completed rail transit throughout. Consequently the railway undercut and destroyed its water-borne rival. Evidence of this could be seen at Blunham, where a former flour mill was once served by a steeply-graded siding and in the considerable market gardening traffic. In one week in 1900, some 200 tons of potatoes were forwarded from Sandy and Potton stations, making use of the 19.00 special from Potton which called at Sandy, Girtford Siding and Blunham to collect vegetables and arrived at Bletchley at 22.00, where the wagons were sorted for dispatch to London and larger provincial towns.

For a moment in 1958 it seemed that the line was destined for greater glory than had been its lot until then. As part of a study to utilize more fully the cross-country connections outside the Metropolitan area, the Cambridge to Oxford line was proposed for development. To enable trains from the Great Northern to gain access to this new trunk line, a reversing loop was planned at Sandy and thirty trains a day each way were intended to use this route. All that was built however was the flyover at Bletchley and then the plan faded away to become another might-have-been.

Passenger traffic was always varied. An account of the opening of the line recorded that few of the passengers on the inaugural journey had ever travelled between Potton and Cambridge or ever would have done so but for the railway. Doubtless they were uncertain whether to do so again when they heard of the fatal accident to a railway employee who fell out of a van as the door on which he was leaning gave way. The opening did, however, provoke *Herapath's Railway Journal* to speculate facetiously on the line's use for varsity matches, as it completed rail transport between Oxford and Cambridge. In much later years, holidaymakers destined for East Coast resorts and for the main line at Sandy made use of the route.

The Bedford & Cambridge started at an end-on junction with the London & North Western at Bedford, which from 1846 to 1862 had been the terminus of the branch from Bletchley. During this time arrivals were dealt with at the northern platform and departures from the southern, where the booking office was located. Both platform lines were covered to form carriage sheds, and a branch ran down to the Ouse, subsequently serving the LNWR coal yard. Alterations in later years moved the main offices to the northern platform but the southern platform existed in its original form for much longer, retaining what is thought to have been the original entrance. The locomotive shed that stood on the north side of the line has now been demolished.

Crossing the Ouse, the line passed the erstwhile Goldington Crossing loop, whose name was a misnomer as it was actually nearer Cardington. Opened in World War I, it closed in the 1920s and stood derelict until 1938, when it was dismantled. It was re-instated in 1940, used for emergencies and removed again after World War II. Willington, further to the east, was not an original station, a single platform with wooden buildings having been opened in 1903. It was followed by a second platform on the north side, where the signalbox stood. The facing points at the entrance to the goods yard were a reminder of the days when there was no passing loop here. If there had been a loop from the outset, the connection would have been a trailing one.

Blunham was an original station, of the typical architectural style of the Bedford & Cambridge, entirely different to the Bletchley to Bedford section. Steps were often used to reach the coaches from the low platforms and oil lamps illuminated the station. Just where the A1 crossed the line, the LMSR opened Girtford Halt in 1938 but its brief life came to an end in 1940. Tickets had to be purchased at a nearby garage. However, the siding for vegetable traffic was open for very much longer, from 1863 to 1951, although it did close temporarily during World War I.

A double-line spur to the Great Northern, north of Sandy, was opened in 1940. As a wartime precaution, a series of these spurs was built to enable trains for the North to be diverted in case of damage to tracks from air attack. After the War it fell into disuse and acted as a store for wagons. Crossing the Great Northern by an overbridge, the line dropped into Sandy where it became double track. Sandy was a three-platform station, the centre island being served on one side by the Great Northern and on the other by the Bedford & Cambridge. Until 1917 staff of both companies served their respective parts of the station and the initials B & C could be seen worked into the spandrels of its part of the station. Before the opening of the direct route from the north to Cambridge via Spalding and March, Sandy was used for traffic to and from the Eastern Counties, because exchange at Peterborough entailed a change of stations. Beyond Sandy, the Sandy & Potton formation was utilised, until the Bedford & Cambridge turned away to pass through a new Potton station en route for Cambridge.

Withdrawal of passenger services was threatened in 1959; instead, an improved diesel service was introduced. The Beeching Report proposed closure only of intermediate stations and population growth seemed to assure the line for the future. However, in December 1963 closure was again proposed, and despite opposition and difficulties in arranging the replacement bus services, complete closure came on 1 January 1968, leaving Bedford St Johns as the terminus for trains from Bletchley. The idea of preserving the entire line between Bedford and Cambridge had been mooted, but discussions with British Rail showed the idea to be impracticable. A public meeting was held at Sandy to investigate interest in purchasing the line between Sandy and Potton. A society was formed, but was unable to raise the purchase price outright and despite the support of Sandy UDC met with little success. Attempts to purchase the line were frustrated by the start of track removal in July 1969 and as alternative proposals proved unsuitable, the Society was eventually wound up.

Captain Peel's monument still stands in Sandy Parish Church. The statue of the hero of the Crimea has seen a great deal but is saying nothing.

Kettering to Huntingdon

The Kettering to Huntingdon line was an unglamorous, workaday branch of the Midland Railway which, although subsidiary to the Midland main line, served the Northamptonshire ironstone industry and provided outlets to the Great Northern and Great Eastern Railways.

The first part was promoted as the Kettering & Thrapstone

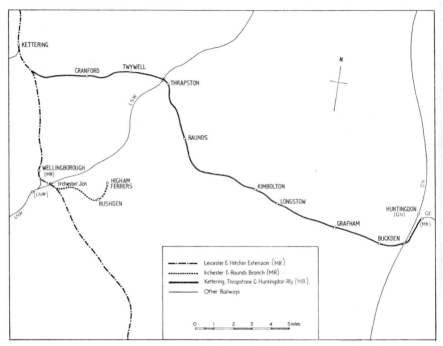

Map of Kettering to Huntingdon and Higham Ferrers branches,
Midland Railway

Railway, authorised to link the two towns of its title in 1862.
Although it was promoted as an independent company, powers
were granted in the Act for it to make agreements for the line
to be worked by the Midland Railway. It must be regarded as a
Midland satellite from the first and perhaps the influence of
the Midland is apparent in the extension, authorised by a
further Act in 1863, which was to be carried out by theKetter-
ing, Thrapstone & Huntingdon Railway and comprised a new
railway from a junction with the original line at Thrapston to a
further junction with the St Ives & Huntingdon branch of the
Great Eastern Railway at Huntingdon. A connection with the
Great Northern Railway at its Huntingdon station was also
authorised by this Act, together with an arrangement for the
interchange of traffic between the Midland and the Great

Page 123 (above) Sarsden Halt, typically GWR, where schoolboys joined trains and a farm was unloaded; (below) Adderbury station in 1972, one of the better-preserved abandoned stations of the region

Page 124 (above) A train for Ashchurch, headed by LMS 2–6–2T No 171, about to leave Broom Junction on 8 September 1949. The island platform has altered little since then; (below) MR 0–6–0 43940 waits to leave Evesham Midland station on a northbound goods, about 1960

Northern. The interdependence of the two projects was shown by the provisions that charges were to be on the basis of the 1862 Act, as if the extension formed part of the original line, and that new shareholders were to rank *pari passu* with the existing ones.

The reasons for the promotion of the two lines can only be conjecture but it seems likely that the original line as far as Thrapston was concerned to aid the extraction of the ironstone deposits that lay in the vicinity. Examples of the deposits found on the Woodford Estate near Twywell had actually been on display at the Great Exhibition of 1851 but it took the coming of the railway to stimulate development in the area. Quarries were eventually worked alongside the line as far as Thrapston, the earliest dating from the opening of the line in 1866. However, the more easterly pits lay on the edge of the workable field and had short lives. The limit of the field is reached at Thrapston, explaining its choice as the original terminus. Beyond, the land is agricultural and, whilst affording some traffic, would not of itself justify the line's construction. However, by continuing to Huntingdon two other companies could be reached and interchange facilities established. By joining the Great Eastern and making use of the running powers it was granted, the Midland could reach Cambridge, an important centre for East Anglia. It would thus seem that the line was originally a local promotion which was taken under the Midland wing, who then added the extension to reach the railway crossroads at Huntingdon.

Against this background, the first goods train from Kettering to Cambridge ran on 21 February 1866 and was followed by the first passenger train on 1 March. Both trains were run by the Midland, as it operated the line from the outset, but the nominal independence of the railway continued until finally absorbed in 1897. Certainly the line cannot have been easy to work because of the steep gradients in certain places, as when it climbed away from the main line at Kettering Junction at 1 in 70. These gradients were perhaps inevitable as the line had to climb from the Ise valley at Kettering across into the Nene valley, and ascend again to upland country before finally descending to the Ouse at Huntingdon. Even so, the earthworks were somewhat skimped and if finance had permitted their being more substantial, the line could have been more easily graded. Added to this was a weight restriction caused by the wooden underbridges between Huntingdon and St Ives, which affected all trains bound for Cambridge. The Midland section proper was not subject to this restriction and any type of locomotive could be used.

So for many years such restrictions brought Kirtley-designed 2–4–0s and 0–6–0s on the passenger trains, which generally worked through to Cambridge. Canon Roger Lloyd in *The Fascination of Railways* gives a delightful picture of one of these 'working museum pieces' and its train arriving at Cambridge, after having 'meandered its way through a succession of villages with intriguing names like Raunds'. At Cambridge, too, the Midland outstationed a locomotive in the hospitality of the Great Eastern shed; for many years this was No 239, with sisters Nos 236–8 at Kettering. These were finally replaced in 1946, when Nos 6400–2, Ivatt-designed 2–6–0s, arrived, the first of the type being sent to Kettering especially for this line. Because of this through working a cultural link grew up between the district served by the line and Cambridge while connections could be made at Kettering, offering a route between East Anglia and the North. Yet even in the 1930s, a commentator bemoaned that 'This might be a possible route to the North, if the main line connections at Kettering were not so bad, and the journey on the branch not so long.' Even for local journeys the line was of doubtful use as the stations were situated some distance from the communities they ostensibly served. Kimbolton station was about $2\frac{1}{2}$ miles and Raunds 1 mile from the centre of the actual villages, an unhappy legacy in the motor age.

An attempt was made to give Raunds a more central station by the Irchester & Raunds branch. This project sprang out of the demands voiced in the 1880s at Rushden and Higham Ferrers for better railway facilities. Merchants and manufacturers, especially in the predominant boot and shoe trade, were no longer satisfied with the outlets provided by the LNWR Blisworth & Peterborough branch and the Midland main line. So agitation for a new branch was answered by this railway, projected to run from Irchester Junction on the Midland main line through Rushden, Higham Ferrers and Stanwick to a junction with the Kettering, Thrapstone & Huntingdon line at its Raunds station. Although the line was opened to passengers as far as Higham Ferrers in May 1894, the section beyond was abandoned and the line terminated a little to the north of Higham station. Local legend attributes the abandonment to the opposition of a landowner, who even went so far as to build some houses in the path of the projected line. Whether this is true or not, the cottages certainly stood in an inexplicably isolated position.

On the Huntingdon line, the pattern of freight traffic was truly miscellaneous until the 1920s, when the ironstone traffic became more predominant. Some evidence of the ironstone traffic could be seen in Butlins Sidings signalbox near Cranford. Latterly this was only a block post controlling a passing loop, but originally served the Burton Latimer pits, opened by Butlin Bevan & Co in the early 1880s, and at one time with a standard-gauge line of their own parallel to the branch. A further complex was found further along the line at Islip, with the largest narrow-gauge railway system in the ironstone industry which remained in use until 1952. The line ran through an area with a large number of workings and their associated railways but these were never really evident to the casual passenger.

In summer, special freight trains were run for fruit traffic from stations such as Histon and Oakington on the St Ives to Cambridge line. These were generally double-headed by two Johnson Class 2 0–6–0 locomotives, one of which had set out from Kettering earlier in the day to set down empty vans for loading at these stations, while the other had double-headed a freight to Cambridge, specifically to return as the second engine on this train. Sometimes extending to sixty or seventy vans, these trains could block movements at Kettering station whilst they came off the branch and were put back into the goods refuge siding alongside the main line. Agricultural produce was also loaded between Thrapston and Huntingdon, principally corn, hay, fruit, vegetables and wheat. A vastly different load was carried in World War II; bombs and supplies for the USAF camps in the area were unloaded in sidings laid for the purpose at Longstow and Kimbolton.

Although the fruit trains ceased at the onset of war, the other special feature of the line did return after hostilities had ceased, the excursion trains. Run on the Easter, Whitsun and August Bank Holidays, these heavy, packed trains, destined principally for Clacton, required double-heading to Huntingdon. There was also a regular Clacton train run on Summer Saturdays.

Few changes were made to the line during its working life but alterations were made to the layout at the extremities. When the direct spur from the Midland to the Great Northern at Huntingdon was lifted in 1883, a new station, latterly known as Huntingdon East, was opened, built to Great Northern designs. This had three platforms and the Kettering service used the outer face of the island platform. In 1935, at the other end of the line, the layout in the Kettering Junction area was altered. A new enlarged Kettering Junction signalbox was built on the opposite side of the tracks from the original one and Pytchley box at the start of the Huntingdon line closed.

The decline of the line was gradual and closure to passengers, although vigorously opposed, came on 15 June 1959. Time passed, leaving today ironstone loading at Twywell, the formation pressed into use as a slip road for the A1 at Buckden and an abandoned formation running through the tumbled landscape between Thrapston and Cranford, a tangible reminder of a once thriving industry and the railway that served it.

CHAPTER 5

The Northampton Uplands

Introduction

Sylvan glades and timelessness are the two embodiments of a country branch and, set in the heart of Oxfordshire, the line from Kingham to King's Sutton had both in plenty. Was this not the country described by the poet, Edward Thomas, in 'Adlestrop'? Great Western ownership added the final flourish, but originally more serious purposes had been intended. Likewise the impecunious SMJ had started life with great hopes, but became an idiosyncratic feature of the local scene, regarded with affection by all who knew it.

Yet in the nineteenth century, they were both built against a background of a recurrent theme, an east-to-west trunk railway. Ideas circulated of a line from the Wash to the Severn for which great advantages were claimed. But the glowing promises failed to materialise and the railway system as a whole remained focused on routes radiating from London. So the lines that were unfortunate enough actually to be constructed, led a precarious existence and instead of arteries of industry remained backwaters of rural calm.

The Stratford-upon-Avon & Midland Junction Railway

The Stratford-upon-Avon & Midland Junction Railway was one of those lines that endeared itself to the inhabitants of the neighbourhood it served even if at times it exasperated them. Affectionately known as the SMJ, Slow and Muddle Junction or Slow, Mournful Journey, it comprised 68 route miles when it was absorbed into the LMSR in 1923, but it had only existed as a complete entity from 1910 and consisted of railways originally constructed by four separate companies.

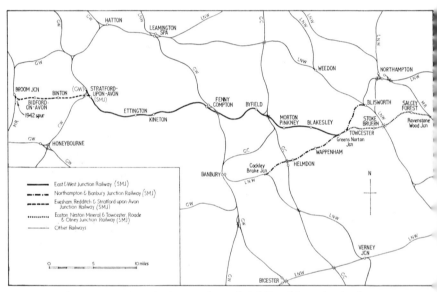

Map of the Stratford-upon-Avon & Midland Junction Railway

At first sight the line did little that was useful, except link the London and Bristol arms of the Midland Railway, and traversed country that seemed unpromising for railway traffic. Indeed, so unsuited was the locality that the independent companies were perpetually facing financial crises and one, the Northampton & Banbury Junction, at one time had the dubious distinction of earning less per mile than any other company in Britain, despite strong competition for that title from its neighbour, with whom it ultimately amalgamated, the East & West Junction Railway. It was said of the latter that it did not earn enough to pay for oiling its locomotives.

However, these railways once presented bright hopes for the future, based on the ironstone of Northamptonshire. In the 1860s the South Wales blast furnaces had exhausted their local ores and it seemed that Northamptonshire ore would be substituted. Obviously railways would be needed to transport the stone and so there was an upsurge in local railway promotion, in the expectation of heavy traffic with its concomitant, good dividends. In addition, support in Stratford was reinforced by the desire of the town to break the stranglehold of the Great Western Railway, which at the time had a monopoly of all rail and water transport in the district. Unfortunately ore shipped from Spain became the principal source for the South Wales iron industry, and the railway promotion bubble burst, leaving the railways with no effective role and financially unsound.

The resulting routes became cross-country links, useful in times of war or other crisis, but normally eking out an existence on limited traffic. In an attempt to attract passengers, the lines publicised themselves as the Shakespeare Route but amalgamation into the LMSR group must have been a welcome relief, as separate existence into the age of motor transport would have been precarious indeed. In fact the LMSR tried to harness the benefits of the motor age to railways for some months in 1932. A Karrier *Ro-Railer* was employed to run on rails from Blisworth to Stratford and then change to road wheels for the drive to the Welcombe Hotel, opened by the company in the previous year. It must have been judged an experiment that failed, as the service was taken off in June 1932.

But to return to the origins of the system. The first constituent of the SMJ was the Northampton & Banbury Junction Railway (N & BJ), granted an Act in 1863 to run from the LNWR main line at Blisworth to Cockley Brake Junction near Farthinghoe, where it joined the Buckinghamshire Railway, over whose line it had running powers into Banbury.

The N & BJ had an authorised capital of £140,000, and its Act gave it power to make arrangements with the LNWR to cover such matters as working the line, supplying rolling stock and providing staff. At this juncture, it would appear that the N & BJ was just another rural line to be leased to a major company. However, in 1865 it received sanction for an extension to Blockley; the full extent of its ambitions was revealed in the next year, when the company obtained an Act for a further extension to Ross-on-Wye in Herefordshire towards its South Wales goal. The line, now grown to 96½ miles of authorised railway, was to be renamed The Midland Counties & South Wales Railway in line with its grand design. Alas, the design was never realised, and Parliament granted permission to revert to the original aims and title in 1870.

Meanwhile another constituent of the SMJ had been born. The East & West Junction Railway (E & W), was authorised in 1864 and ran from Greens Norton Junction, one mile west of Towcester, to Stratford-upon-Avon. Running powers were granted over the N & BJ from Greens Norton Junction to Blisworth. This line again expected to carry ore to South Wales, in conjunction with the London, Worcester & South Wales, a project authorised in 1865 to run from Stratford to Worcester. No doubt another line would have been projected from Worcester onwards to South Wales but in 1866 these plans came to naught. Concurrently the E & W was in financial difficulties and an Act of 1874 authorised the issue of debentures to try to rectify matters. Despite 'the confidence felt in the soundness and success of the undertaking' declared by the prospectus, little money was raised by this issue and a Receiver was appointed in 1875. No passenger traffic was to be carried from 1877 to 1885.

In the 1874 prospectus, mention was made of another of the SMJ's constituents, the Evesham, Redditch and Stratford-upon-Avon Junction Railway (ER & SJ). Authorised in 1873, this 7½ mile line ran from Stratford to Broom on the Evesham & Redditch Railway. The ER & SJ was promoted and built by the same people who controlled the East & West and the E & W were to work this extension. Running powers were granted throughout between Redditch and Evesham by the ER & SJ Act but, apart from the five chains into Broom station, were not used. With the opening of the ER & SJ in 1879, through communication from Blisworth to Broom, forty five miles, was achieved.

Regardless of the financial morass into which the E & W and its leased line had sunk, an Act for the final and cumbrously named constituent of the SMJ was obtained in 1879. This, the Easton Neston Mineral & Towcester, Roade & Olney Junction Railway, ran from Towcester to Ravenstone Wood Junction on the Midland Railway's Bedford & Northampton branch. The company was given powers to run over the E & W and the ER & SJ, and its Act gave tentative powers for a direct line to be built between the E & W at Greens Norton Junction and the new line, independent of the N & BJ; if the latter were to give written notice of their intention to lay a second line between Greens Norton Junction and Towcester within eighteen months of the passing of the Act, these powers for an independent line were to lapse.

Matters progressed slowly; an Act of 1882 reduced the capital and authorised a change of name to the Stratford-upon-Avon, Towcester & Midland Junction Railway (S & MJR). A further Act of 1883 authorised the company to improve the East & West Junction and provided that the two companies should be managed as one concern by a joint committee. Finally, after further difficulties, the Towcester to Ravenstone Wood Junction line was eventually opened for goods only in 1891. In expectation of traffic that never came, stations were provided at Salcey Forest and Stoke Bruern. On the first train one person alighted at Salcey Forest but nobody joined, whilst at Stoke Bruern one alighted and seven joined the train! By March 1893, the local paper reported, the company incurred a loss of about £40 per week in running the service and it was reckoned something extraordinary to get twenty passengers a week.

Eventually in May 1898, a Receiver was appointed for the S & MJR, joining the ER & SJ whose Receiver had been appointed in 1886. In order to clarify the ownership of these lines, the three companies promoted a Bill in 1901, which also enabled them to sell the lines. However, no willing purchaser was to be found and so the joint committee had to struggle on with their burdensome inheritance. An overdue rationalisation was effected in 1908 when the three railways, the E & W, the ER & SJ and the S & MJR, were amalgamated into the Stratford-upon-Avon & Midland Junction Railway, which commenced operations on 1 January 1909. Subsequently the SMJ purchased the N & BJ, which was formally amalgamated on 1 July 1910.

At the time of this second amalgamation the Traffic Manager and Engineer was Russell Willmott, who had been appointed in 1908. He succeeded in reviving the railway, and *The Railway Magazine* was able to report in 1910 that the growth of grass and weeds that gave the E & W track a somewhat derelict appearance had been uprooted. However, it noted that a railway which provided valuable inter-communication and cross-country facilities did not necessarily obtain a great deal of important and valuable traffic and for this reason the history of the line had been chequered.

Indeed, with its many junctions to other railways, the SMJ did offer a great number of potential interchange points but none were greatly used over a considerable period of time. Starting from the eastern end the first junction was at Ravenstone Wood with the Midland. By an arrangement of 1889 running powers were granted from Ravenstone Wood to Olney, where the SMJ had the use of the station and all its facilities. The actual junction box was situated in woodland and sufficient land was purchased for sidings to be laid out. However, all that was constructed was a junction between the single line SMJ and the Northampton-bound line of the Midland, at the summit of the 1 in 80 grade of the SMJ line.

The next junction came at Roade, after the line from Olney had crossed the LNWR main line by a lattice girder bridge, and was a connecting spur to the LNWR at Roade station. A bay platform was built on the down side of the station for services via the SMJ. The spur was little used and, although opened in 1891, it closed in 1917; as part of the War effort, the materials were taken up to be re-used elsewhere.

The high point of the Ravenstone Wood to Towcester section, after regular passenger services had been withdrawn, was the Easter Monday Race Special, the only passenger train to use this section in the year. From 1927 to 1939, these trains ran from St Pancras to Towcester and back, and sometimes required a Midland locomotive as banker on the severe climb from Olney to Ravenstone Wood Junction. Not for nothing was the Bedford and Northampton line known as 'over the Alps'. The races were always the occasion for every available SMJ locomotive to be pressed into service and coaches, sometimes ex-North London four-wheelers, hired.

Two junctions domestic to the SMJ system were in the Towcester area, Towcester Station and Greens Norton Junction. The former was a quarter of a mile outside the actual station where the Blisworth and Olney lines met. This junction was opened in 1891 and the 10½ mile section from Ravenstone Wood was worked as one block section. Alterations were made to the layout at Towcester in 1910 as part of the abolition of Greens Norton Junction. Originally a physical junction, this was closed and the hitherto double track section became parallel but single lines to Banbury and Stratford respectively.

A further junction with the LNWR at Blisworth was originally made by the Northampton & Banbury Junction. Here the N & BJ had separate platforms controlled by its own signalbox, known latterly as Blisworth SMJ, with a siding connection to the LNWR under the control of a ground frame. Use was made of this connection by the LNWR to run complete trains, 'Shakespeare Specials', hauled by 2-4-0 'Jumbo' locomotives between Blisworth and Stratford. Inaugurated in 1890, these trains at one time ran each Saturday in Spring and Summer and later East & West locomotives took over the part of the run on their system. Still later, in LMSR days, an express was put on between Blisworth and Stratford calling at Towcester only, comprising one bogie composite coach hauled by a Midland o–6–o locomotive, to connect with the stop made at Blisworth by a Birmingham express.

At the other end of the N & BJ, Cockley Brake Junction, where the SMJ joined the Buckinghamshire Railway, was the end of another extensive block section from Towcester, at 11¼ miles one of the longest in the country at the time. Running powers took the line into Banbury, which was to have been the springboard for the westward extensions. Instead the service terminated at Merton Street station in Banbury, which remained largely in its original condition until the end.

Reverting to the E & W, the next junction from Greens Norton, if such it can be called, was at Blakesley. Here, during the 1910s and 20s the fifteen-inch gauge Blakesley Hall railway ran into its rustic terminal at the back of the down SMJ platform, from its other terminus at Blakesley Hall. Built by C. W. Bartholomew, its role was part business, bringing stores up to the Hall, and part pleasure. It was worked for a long time by a Bassett-Lowke 4–4–4 locomotive with a steam exterior but driven by an internal combustion engine. After Mr Bartholomew's death in the 1930s, the line was less frequently used, mainly for school outings and sometimes at the Blakesley Flower Show.

The next junction was in fact two in one; two spurs to the Great Central at Woodford, one facing towards London and the other away from it. The Great Central espoused the E & W, not only as a valuable link in its network of feeding lines but also as part of an independent route to Birmingham, a dream left unrealised because of a later entente with the Great Western.

After crossing the Great Western's Birmingham line at Fenny Compton, a connection trailed in from the right. The junction was remodelled in 1960 as a facing junction providing a direct connection controlled by a new signalbox, in order to cater for the iron ore trains from Banbury to South Wales. The initial ambitions were thus fulfilled to some extent at this later date. In order to alleviate congestion at Banbury and to obviate banking on Hatton bank, trains were diverted to the SMJ between Fenny Compton and Stratford, requiring junctions at both places.

The section from Fenny Compton to Burton Dassett is now the only part of the SMJ still in use, although it is now run by the army as the rail access to the Central Ammunition Depot at Kineton. At Burton Dassett, west of the road bridge, the SMJ made a further junction, this time with the Edge Hill Light Railway promoted in association with the SMJ to tap the ironstone deposits in the vicinity of Edge Hill. The line was opened in 1919 but was not used from 1925, when the quarries fell into disuse. The line was partially rope-worked and an uncompleted extension was left just as the tools were dropped. Pride of place went to two ex-LB & SCR Terrier tanks, *Deptford* and *Shadwell*, which still lay derelict on the line in 1942, at a time when scrap was valuable. The line never operated again but took a long time dying, becoming enmeshed in legal problems.

At Stratford-upon-Avon, where the head offices of the line were sited, there were eventually three junctions, two with the GWR line and the other with the ER & SJ. The first junction with the Great Western was made by a spur twenty chains in length from Old Town station, facing the Birmingham direction and this formed one of the ends of the E & W. The other junction with the Great Western was southward-facing, south of the GWR Stratford-upon-Avon Racecourse Platform. This was laid in 1960 as part of the programme of works already mentioned. Previously trains from Woodford to South Wales travelled as far as Broom Junction on the SMJ and these were diverted over this spur after its completion. A new signalbox, Evesham Road Crossing, was established to control the new link and took over the work of Evesham Road Level Crossing, SMJ Junction and Old Town signalboxes, although a ground frame was left to control operations at the SMJ Old Town station. Sidings were established at Honeybourne for trains from the SMJ to change locomotives or crews.

The final junction was with the Evesham, Redditch & Stratford-upon-Avon Railway that took the East & West onwards to the west and from which passenger services were temporarily withdrawn on 16 June 1947 and the line permanently closed to passengers from 23 May 1949. This climbed from Old Town station to cross the GWR at right angles by an overbridge and led into 'the fair Arden district, where cluster the haunts of the Poet's [Shakespeare's] boyhood' as the *Shakespeare's Country* guide of the E & W said in 1886.

Whether Bidford was drunken, or Broom beggarly, as the couplet in the guide represented them, they brought the line to its final junction at Broom, where the SMJ joined the Evesham & Redditch Railway, running in by a northward facing junction. The completed SMJ thus formed a link between two Midland lines but the junction at Broom, as it were, faced the wrong way. It took the impetus of World War II to justify the provision of a south-to-east spur, opened on 28 September 1942. This entailed a new signalbox, Broom East, to control the West Junction and the South curve, which was opened on 17 May 1942. As a link between Midland lines, the SMJ saw banana trains from Avonmouth to St Pancras and a nightly, Sundays excepted, freight from St Pancras, nominally terminating at Broom but continuing to Bristol St Philips with a corresponding return working.

As might be expected, the SMJ and its constituents purchased locomotives on financial rather than engineering grounds. Of the thirteen that the LMSR took over in 1923, none saw 1931. Eleven of the thirteen were Beyer Peacock 0–6–0s, built between 1880 and 1908, while the other 0–6–0 had been purchased secondhand from the LBSCR. The last locomotive to go was a Beyer Peacock 2–4–0 of 1903; renumbered LMSR No 290 it was withdrawn in 1924. As the SMJ locomotives were non-standard types of moderate power with a good many years service, they were rapidly replaced by former Midland 0–6–0s. Coupled to some of that company's coaches, they gave the SMJ quite a Midland flavour in the 1930s.

Operations commenced on the N & BJ with hired locomotives. The company had ordered two 0–4–2 tank locomotives and two 0–4–2 tender locomotives from Neilson & Co but could not pay for them, and they never came to Northamptonshire. Although arrangements were made with the LNWR to work the line, the N & BJ still yearned to operate its own railway. Accordingly it acquired former South Staffordshire Railway 0–6–0 No 21 from the LNWR in December 1872, an 0–4–2 tank from the same source in April 1873 and an 0–6–0, again from the LNWR in 1873. The poor equipment possessed by the small sheds at Blisworth and Towcester and the general difficulties of operating locomotives persuaded the company to enter into another working agreement with the LNWR from 1 November 1876.

The first train on the E & W was hauled by an 0–6–0 saddle tank, which had belonged to the contractor building the line. The E & W bought the locomotive and changed the name from *Crampton*, the contractor's name, to *Kineton*. In 1873 three 0–6–0s and three 2–4–0 tanks were ordered from Beyer Peacock. Although acquired on hire purchase, money could not be found to complete the transaction and they had to be returned to their makers. The E & W next purchased *Ceres*, a 2–4–0, and *La Savoie*, an 0–6–0; both came from a French railway and were bought from Thomas Brassey & Sons, the railway contractors. Truly international in outlook and always looking for a bargain, the E & W acquired two Fairlie engines in 1876 that had been originally intended for a Mexican railway. No 1 was a double-boiler 0–6–6–0 and No 2 was a single boiler 0–4–4 tank, named *Robert Fairlie*. These and the other E & W locomotives were maintained at the shops and shed at Stratford-upon-Avon.

Passenger rolling stock consisted mainly in the earlier years of four-wheeled vehicles, but these were gradually replaced by six-wheelers fitted with electric light. Great Central stock was also seen on the line in later years on the through coaches between Stratford and Marylebone. In 1910 the livery of the carriages was chocolate with cream upper panels, whilst the locomotives were painted black lined out in yellow. The Westinghouse brake was standard on the E & W but several locomotives were fitted with the vacuum brake.

Closure to regular passenger services came piecemeal: Olney

to Towcester on 31 March 1893; Stratford to Broom on 23 May 1949; Blisworth to Banbury on 2 July 1951; and the final section from Blisworth to Stratford on 7 April 1952. Thenceforward the freight-only SMJ dealt particularly with coke and steel trains but gradually freight services were withdrawn, ultimately concluding in 1967.

Now nothing substantial remains of the SMJ, a line conceived in the expectation of riches but living in an atmosphere of financial stringency. None the less the line is remembered with affection in the area it served and apocryphal stories circulate of wages being paid in the form of chits valid in local stores, accompanied by dark hints not to change them too early in the week; of freight trains too heavy to climb the banks, needing to be split and taken up in two parts; and of everybody's wages being doubled in December 1922 to make the railway appear more important in the eyes of its fellow constituents of the LMSR formed the next month!

King's Sutton to Kingham

Last trains are sad affairs, but in the 1950s and 1960s they became a common feature of the rural scene. Yet when each line was opened it reflected the hopes and aspirations of the local community, and was expected to last for as long as could be foreseen. The Banbury & Cheltenham was no different in essence from many others, but as it ran across sparsely-populated Oxfordshire and Gloucestershire, its stopping services were early candidates for withdrawal. Accordingly 2 June 1951 saw the last stopping passenger train to run throughout from Kingham to Banbury.

After this, passenger services were cut back to run from Kingham to Chipping Norton only, a state of affairs that had existed sixty-four years earlier. Originally the only railway in the area was the Oxford, Worcester & Wolverhampton, which opened its line from Oxford to Evesham in 1853. Two branches sprang out from Kingham, to Chipping Norton in the east in 1855 and to Bourton-on-the-Water in the west in 1862. By

Page 141 (above) A unique view of GWR 0–4–2T 203 after arrival at Alcester on a branch service from Bearley, about 1901; (below) the Old English style of Oundle station is well brought out in this view of ex-LNER Class B1 4–6–0 61006 *Blackbuck* with the 17.10 from Northampton Castle on 15 May 1957

Page 142 (above) Uppingham station shortly after opening, with Station Road looking very new; (below) the same station on 9 January 1960; 0–6–0T 47300, not motor-fitted, had to run round its single coach for the return journey to Seaton

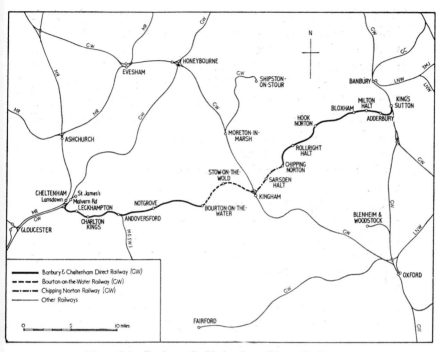

Map of the Banbury & Cheltenham Direct Railway

extending these branches to King's Sutton and Cheltenham respectively, the Banbury & Cheltenham Direct Railway, projected in 1873, formed an east–west line. Until 1906 through trains had to reverse at Kingham but a loop directly linking the two lines was opened in that year.

Kingham, or Chipping Norton Junction as it was known until 1909, was therefore an important station and had originally been intended to form a focal point for the area. As part of this plan, James Haughton Langston, who lived at Sarsden House, built a large hotel called the 'Langston Arms'. Situated adjacent to the station, it was connected to it by its own entrance from the station footbridge. Nowadays the cattle market next to the hotel is served by road vehicles, instead of the rail transport it used in its earlier days.

Close to Kingham Station Box, one of the four that controlled the station and its approaches, was the single-road engine shed. This was a sub-shed of Worcester and was to house BR Standard Class 2 2–6–0 No 78001 in the days when the service was truncated at Chipping Norton. Nearby the junction with the loop at Kingham East Box had once seen the Ports to Ports Express. This had originally been sponsored by the Great Central and was introduced in May 1906 to run between Cardiff and Newcastle. It survived although in a somewhat modified form until 1939, even though this route was not the most obvious to select, nor owing to its steep gradients, the easiest to work.

Undoubtedly this tortuous nature was due in part to the piecemeal construction of the line. Undaunted by this handicap, the promoters advanced a great number of benefits that were expected to accrue from its building. The iron ore deposits that lay alongside the line would be developed, access would be improved for coal from South Wales, cattle would be better transported to Banbury market and Gloucester timber would be more easily obtained in Banbury. Great expectations, but progress with the work proved more difficult. Work on the line, which had started in 1874, was suspended between 1878 and 1879, owing to the financial crisis of 1878, and the section between Chipping Norton and King's Sutton was not finally opened until 1887.

The first stop on this arm was Sarsden Halt, which served Churchill, the birthplace of Warren Hastings. Again, James Haughton Langston was probably the instigator of the name of this halt, as Sarsden village is three miles away. Goods traffic here was varied; anything which was required by Kingham Hill School would be brought here and once a train unloaded the contents of an entire farm, transported from Devonshire to Oxfordshire in a day. Many milk churns must have passed through Sarsden Halt, and each morning the valley rang to the sound of carts bringing the churns to be loaded on the milk train.

Further up the valley of the Kingham Brook was Chipping Norton, the terminus from 1855 to 1887. When the Banbury

& Cheltenham was built, a new station was erected on the extension, which left the former terminus isolated on a short spur. Subsequently the erstwhile station became part of the goods yard. Amongst the sidings here was one for Bliss's Mills. In 1873 William Bliss employed 800 people and was spending £60,000 on building 'one of the handsomest mills . . . in the kingdom'. As a leading citizen of the town, he had been intimately concerned with the promotion of the earlier Chipping Norton branch; later he claimed that the two branches incorporated in the Banbury & Cheltenham were conceived as part of a cross-country route from the outset. However, when questioned, he conceded the damaging admission that, although he was in favour of the Banbury & Cheltenham, he was not prepared to invest in it. His friend, Samuel Peto, played a considerable part in the promotion of the Chipping Norton branch, subscribing a third of the capital. His firm, Peto & Betts, constructed the branch during 1855 and some wagons used on the contract eventually found their way to the Balaclava Railway, a military line constructed during the Crimean War.

The Banbury & Cheltenham station at Chipping Norton was built on a curve so sharp that the staff were instructed to exercise great care when shunting coaches there. Under the road bridge, the single track disappeared into a tunnel to leave the valley in which Chipping Norton lies. In later years the 750yd tunnel was to be suggested as a bomb proof shelter in case of nuclear attack!

After emerging from the tunnel on a rising gradient of 1 in 80, the line ran along a section of heavy earthworks. Looking to the north-west, across the lonely upland valley, passengers could see the Rollright Stones on the crest of a lofty ridge running parallel to the line. Their great antiquity was not matched by Rollright Halt, which served the people of Great Rollright. Onwards the line continued its way along the Swere Valley to reach the summit level of the line at 600ft and, after a mile, the eleven-mile descent at a ruling gradient of 1 in 100 began. Soon the line turned northward, passing through the 490yd Hook Norton tunnel and approached two impressive viaducts. Carrying the rails 85ft above one valley and 60ft above the other, these viaducts claimed the lives of two workmen who fell to their deaths during construction. The viaducts and tunnel were built instead of open cutting to save time in construction, and to bring the line nearer to Hook Norton. Originally it had been intended to pass through Swerford instead of Hook Norton but the change of plan, costing an extra £25,000, was approved by Parliament in 1881.

Hook Norton was once a centre of the wool industry, as can be seen from its Wool Church, but in the nineteenth century the extraction of iron ore became predominant. One of the concerns formed to exploit the deposits was the Hook Norton Ironstone Partnership who unfortunately became bankrupt. As the principal creditor, the Great Western Railway, who had absorbed the Banbury & Cheltenham Direct in 1897, came into possession of the ironstone undertaking's locomotive *Hook Norton*, which was an 0-6-0 tank, built by Manning Wardle & Co in 1889. It was transferred to Weymouth to work boat trains on the harbour tramway, where it survived as GWR No 1337, until 1926.

After crossing the country where iron ore deposits had been worked regularly after the coming of the railway, the line reached Bloxham. Here the railway left two tangible reminders of its presence, the 'Railway Tavern' in Queens Street, now closed and used as a private house, and the footbridge spanning the line, that had to be built to maintain the private footpath of Dr Hyde. But although people said Bloxham would miss the train, by 1963 it was scarce remembered. After all, Bloxham was only three miles from Banbury by road, but ten miles by train.

After calling at Milton Halt, trains ran into Adderbury, where the single track with passing loops became double. At first Adderbury was considered to be too near the end of the line to make the construction of a station worthwhile, but the importance of the ironstone industry caused the provision of a small station for the village by the time the line opened. Just short of the junction at King's Sutton, an authorised southward facing spur would have curved away to join the Oxford to Birmingham line.

However, on 2 June 1951 all this was to change. Driver Townsend and Fireman Baker stood ready with 0–6–0 pannier tank No 5407. The one-coach push-and-pull unit led for the trip to Banbury and Driver Townsend, sitting in the driving compartment, was to be kept busy, raising his cap to the villagers who turned out to wave farewell. Outward signs of the passing of the service were a Union Jack, a laurel wreath and a board reading '1887 Last Train 1951'. Among the mourners were a party from Bloxham School and the Locomotive Superintendent from Banbury, but they were to be joined by a varied company as the journey continued. When Fireman Baker had removed a large number of schoolboys from the locomotive, the journey into history started. He was determined to enter and leave each station in fitting style and added the noise of the whistle to the explosion of fog detonators. At Chipping Norton the train stopped for ten minutes. 'Chippy Dick', one of the many local nicknames for the train, was making his last run today and was surrounded by press reporters and photographers. A little to one side the stationmaster plotted with a ganger to give 'them boys from the school' a scare. He dispatched the ganger hotfoot to place six detonators further along the line and the loud report they produced gave the twenty boys a rude awakening.

As the train ran across Hook Norton viaducts, it was spotted by Signalman Moulder. 'Here it comes for the last time', he said as he pulled back a lever and prepared to exchange the blue token the engineman had carried from Chipping Norton for the red token they would take to Bloxham. When 'The Hooky Flyer', as the train was known locally, reached Bloxham, it was met by a crowd of about 200 and a group from Bloxham School's Cadet Corps drum and bugle band who were there to give a musical background to the event. One of the passengers to join the train here was 77-year-old George Manning, who as a schoolboy had bought the first ticket from Bloxham to King's Sutton on 6 April 1887. He also bought the last ticket and was allowed to retain it as a souvenir when he reached Banbury. He recalled that on his first trip, made to drive a pig home, the train was composed of four coaches and three classes, in hope or anticipation of future traffic. On his last trip, the train departed to the sound of 'One More Mile to Go' played on a bugle. Finally the cortège passed over the junction at King's Sutton and joined the Birmingham line, over which it continued as far as Banbury. 'The Hooky Flyer was dead.

CHAPTER 6

The Vale of Evesham

Introduction

The Vale of Evesham is very much a transitional area at the crossroads of the South-West Midlands. To the north lie the Midland Plain and the industrial areas of the Black Country. To the east and south-east are the historic towns of Warwick, Stratford-upon-Avon and many beautiful Cotswold villages, while not far away to the south are Gloucester and Bristol, with the Malvern Hills and Welsh borderlands to the west.

Evesham lies almost centrally within its Vale on the banks of the River Avon, not a great distance from Tewkesbury where the Avon joins the Severn, and is the centre of the fruit-growing industry for which the Vale is famed. Geographically the region has much of interest, and so too have its railways. This chapter includes only two, the first being from Redditch to Ashchurch via Alcester, Broom and Evesham, the second from Alcester to Bearley.

Redditch to Ashchurch—The Midland Loop

Redditch to Ashchurch is the closed portion of a line which originally formed the Midland Railway loop from Barnt Green

to Ashchurch. One of the first major railway coups was enacted
by the Midland when it purchased the Birmingham & Gloucester and Bristol & Gloucester Railways in 1846 from under
the noses of the Great Western directors, achieving direct access
into the heart of GWR territory. The direct line, opened

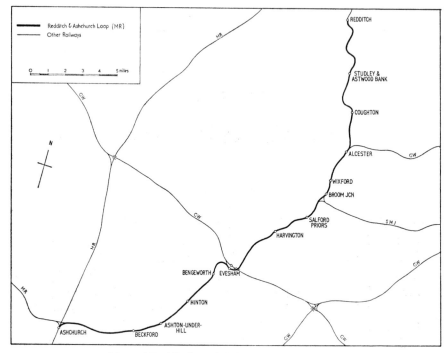

Map of Redditch to Ashchurch, Midland Railway

throughout between Gloucester and Birmingham on 17
December 1840, became the shortest route from the south-west
to the Midlands and, as a consequence, a very valuable access
line.

The direct line, however, had several drawbacks, one being
the difficult Lickey Incline, but more important from the local
traffic viewpoint was that it bypassed most of the towns of any
importance in the Vale. It was evident that in due course some
form of rail communication more directly related to the local

needs of the Vale would be required, and a number of proposals were put forward. Three of the towns, Evesham, Alcester and Redditch, lay in the Avon and Arrow valleys and offered immediate prospects for rail connection. This eventually resulted in the Midland Railway's loop line, traversing the Vale in a north-to-south direction, but it took three separate companies to carry it through! The first arm of the loop was provided by the Redditch Railway, authorised by an Act of 23 July 1858 to construct its single-track branch from Barnt Green, on the Birmingham & Gloucester Railway, to Redditch.

Redditch is a town very much in the throes of change and development, being today a designated New Town and overspill of Birmingham, and the line from Barnt Green to Redditch remains open to allow for commuter traffic to the City. The town grew up initially around skilled metal industries, such as fishing tackle, needle and spring manufacture, and as such represents the southernmost extremity of the West Midlands industrial area, forming the gradual transition to the quiet agricultural lands of the Vale. The Redditch Railway originally terminated on the northern edge of the town, but a more convenient site closer to the town centre was chosen when extending the line southwards. This station, however, was demolished for part of the new shopping centre for Redditch new town and yet another site 100yd to the north has now been adopted for the terminus.

At the southern end of the Vale, the Midland looked with covetous eyes upon Evesham, already served by the Oxford, Worcester & Wolverhampton Railway which had opened its station in 1852. A branch from Ashchurch to Evesham was accordingly authorised by an Act of 7 June 1861, passed almost two months before the GWR leased the OW & WR. Four years were allowed by the Act for completion, and the line to Evesham opened on 1 October 1864, having a station only a matter of yards from that of the GWR and sharing the same approach road.

Meanwhile, moves were afoot for linking Evesham with Redditch and plans were made by the independent Evesham

& Redditch Railway, authorised on 13 July 1863, to link with both the advancing Midland and the existing GWR at Evesham. From its Act which stated:

> An Act for making a Railway from the Ashchurch and Evesham Railway of the Midland Railway Company, in the Parish of St. Lawrence, Evesham, in the County of Worcester, to the Redditch Railway at Redditch, with a branch to the West Midland Railway. . . .

it is apparent that the driving force behind the line came from the south, to provide better access to the Birmingham market for products of the Vale.

Construction work began from the southern end and reached Alcester to allow the line to be opened for goods on 16 June and passengers on 17 September 1866. North of Alcester, work was more difficult, largely because of a tunnel south of Redditch station, approached at both ends by deep cutting. The southern approach to Redditch was in itself particularly arduous, with a long climb at a ruling gradient of 1 in 120, and locomotives were often quite short of steam by the time they had completed the journey. In January 1881, a particularly heavy blizzard caused snowdrifts which completely blocked the cutting to the northern tunnel entrance, reputedly halting trains for a week, while instances of night goods trains stalling on greasy rails on the incline could often awake half the town!

The final section of line was opened on 4 May 1868, with a new station at Redditch. The line became effectively the Midland loop from that date as both the Redditch and Evesham & Redditch Railways were worked from the outset by the Midland, the Redditch Railway having been taken over by the Midland on 1 January 1865, though the E & RR remained nominally independent until 1 July 1882. From 1868, therefore, the Midland held the monopoly of north to south communications across the Vale, and the GWR the less strategically important east-to-west route, as far as the internal economy of the Vale was concerned.

Apart from Evesham and Alcester, the latter becoming the

terminus of the GWR branch from Bearley, the other point of interest on the route of the E & RR was Broom. This was to become the junction with a further interloper to the area, the Evesham, Redditch & Stratford-upon-Avon Junction Railway. Strangely perhaps, the hamlet of Broom never seemingly benefited from proximity to its railway junction and, apart from Broom Mills, remains a relatively quiet, rural locality. Broom Junction was scarcely worthy of the importance its name implied being an island platform with the minimum of facilities. It was situated in a rather isolated spot about a quarter of a mile west of the village on the opposite bank of the River Arrow!

Ashchurch was a complicated junction station of a somewhat unusual layout. The platforms for the main line between Birmingham and Gloucester were parallel, but both branches to Evesham and Tewkesbury had curved platform faces turning outwards from the south within a triangle completed by a line linking the Evesham and Tewkesbury branches which crossed the main line by a flat crossing just to the north of the station. This line permitted through running to Tewkesbury for Midland trains from the Evesham branch but was little used.

Services north of Redditch were more of a commuting nature, but the remainder of the route served primarily local needs. On the double-track section between Ashchurch and Evesham the stations at Beckford, Ashton-under-Hill, Hinton and Bengeworth were constructed of stone, whereas those to the north of Evesham were built of brick. These stations were substantially built, and a journey along the entire loop through the Avon and Arrow valleys took the passenger through some very pretty station settings and countryside.

The local goods traffic, rather than the long-distance freight which also used the loop, was primarily of fruit and vegetables on outgoing goods trains and coal and fertilisers on incoming services. During the season a number of special fruit trains of up to sixty wagons consigned to all parts of the country would often delay the passenger services over the loop. Grain for the mills at Broom and Great Alne was also delivered by rail, much of it being imported via the Port of Bristol. Evesham was the centre of the fruit traffic and always had a busy yard and transfer traffic with the GWR. Salford Priors was another station of interest as there was a private siding to a firm which repaired steam traction engines for agricultural use. Wixford had a small goods yard with facilities for a large pig farm at Oversley Castle, while Coughton was built mainly to serve the needs of the gentry at nearby Coughton Court. Many of these stations on the loop still remain today as private dwellings.

The line played an important role in the livelihood of the Vale and it came as something of a shock when BR suddenly announced withdrawal of services between Redditch and Evesham from 1 October 1962 due to the unsafe condition of the line. The southern section between Evesham and Ashchurch only survived for passengers until June 1963. From October 1962, BR provided the service using hired Midland Red buses which called only at the stations. Goods trains between Redditch and Alcester continued to operate until 6 July 1964.

Passenger trains over the Midland loop in the nineteenth century were largely operated by Kirtley and Johnson 0–4–4 and 2–4–0 tank engines, but in the early years of the twentieth century, larger Deeley 0–6–4 tanks came to the line and provided the staple motive power until replaced by Stanier Class 3 2–6–2Ts. These were in turn superseded by Fowler 2–6–4 tanks and Ivatt Class 4 2–6–0s, while several classes of BR standard locomotives could also be seen from time to time. On 25 April 1960, diesel multiple-units were introduced between Birmingham and Redditch, at which point there was a transfer to steam, and trains south of Redditch were sometimes operated thereafter by 'Jinty' Class 3F 0–6–0Ts. As a result of the emergency withdrawal of the intermediate section of the loop between Redditch and Evesham in 1962, it became impracticable to continue to operate the remaining steam-hauled services to Evesham from Ashchurch by LMSR locomotives and to fill the vacuum created ex-GWR 0–6–0 pannier tanks from Cheltenham shed were introduced for the nine-month period prior to final withdrawal of passenger services between Ashchurch and Evesham.

Goods traffic also had varied motive power, with various Kirtley, Johnson and Deeley o–6–o tender locomotives hauling early goods services. In the twentieth century, Midland Class 4F o–6–os were introduced and became mainly concerned with this traffic, although Stanier Class 5 4–6–o, Class 8F 2–8–o and in latter years BR Standard Class 9F 2–10–o locomotives played a role on heavier goods traffic. South of Broom, goods services from the SMJ also brought additional variety of motive power and, after the introduction of South Wales traffic in 1951, Austerity 2–8–os could regularly be seen working on these freights. With the withdrawal of these services in 1960 and the ending of the Washwood Heath to Gloucester freights which previously used the loop, section by section services across the Vale by the loop finally came sadly to a close.

Alcester to Bearley—The Alcester Railway

The Alcester Railway was 6½ miles of interest and character and it is surprising that more has not been published on it. It was very much a 'typical' GWR branch, but with a personality perhaps special to the Vale.

The line was authorised as the Alcester Railway by an Act of 6 August 1872, being a branch from the Stratford-upon-Avon Railway at Bearley to Alcester on the Evesham & Redditch Railway. From the outset it was dominated by the GWR which was to operate the line for the company after it was opened on 4 September 1876. The GWR also took over maintenance of it on 4 September 1877, before finally absorbing the company in 1883.

As built, the branch had a single intermediate station at Great Alne, but a halt was opened at Aston Cantlow on 18 December 1922 when the line was re-opened after having been closed during World War I. Aston Cantlow was a single platform constructed from sleepers, with a small wooden shelter. Great Alne, on the other hand, was far more substantially built, with a large station canopy, and is little changed today although it is now used as a private residence. Great

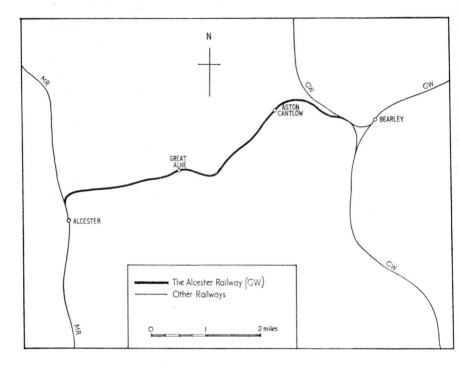

Map of the Alcester Railway

Alne was also of interest from two other aspects. First, it was site of flour mills which have been established on the banks of the River Alne since medieval times at an especially pretty spot. Secondly, the village was chosen by the Maudslay Motor Company for a motor works after having to move from Coventry during World War II.

The mills were served by private road, owned by the railway, which left the village at the east end by the old Boot Inn (now demolished) and crossed the line by a level crossing. About 75 per cent of the grain was imported mainly through the Port of Bristol and for many years came to Great Alne by rail, as did the remaining 25 per cent unless grown within a twenty-mile radius of the mills. Most of the flour, meal and finished products

156

were delivered by horse-drawn transport, but some was sent further afield by rail to places such as Birmingham.

The opening of the Maudslay Works was perhaps an even more interesting tale. In 1940, the company was directed by the Government to move out of Coventry for strategic reasons. The site selected was the grounds of the former manor house at Great Alne in the woods towards the Alne Hills to the north of the village. This offered both security during the war and the promise of longer term development as a factory community. Owing to the wartime conditions, the employees were not permitted to change their employment and as a result were obliged either to travel from Coventry or find alternative accommodation. Passenger train services over the branch had ceased officially from 25 September 1939 but because of the large number of employees who had to travel daily from Coventry the branch was quietly reopened between Bearley and Great Alne for the unadvertised special train which brought the work force to the factory. The journey was achieved by normal service train from Coventry to Leamington where the special train was joined. This travelled via Hatton and Bearley Junctions arriving at Great Alne at 08.00 and departing in the evening at 17.30 often not arriving back at Coventry because of day-time service disruptions until 20.00. These unadvertised services continued until 3 July 1944, when the journey was transferred to road by hired buses.

The rather chequered career of the branch requires a little additional historical detail. During World War I, the branch was closed from 1 January 1917, and the track was lifted and sent to France. Local stories, however, say that the ship carrying the rails was torpedoed in the English Channel where they say the rails remain to this day! After the War the GWR decided to relay the line and the section from Bearley to Great Alne, including the new halt at Aston Cantlow, was opened again on 18 December 1922. Great Alne to Alcester was reopened on 1 August 1923.

As built, the branch left the Midland a short distance to the north of Alcester station which originally had separate booking halls for both Midland and GWR passengers! The busy yard at Alcester dealt mainly in coal, timber and steel traffic for the small factories of the town while the local co-operative society had a private cattle siding for its abattoir. At the junction, the GWR built a small shed for the branch locomotive. Passing beneath Ryknild Street, the original Roman road on which Alcester grew up, the branch crossed the River Arrow by means of a sturdy girder bridge and proceeded to climb to Kinwarton, on a rising grade locally known as Gerrards Bank. If the train was a mixed one with both an auto coach, coal trucks, and vans, the climb was something of a feat for the diminutive GWR 0–4–2 tank usually employed on the branch. When the line was under construction near this point, the wife of a former incumbent of Kinwarton Rectory was opposed to the railway and it was her practice to go out at night and remove the surveyors pegs placed along the projected line of route. Eventually she was dissuaded and construction of the line in the area proceeded! Shortly after the summit, the line crossed the B4089 road and after traversing a level crossing, ran into Great Alne. The line then followed the meandering course of the River Alne, which it crossed near Aston Cantlow. Having been travelling in a north-easterly direction for almost two miles, the line curved into an easterly course as it approached the railway-owned Stratford-upon-Avon Canal.

On 26 July 1901, the GWR obtained authority to construct a line from Tyseley to Bearley, where junction was to be made with the former Stratford-upon-Avon Railway giving the GWR more direct access to Stratford. When opened to goods at the end of 1907 and passengers on 1 July 1908, a junction was also made with the Alcester Railway at a point just east of where the line passed beneath the Edstone Aqueduct of the canal and a triangular junction permitted the Bearley trains to reach their terminal station.

At the junction with the Alcester Railway, the branch train was able to take water from the canal by means of a pipe from the aqueduct and the trouble caused when fish were caught in the tanks also occupied a high position in local folklore!

Page 159 (above) The first LNWR station at Market Harborough, which was replaced in 1885. The Midland branches off to the left, and the Rugby line to the right; (below) in 1896, the bricklayers start to construct the island platform at Woodford, and the abutments of the rail overbridge

Page 160 (*above*) On 26 October 1963, in the twilight days on the
Great Central route, Royal Scot 4–6–0 No 46125 *3rd Carabinier* enters
Brackley with the 14.38 Marylebone to Nottingham train; (*below*) the
latter-day pride of the Great Central route—Class A3 4–6–2 No 60102
Sir Frederick Banbury leaves Rugby with the up Master Cutler, passing
the exit from the up goods loop, in the 1950s

Although the branch was closed to all traffic from 1 March 1951, the water pipe and cistern could be found until comparatively recently. After closure the branch was used as a storage siding for redundant wagons before eventually being lifted, although the trackbed and features of the line remain well defined to this day. 'The Alcester Coffee Pot', as the branch train was affectionately known locally, was generally hauled by a small 0–6–0T or Dean or Collett 0–4–2 tank engine. In the nineteenth century, an outside-framed Armstrong 0–6–0T was usually employed but in 1901 the engine was 0–4–2T No 203, while from 1923 until about 1936 No 537 worked on the line prior to the arrival of No 4848 (later 1448) which was the regular locomotive during the final years of operation.

CHAPTER 7

The Nene and Welland Valleys

Introduction

Nestling at the foot of the hill from the village, under the shadow of Harringworth Viaduct, stood Seaton station. At any time in the 1950s it must have presented a timeless sight, a country junction where three lines met and what few passengers there were could make their connections. Summer must have seemed everlasting.

In 1851 the Rugby & Stamford Railway was opened; later, in 1879, came the line to Wansford with a service ultimately extending to Peterborough and finally in 1894 the Uppingham branch. But inexorably the axe fell during the 1960s and by 1966 the last passenger had departed. Seaton station still stands but where trains once ran, cars are scrapped. *Sic transit gloria mundi.*

Blisworth to Peterborough

The level of the proposed railway will differ so little from that of the natural ground over which it will pass, that it may be executed at much less expense than other railways in general, provided that the company who are to form it be allowed to use level crossings for the roads which will be intersected by their line, which are so numerous, that if bridges over all or most of the roads be made a *sine qua non*, it will be a complete veto to the undertaking.

In these terms General Pasley reported on the desirability of the twenty-six level crossings on the Northampton & Peterborough Railway, to which many objections had been raised. The owners of the Peterborough & Wellingborough turnpike,

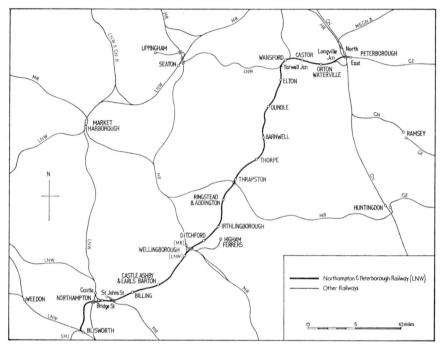

Map of the Northampton & Peterborough Railway

for example, had stated that the proposed railway was not in the public interest and even if it was, no circumstances justified crossing the turnpike on the level. As a result of the controversy, provisions as to these crossings were included in the authorising Act. 'Good and sufficient' gates were to be erected, opened and shut by 'proper persons' and although they were normally to be kept shut against the road, the Board of Trade could insist on them being kept shut against the railway. Furthermore, when the railway crossed a turnpike road on the level adjoining a station, trains were limited to a maximum speed of 4 mph.

Level crossings were inevitable on a line that followed the Nene valley for most of its course, a good example of geography dictating the course of communications. The river was of course the first means of connecting the towns of its valley, but the railway was regarded as much more preferable once it was seen to be practicable. So in the autumn of 1842 a group of Northampton citizens approached the directors of the London & Birmingham Railway with the proposal to construct a branch from Blisworth to Peterborough. One factor which may have influenced them was the by-passing of the town by the main line. An old *canard* attributes this to the opposition of the people of Northampton, who feared the disturbance that a railway would create, but a more likely reason is the gradients that such a line through Northampton would have entailed. Robert Stephenson was supposed to have said that he could easily get the line into Northampton but it would be a different matter to get it out again. By following the Nene valley a railway could leave the town, and reach the valuable prize of Peterborough, whilst Northampton could enjoy the benefits of being on a railway, albeit a branch.

Upon investigation the London & Birmingham found that not only did the line possess a favourable course, with the likelihood of local traffic, but also would indirectly serve Boston and Lynn, together with the greater part of Lincolnshire. Indeed the Parliamentary Select Committee also heard of great support from Yarmouth and the Eastern Counties for this line to connect them with the 'manufacturing districts' and further support from the Black Country. But the Chairman of the London & Birmingham put it more succinctly.

Still it is as an accessory to the London & Birmingham Railway that it is of value, as a line of communication which will put us in possession of traffic which we have not hitherto possessed. I should, however, be misleading you, if I held out the prospect of its being lucrative, independent of the London & Birmingham Railway.

It was just this attitude to which Earl Fitzwilliam objected, and explains his opposition to the railway. He felt that this line would discourage the construction of a northern line of railway via Cambridge and Peterborough by the impecunious Northern & Eastern Railway. The Northampton & Peterborough would add twenty-five miles to a route via Cambridge to London and the noble Earl thought that the support the line had gained in Peterborough was based on the expectation of profit with little exertion required for its attainment. Strong words, but they did not prevent the company from obtaining its Act.

Further difficulties were presented by the Dean and Chapter of Peterborough Cathedral, who had the privilege of holding the Bridge Fair in a meadow where the railway was to terminate. Naturally they objected to any interference with the fair, from which they received valuable tolls, but eventually a compromise was reached; the railway was to terminate to the west of this ground. Meanwhile the Eastern Counties Railway had proposed a branch from Ely to Peterborough and it was eventually agreed that the London & Birmingham should have the use of the ECR station for its trains from Blisworth. The Midland Railway's Syston & Peterborough line also came to use this station and its temporarily isolated section from Stamford to Peterborough was worked by the LNWR, as successor to the L & B, until the ECR took over. LNWR locomotives and coaches were thus seen in Stamford six years before its legitimate service on the Rugby & Stamford began.

Robert Stephenson had ultimate responsibility for the engineering of the line, familiarising himself with the lie of the land by walking over its entire length. Under his direction it was laid out by George Bidder, who described the works on the line as generally light. Since the average fall of the valley was between 6 and 8ft per mile, the gradients were good. The steepest were 1 in 100 at Blisworth, where there was also a 9 chain radius curve, and 1 in 180, adopted to pass Lilford Park without interfering with ornamental property. The 1 in 100 was anticipated to cause little difficulty in working the line, firstly because traffic was expected to be light and secondly assistance could be given if necessary.

Nearly half of the route passed through water-meadows, valuable agricultural land. Some doubt was thrown on the value attributed to the required land, as the Land Agent had only 3½ days for his valuation, and had to use a gig to cover the ground rather than walk the course. No appreciable difficulties were expected from the flood waters of the Nene, which was crossed eleven times, although provision was made for the river over-flowing; even so, flooding damaged the line in 1847, 1852 and 1947. The Act provided that whenever the river was crossed, the railway should be constructed on piling for a minimum of 100yd, including the bridge.

The river could not be followed all the time as there were a variety of obstacles, natural and man-made. Near Wansford the Nene takes an acute bend, and to avoid it a tunnel was constructed, 681yd long. Between Barnwell and Thorpe Waterville the line took a wide sweep through Wigsthorpe to avoid a deeper cutting, which would have had to be built on the more direct course so as not to disturb Lord Lilford. This diversion was four miles long and entailed a lateral deviation of 1½ miles. Had it not been made, it was estimated that the route would have been ⅓ mile shorter and £25,000 extra expenditure would not have had to be incurred. Further controversy over the course was caused by its close proximity to Delapré Abbey in Northampton, the property of Edward Bouverie. To counter his objections, the railway company pointed out that the river was very busy with barges and 'the nuisance of loitering navigators' destroyed his amenities. However, the Act specifically allowed deviations through his estate to meet his wishes.

Perhaps the greatest spleen was vented by Lord Fitzwilliam. Having failed to defeat the railway he determined to throw obstacles in its way. He requested one deviation to avoid Alwalton Meadow, to which there would have been scarcely any opposition, and another of 300yd to keep the railway away from the line of Alwalton Castle, a request which would have failed Standing Orders. He suggested a further alteration, leaving the railway as built between Fotheringhay and Elton and following the road from Oundle to Peterborough, rejoining the line near Orton Waterville. It would have entailed rough country and cost an extra £120,000. Not only this, it increased the distance to Stamford, served by Wansford station, by two miles. As a coup de grace, he wished the line to be diverted to clear a fox cover.

The railway was proposed and built as double track from Blisworth to Northampton and single onwards to Peterborough, with a crossing place at Thrapston. Trains would be timed to meet at Thrapston so that their locomotives could be changed. Single-line tokens had not been evisaged then and it was proposed to confine locomotives to their respective sections. 'It is obvious that unless it was possible for an engine to run against itself there can be no collision'. Four journeys a day were proposed, and it was confidently expected that it might be increased to seven or eight, still in safety. Much discussion revolved around the safety of single-line working and George Hudson was called for his advice. The oracle did not confine himself to this subject alone, as he spoke about level crossings, the transport of cattle and gave advice of all kinds.

Excitement mounted when the locomotive was placed on the rails on 19 February 1845 at Thrapston station, having first passed through Northampton, drawn by sixteen horses. All was made ready for the opening to passengers. The section from Blisworth to Northampton opened on 13 May and the section onwards to Peterborough on 2 June 1845. On 31 May the L & B Directors and a large party of friends attended the formal opening. *Herapath's Railway Journal*, having received no invitation and feeling somewhat snubbed, spoke of these friends 'of which we have not the honour to be in their number, and therefore cannot speak of the beauties of the line, nor of the good things they enjoyed'.

A special train ran on Monday 2 June conveying the Directors accompanied by the Mayor, Corporation and other inhabitants of Northampton. Composed of fifteen first class carriages, it ran the forty-seven miles to Peterborough in about 2½ hours inclusive of stops, which in total took about fifty minutes. 'The progress of the train was a sort of spectacle for the people of the district through which the line passes, every station and village being crowded with wonder-struck gazers.'

The rapid increase of traffic induced the company to make the single-track section double by 1846, and in 1847 authority for a cut-off line was obtained. This would have run from Wellingborough to Bletchley to shorten the route to the south by about eleven miles. However, the Great Northern Railway route was still about twenty-three miles shorter and the proposal hardly seemed worthwhile. It would have served Newport Pagnell and Olney but no attempt was made at its construction. Similarly powers for a link from Weedon to the branch near Northampton were allowed to lapse.

Early passengers would have left 'the commodious booking offices and sheds of the Blisworth station' and crossed the main line. Here the LNWR Rules stated that 'the Policeman' was always to keep the red signal turned on to the Peterborough line, except when he had ascertained the main line was clear, when the red signal was to be displayed to the main line and the train let off the branch. A couple of miles further on, just after the curve below Hunsbury Hill, a contemporary guide advised passengers that they could gain the best view of Northampton. The station here, later called Bridge Street, had an 'engine house', sheds for carriages and goods, cattle and sheep pens while Messrs Worster & Co, Chaplin & Horne, and Pickford & Co had separate establishments. In 1866 the Midland made a connection from their Leicester & Hitchin Extension at Wellingborough to the Northampton & Peterborough and reached Northampton by running powers. Their passenger station was originally sited near Bridge Street but on the opening of the Bedford & Northampton line in 1872, services were transferred to that railway's station at St John's Street. A further piece was added to the jigsaw by an Act of 1875 which authorised a link between the Northampton & Peterborough and the Northampton & Market Harborough Railway components of the LNWR to enable trains to run from Bridge Street to Castle stations. On its opening to passengers in 1882 all but one train on the Peterborough line were diverted to run to and from Northampton Castle instead of Blisworth.

Peterborough passengers travelled onwards through the 'first class' station at Wellingborough as well as others of lesser worth, and at Wansford they might have seen one of the coaches and omnibuses, which would take about an hour on the journey to Stamford.

At the outset three trains a day each way, soon increased to five, covered the 110 miles to Euston in 4½ hours. By the 1870s this had increased to six passenger trains throughout each weekday with one on Sundays. Additionally, there were five short workings each way on weekdays between Blisworth and Northampton. In the 1870s too, Peterborough had direct goods services to Rugby, Birmingham and Camden amongst other places.

The London & Birmingham coke ovens had been sited at Peterborough, but with the replacement of coke by coal as a locomotive fuel, they fell into disuse. Their site was used for a locomotive shed, opened in 1880, and on the eve of grouping in 1922 housing fifteen locomotives. Turning a Prince of Wales 4-6-0 here presented quite a problem. As the locomotive and tender together were too long for the turntable, each had to be turned separately. In 1932 the locomotives and men were transferred to the former Midland shed at Spital Bridge and the shed closed. A further change of management, British Railways, brought all Peterborough sheds into the Eastern Region and a mixture of Eastern and London Midland region types as locomotive power.

May 1845 had brought excitement; May 1964 brought melancholy. The last trains ran on Saturday 2 May and No D5800 set out at 17.05 from Northampton Castle for the forty-five mile run to Peterborough. On its way it passed ex-LMS Class 5 No 44936 with the 18.00 Peterborough East to Northampton, and when it drew into Peterborough almost a hundred and twenty years of history were at an end. Now moves are afoot to use part of the route for a steam railway.

Running through the Nene Valley Park, it would be one of the recreational amenities of Greater Peterborough. A Northampton & Peterborough guide of the 1840s said 'the entire line of country through which the line passes is an attractive one'. The wheel has turned full circle.

Rugby to Stamford and Peterborough

A place replete with shadowy shapes, this Mugby Junction in the black hours of the four and twenty. Mysterious goods trains, covered with palls and gliding on like vast weird funerals, conveying themselves guiltily away from the presence of the few lighted lamps, as if their freight had come to a secret and unlawful end. Half miles of coal pursuing in a detective manner, following where they lead, stopping when they stop, backing when they back.

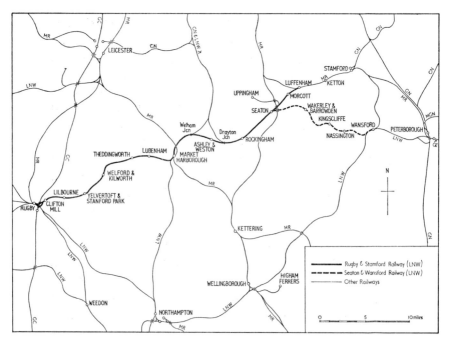

Map of the Rugby & Stamford Railway

In these graphic terms Charles Dickens described Rugby in the Christmas number of *All the Year Round* in 1866, an edition which sold 70,000 copies in America in less than a fortnight, and a quarter of a million in England.

The stories it contained revolved around people and places connected with Mugby (or Rugby) but the piece is probably best remembered for Dickens' spirited attack on the refreshment room, 'What's proudest boast is, that it never yet refreshed a mortal being.' 'Our Missus', the *grande dame* in charge, had travelled to France to see how things were done there, secure in the knowledge that it was bound to be inferior to anything England could produce. Upon her return she gave her impressions to the assembled staff and a horrible tale it was. Not only were there eatable things to eat and drinkable things to drink, convenience, elegance and moderate charges, but even worse 'attention, common civility, nay, even politeness'.

To be fair, the story was an amalgam of all Dickens' experiences in refreshment rooms, but his satire resulted in troops of passengers alighting at Rugby to purchase refreshments, just to see 'Our Missus' and her young ladies. The refreshment room they patronised was not the present one, which dates from the rebuilding of 1886, but rather the one in the second station of 1840. It stood to the south of an underbridge leading to Brownsover Mill, and was built entirely of wood. Around 1850 a bay was added to accommodate the trains of the Rugby & Stamford Railway, the up platform being extended to the end of it.

Essentially a satellite of the London & Birmingham Railway, the Rugby & Stamford encountered opposition in Parliament from a rival project, the Rugby & Huntingdon, but the latter's hopes were dashed when the preamble to its Bill was declared unproven. Among the procession of witnesses which appeared to convince the legislature of the value of the Rugby & Stamford was its engineer, Charles Liddell. He expected no peculiar difficulties in the engineering works of the 34 mile line, as the works were light and the steepest gradient was 1 in 140. None of the gradients would require a second locomotive to assist, while the sharpest curve, with a radius of three furlongs, was at the junction with the London & Birmingham at Rugby. However, the gentle course of the line meant that sixteen roads had to be crossed on the level. Adjoining one of these roads, at North Kilworth, the authorising Act required a station be built.

In 1840 the system of inspection by an officer of the Royal Engineers prior to a line's opening to passengers had been introduced, and Captain Wynne duly inspected the section from Rugby to Rockingham on 18 April 1850; he reported that the line was laid single as far as Market Harborough and double thence to Rockingham. All the works were of sufficient strength and the slopes of the cuttings and embankments stood well. However, he objected to a single signal post at Market Harborough as giving insufficient protection together with the lack of proper pointwork and recommended that the opening should be postponed. By the time that Captain Laffan arrived on 27 April 1850, a second signal had been added at Market Harborough and proper pointwork installed. The company proposed to work the line with only one locomotive, obviating risks of collision on the single line, and the Captain advised that the line could be opened. The section from Rugby to Market Harborough was opened on 1 May 1850 and on to Rockingham on 1 June.

Captain Wynne returned in 1851 to inspect the section from Rockingham to Luffenham. He found no signalling installed at the junction with the Syston & Peterborough line of the Midland Railway, which was to be used to reach Stamford. Nothing appeared to be happening to erect the signals, a state of affairs for which the Midland, whose task it was, were blamed. However, on his return, satisfactory arrangements had been made and, subject to regulations for a temporary length of single line at Rockingham, he considered that the line could be opened.

The opening of the final section on 2 June 1851 was not marked by any kind of celebration, and the first train apparently attracted very little attention. The *Stamford Mercury* of 6 June 1851 reported that traffic had been very moderate and probably would continue to be so until the new route was better known. Perhaps to make it better known, the LNWR offered return tickets, available for fifteen days, at 14s 6d (72½p) first class, 11s 6d (57½p) second and 7s (35p) third class to go to the Great Exhibition in London.

Twenty years later, the LNWR had turned to thinking of its route between Peterborough and Birmingham, and did not much like what it saw. All traffic had to pass via the Blisworth & Peterborough line to Blisworth and then go down the main line, a distance of 96¾ miles. Even passengers using the Midland route via Leicester had to travel 92½ miles. If a line were to be built from the Blisworth & Peterborough to join the Rugby & Stamford, a new, more direct route could be secured. Such was the background to the Seaton & Wansford Railway, which provided this twelve-mile link. This did not have the gentle profile of its elders but its steepest gradient was probably inevitable, given that it had to climb across from the Nene to the Welland valley.

The opening of this line to passengers on 1 November 1879 attracted more attention locally than had the Rugby & Stamford, 139 people joining the first train from Rugby, the 10.09 from Kingscliffe. The station here was curiously at odds with its surroundings, the only brick building in a grey stone village. Five trains a day each way were provided and this line soon became the tail that wagged the dog; the Seaton to Stamford section began its slow decline. In the same year that the Seaton & Wansford had been authorised, the Great Northern had obtained powers for a link from Fletton Junction on its main line to Longville Junction on the Blisworth & Peterborough. By using this one and three quarter mile link and the Seaton & Wansford, it could reach Drayton Junction, where it diverged on to the GN and LNW Joint Railway, eventually to reach Leicester (Belgrave Road). This service commenced in 1883 and lasted to 1916.

Meanwhile developments had been taking place at Market Harborough. When the Leicester & Hitchin Extension of the Midland had been built, it had been content to join the LNWR at Great Bowden, to run through and use its station and then bear off again. At the time it seemed a useful expedient, but with the increase in traffic it became more and more awkward. It was finally ended in 1885 when the 'Market Harborough New Line' was opened. This left the Midland's old course at

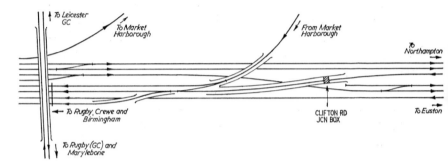

Diagram of Clifton Mill Junction, Rugby

Great Bowden, climbed at 1 in 165 to cross the Stamford line and then fell at 1 in 200 to enter the joint station where its tracks were level with the LNWR. It rejoined the old line at Little Bowden Junction. The joint station had two station-masters, one LNWR, who also represented the GNR which was allowed to run into the town, and one Midland. The LNWR staff maintained with all the authority of the Premier Line that, 'whereas the LNWR had been built by engineers, the Midland was built by mountaineers', an allusion no doubt to the sawtooth profile of the Midland main line. Whether this furthered harmony between the two staffs must remain un-answered but there could be no doubt about the harmony of the station building. Constructed in a revived Queen Anne manner, it has been aptly described as 'perhaps the most pleas-ing of all Leicestershire stations'.

Back at Rugby something was at last being done about a new station. Opened finally in 1886, it was basically a huge island platform with bays let into the ends and in one of the bays at the south end, today's platform 7, the Stamford trains found a home. Firmly grasping a thorny problem, the LNWR determined to provide a system of junctions at the south end so that trains converging on the main line, Stamford and Northampton lines would not foul each others' paths. Thus Clifton Mill Junction took shape and required alterations to the down Stamford line. Its new course diverged just after leaving Clifton Mill station and after taking an 's' bend, passed under Clifton Road between Clifton Vicarage and Vicarage Hill, crossed the River Avon on a viaduct and also crossed the up Northampton line. It then passed over the up main line, joined the down Northampton line, and then descended to the level of the other lines. Alterations were made at the time of electrification but the basic pattern remains, as illustrated in the diagram opposite.

On 5 July 1885 about 300 men were engaged in track alterations, so that the trains could run into the down side of the new station. After the mid-day trains had left the old down side, the next train was the 18.45 arrival from Market Harborough. One thousand five hundred people assembled on the platform to see it arrive and some 200 people walked out to Clifton Mill to join the train there. Driven by the assistant locomotive superintendent, the footplate was crowded with officials.

With the opening of the new line in 1879, through coaches were introduced from Birmingham to Harwich. In 1909 they had become a train leaving Birmingham at 16.00, and Rugby at 17.10 taking an hour and twenty minutes to reach Peterborough, with an ultimate arrival at Harwich at 21.30. Although the service to Harwich ceased in 1939, the trains were still dubbed the 'Contys' and a descendant ran between Birmingham and Yarmouth, a route also taken by holiday specials. A night mail was run from Rugby to Peterborough to connect with West Coast Postal Services. Local trains were run between Market Harborough and Rugby in the mornings and evenings to provide transport to and from the works, particularly AEI, in Rugby.

Welford & Kilworth station presented an idea of the line in the 1930s. Situated in a vale, at a road crossing, it had been advertised as the station for Lutterworth, as Welford & Lutterworth, before the opening of the Great Central. Cattle came

175

from Ireland and Devon, sheep from Hawick and Knighton and cattle cake from the docks at Liverpool, Hull and London. Farm machinery, seed and fertilizer were other kinds of agricultural traffic and Monday was known as rodeo day, as eight to ten cattle wagons had to be loaded for dispatch to Rugby.

Grain was another staple traffic for which the railway hired out sacks. As from 5,000 to 10,000 sacks could be in use in one season, it required quite some effort by the staff to keep track of them. The farmers acquired the reputation of slow payers, probably because they in turn were always pressing the purchasers of their grain. Parcels traffic was also dealt with, and cartage was hired for those that had to be delivered. From across the road, United Dairies would forward two to four tanks of milk a day depending on the season, and would receive in return machinery, milk cans, churns and coal.

Coal was also received in the station yard by merchants such as J. Ellis & Son and farmers would join together to receive a wagon of coal. Building materials and roadstone were also to be found, as was sugar beet in season. Arrangements were made with farmers that their beet should be forwarded in a certain week, so that last minute exchanges between the farmers meant headaches for the railway staff. Roses, eggs and beer completed the freight scene. Whilst passenger traffic was in the main to and from Rugby and its works, some went to Market Harborough and a few to London, with some holiday traffic.

A peculiar traffic which originated at Welford was water churns for the level crossings, signal boxes and stations that did not have a mains water supply. After the withdrawal of through freight trains in 1965, the Birmingham express stopped at South Kilworth crossing just to set down water. So in Summer many faces peered from open windows to try to find the reason for the stop in the middle of open country.

The Great Northern Leicester to Peterborough service had brought Stirling and Ivatt singles to the eastern arm of the line and LNWR Jumbo 2-4-0s were also to be seen. Relegations from main line services in the 1930s brought Experiment and Prince of Wales 4-6-0s and Precursor, Renown and George V

4–4–0s. The hold of steam was temporarily relinquished in the early 1950s whilst No 10800, the third British main line diesel, used the route as a proving ground. The year 1957 saw the introduction of diesel multiple-units on the Rugby to Ely through train, but most services remained locomotive-hauled, as the large amount of fish and parcels traffic had to be conveyed in vans attached to the trains. Gradually from 1960, Stanier Class 5 4–6–0s, LNWR Class 7F 0–8–0s, Ivatt 2–6–2 tanks and their progeny BR Standard Class 2 2–6–2 tanks, gave way to diesels, such as the Brush Type 2 A1A-A1A (Class 31).

Of the three lines that left Peterborough for the west, the former Midland route to Leicester through Stamford was selected to carry all traffic, so the Rugby to Peterborough line and the associated Seaton to Stamford shuttle gradually declined. Local freight trains had been finally withdrawn in 1964 and closure notices were posted in October of that year. The date of withdrawal had been announced as 4 January 1965 but this was postponed to hear objections. However on 4 January thieves, perhaps anticipating closure, stole 75yd of telephone wire between Seaton and Wakerley & Barrowden stations. On 4 October the Seaton to Stamford shuttle changed from steam to diesel; for its last week it had been the sole-surviving steam push-and-pull train in Britain. Deliberations dragged on, until permission was granted by the Minister of Transport on 30 December, with final closure on 6 June 1966.

After the line closed, it was used to shoot the film *Robbery*. Perhaps the title echoed what the local community thought!

Seaton to Uppingham

Uppingham is principally known for its school. Founded in 1584, the school exercised a considerable influence in the area, and so on the railway that served it. Local lore attributes the coming of the railway to the school and the changes that affected it to the same source. One influence was certain, the school specials, which provided a contrast to the branch train on the three-mile meander from Seaton to Uppingham. Although the journey only took nine minutes, once reduced to six, it entailed a climb from 170 to 375ft above sea level and this could produce severe bouts of slipping on a frosty morning.

In September 1860, Edward Thring, the headmaster who did much to develop and expand the school, had noted in his diary

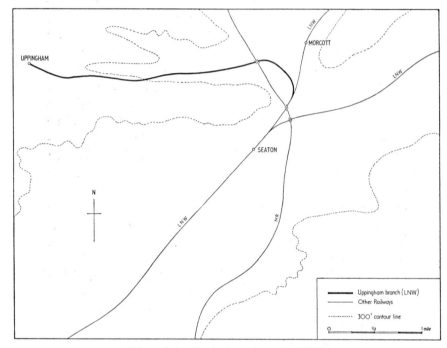

Map of the Uppingham branch, LNWR

'some talk of a branch railway to Uppingham' but nothing happened until 1890. At that time the school and market were served by Manton station on the Midland Railway and Seaton & Uppingham on the London & North Western, from where Mr Woodcock plied with his horsedrawn 'station fly'. Some indication of the state of communications in the district at its worst was given in February 1892, when vehicles were prevented from movement by snow falls, and because of obstructions on the LNWR, the omnibus due to reach Uppingham at 18.45 did not arrive until an hour before midnight.

So keen were the inhabitants of Uppingham to have their own railway and improve communications that they contributed £1,000 for the purchase of land. Lord Norton must have assisted the development of the line, for at a dinner held to celebrate the opening, the chairman spoke of the great interest and support that his Lordship had given the railway. He even gave it as his opinion that it was in no small measure due to Lord Norton that the LNWR were induced to build the line. However, the Chairman of the LNWR, when mentioning the opening of the line, took the opportunity to criticise the Board of Trade. He complained that, although only one locomotive could be run on it, the line had to be signalled as if there were heavy traffic over it. Such requirements were one of the reasons why railway companies had not been over-anxious to make shorter lines to bring traffic on to their main routes.

By the authorising Act the Great Northern were given running powers to Uppingham, in connection with the service they provided from Peterborough to Leicester, but these were not exercised. Furthermore, the Act laid down to some extent the course the line was to take. Certain fields of George Rowley in the parish of Morcott were not to be entered, no deviations from the centre line shown in the plans were allowed on Edward Monckton's land except by his written consent, and the line was to be taken through a specified arch of a viaduct on the Midland's Kettering & Manton Railway. In later years the maintenance gang for the viaduct was based at Seaton. Construction commenced on the circuitious route in November 1891. Trains would have to start from Seaton, running towards the north-east, and curve around to reach the valley up which the line ran to reach Uppingham.

There were three level sections, but also four sections at 1 in 60, and much cutting and embanking was necessary. The bad weather of 1892 delayed the works, as did a number of landslips which cost nearly half the total expenditure on the line. The contract was awarded to W. Radcliffe whose tender, one of fourteen opened, was for £13,830, comparing favourably with the engineer's estimate of £16,000. When the final reckoning came to be made in 1894, the total cost of construction excluding land was stated to be £30,000 and, whether through difficulties with this contract or not, the affairs of the contractor were placed in the hands of a receiver in 1894.

Although there was no opening ceremony, a dinner had been arranged for the evening of Monday 1 October 1894, the first day of scheduled passenger services, to celebrate the event but it was postponed owing to the death of Mrs Selwyn, wife of the Headmaster of Uppingham School. However, on Thursday 8 November fifty to sixty people sat down at the 'White Hart'. Even on that first day some of the thunder had been stolen by three special trains which brought the boys of the school back after their midsummer holidays on 29 September. So the inhabitants that assembled to see off the first train to Seaton at 09.00 had no oratory to distract their attention. None the less a link with the school had been forged, a link that was to last to the end.

Special trains were run at the beginning and end of term and these continued after the line had closed to regular passenger traffic on 13 June 1960. The Easter vacation in 1963, for example produced two special trains leaving Uppingham at 06.30 and 07.15. The first called at Market Harborough, Northampton Castle, Bletchley and Watford to give an arrival at Euston at 09.45, whilst the second ran as far as Rugby. Connections were given to places as diverse as Edinburgh, Shrewsbury, Oxford and Lancaster. Similar services ran when the school re-assembled, when the special left Euston at 16.00 and reached Uppingham at 19.20. Such a diversity of destinations meant that enquiries had to be made of the Fares Office at Euston for many tickets, and the amounts were duly entered in a book whose pages must have contained many stations and routes. Luggage was sent in advance of these trains and the transfer at Seaton was cursed by the station staff, who also remember that the passengers on the school specials produced cigarettes, drink and cards by Seaton, which disappeared before Uppingham during journeys in the opposite direction. Industrial visits produced similar but more disciplined trains.

The influence of the school was said to be behind the closure of the only industry the line served, the ironstone quarry to the south-west of Uppingham. Three locomotives were used on the mineral branch, 0–4–0 saddle tank No 1 *Uppingham* and two 0–6–0 saddle tanks, *Adderley* and *Uppingham*. This branch left the line just to the west of the overbridge carrying the Uppingham to Seaton road, running westwards to pass under the A6003 road and reach the quarry. The parapet of the bridge under the A6003 is still visible on the west side of the road and the erstwhile quarry is now a rubbish tip. Opened in 1912 by James Pain, a local industrialist, the quarry was worked during World War I but such was the opposition of the school that after the war it purchased land which Pain had hoped to use for quarrying to use as playing fields. The depressed nature of the industry lead Pain to abandon the quarry in 1924 but its railway was not dismantled until the early 1930s.

Passenger services were provided by push-and-pull sets. Normally the locomotive led to Uppingham and trailed on the return journey to Seaton. The diagrams provided that the set that ran the Uppingham service also undertook the Seaton to Stamford workings. To cater for the locomotive, a one-road shed was provided at Seaton. This came under the Rugby Motive Power District and on the occasions when non motor-fitted engines were sent as replacements, they could cause delay while they ran around their trains.

A great variety of tanks could be seen at Seaton, up to five types in a day, but one which did not endear itself to the staff was No 41279. This 2–6–2 tank was received new from Crewe in 1950 and was never right according to the men on the line. In the late 1950s some further variety was brought to the scene by two types of locomotive that were based at Spital Bridge locomotive depot in Peterborough. The first were LMSR-built 4–4–2 tanks based on a London, Tilbury & Southend Railway design, of which No 41975 was the principal example, and the second former GNR Class C12 4–4–2 tanks in the shape of No 67368 and No 67362. The motive power highlight came with the school specials, which were usually double-headed to Uppingham where it was customary to halt the train opposite the goods shed to detach the pilot. The train engine would then haul the train into the platform, detach and run around to lead the cavalcade away.

Operations at Uppingham must have had their lighter moments and fly-shunting, although proscribed by the railway company, was practised in the goods yard to save time. With its platform that would take about five coaches and a goods yard dealing with coal, fish, agricultural and occasionally bullion traffic, it must have been in the *Stamford Mercury*'s words 'an appreciative boon to a town hitherto not enjoying direct railway communication'. Many people must have walked down Station Road, specially built for the railway, to catch the branch train, although if no passengers or goods awaited the branch train, local people said it would not make the trip up from Seaton.

When opened, the single line was worked on the block system, but later a staff and ticket system was employed. Originally the Uppingham branch joined the Stamford line at Uppingham Junction about half a mile to the east of Seaton station but simplification in the inter-war period saw the removal of the junction and the reduction of the Stamford branch to one track. Consequently two separate single lines left Seaton and the Uppingham line bore off at the site of the erstwhile junction. This produced a complex-looking signalling system at Seaton with three-arm signals apparently controlling two lines on the down platforms. The left arm controlled the Uppingham line, the middle Stamford and the right arm the Peterborough tracks. Added to this, the box had three signalling systems, absolute block on the double lines to Rockingham and Wakerley, electric token to Luffenham and staff and ticket to Uppingham.

The link with Uppingham school remained to the end. The Headmaster at Speech Day in 1960 referred to the withdrawal of passenger train services which was regretted by local residents but the Boundary Commission recommendation that Rutland should loose its identity was of greater concern. Goods and school specials continued until 1 June 1964 when final closure came. As far as is known, little burning and scrub clearance was done during the seventy years of operation and several species of plant occur along its course that are absent from other lines in Rutland. So the lasting monument to a railway and its work is a different flora than that which might have otherwise occurred.

CHAPTER 8

The Great Central Railway

Introduction

Tycoons are not exclusive creatures of the twentieth century; they also existed in the nineteenth. Whereas today they are to be found in the worlds of oil, property and retailing, some were then to be found in the sphere of railways. To some extent this was inevitable, given that railways were one of the first large-scale organisations to emerge in business, and certain men became public figures. Engineers such as the Stephensons and Brunel were of this ilk but they tended to be more predominant in the early years. Later, commercial tycoons took their place in the limelight and, though relatively late in time, Sir Edward Watkin was one of the most notorious. This *enfant terrible* of the railway world was sometime Chairman of the Manchester Sheffield & Lincolnshire, Metropolitan, South Eastern, and East London Railways, as well as a Member of Parliament, a Magistrate and High Sheriff of Cheshire.

Under his leadership the Manchester, Sheffield & Lincoln-shire Railway expanded from provincial status to a trunk line from the north to London. When he retired from the MS & L

Chair in 1894, *The Economist* remarked 'His retirement will deprive the business world of much that is interesting, the gain being, however, the accession of a larger measure of peace'. By contrast to today's tycoons, who employ modern manage-

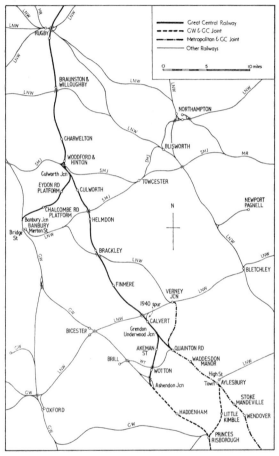

Map of the Great Central Railway, Rugby to Quainton Road Section

ment techniques, Watkin ruled almost as an absolute monarch intent on expanding his kingdom.

In 1864 when he assumed the office of Chairman, the Manchester, Sheffield & Lincolnshire was a west-to-east link across the Pennines, extending to Grimsby in Lincolnshire, and with origins in the Sheffield, Ashton-under-Lyne & Manchester Railway of 1837. It assumed its new name in an amalgamation of 1846, and by 1864 comprised 161 miles of railway. Through the years that Watkin was in command it grew until in 1892 it amounted to 300 miles constructed, 78 miles in course of construction, and 205 miles of lines jointly owned with other companies. Indeed, joint ownership seems to have been one of the cornerstones of Watkin's policy, although more as a means of reaching a *modus vivendi* with other companies than based on a genuine desire to co-operate.

Yet in 1890 the MS & LR was still a west-to-east system, concentrated in its original area of operations. Watkin hankered after trunk status, and wanted to build his own route to the Metropolis, so he unveiled the plan he had conceived for the London Extension of the MS & LR. It was to run from Annesley, north of Nottingham to Quainton Road, north of Aylesbury. At the latter place it joined the Metropolitan, whose tracks it used for the run into London, branching off at Canfield Place Junction in Hampstead to reach its own terminus at Marylebone. After a second attempt, the plan was authorised by Parliament in 1893 and the Extension was ceremonially opened in 1899. Meanwhile, Watkin's health declined and he retired from the Chair in 1894, subsequently dying in 1901. His legacy remained to the twentieth century but the extension finally closed in 1969, never really having achieved the hopes that were expressed at the time of its construction. Now, apart from one small section it lies abandoned, adding a further element of unreality to the un-worldly landscape through which it ran south of Rugby. Looking at the scene of desolation today two questions remain—was its construction necessary? what effect did it have on the country it traversed? To answer the first the whole project needs to be reviewed, but for the second only the section between Rugby and Quainton Road will be considered, together with a particular study of Woodford Halse.

Whim or necessity?

In any consideration of the London Extension, the absence of the papers of Sir Edward Watkin is a great handicap, although in mitigation it can be stated that he did not often commit his policies to paper. Watkin in any event must be considered the prime mover in the scheme, and the general view held is that he planned the extension as part of a grand design to link the north with London, and then, by means of the Metropolitan and South Eastern companies, to run trains on to the Channel, where his proposed Channel Tunnel Company would take them across to the Continent. To support this idea of an integrated project, Watkin did say '. . . if this line is made, it will make the Metropolitan and South Eastern parts of a through system running right through the country— a sort of backbone for the commerce and industry of this country.' Furthermore, by the MS & LR Act of 1893 the Metropolitan and South Eastern were permitted to subscribe up to £200,000 and £300,000 respectively in shares of the MS & LR.

Much was also made at the Select Committee hearings of the Bill of the idea of the Metropolitan being extended slowly northwards and the MS & LR southwards with the eventual aim of joining. But in 1889, when the MS & LR obtained powers for the construction of a line to Annesley, from where the London Extension was later to spring, it promised the Great Northern that it would not apply for another extension southwards. Meanwhile the Metropolitan was concerned with a project to push towards Worcester but failed to obtain the requisite Act in 1890. *Faute de mieux*, the idea of this link between the Metropolitan and MS & LR was advanced and gained ground rapidly. It is important to remember that Watkin was concerned in a railway empire of his own and was virtually dealing with himself in another guise. Little information exists but the real reason for the line's promotion may not have been so dispassionately arrived at as it was presented.

187

But having established a reason why the extension was required, the MS & LR set about advancing the expected benefits. Watkin considered it was absolutely necessary for the MS & LR to obtain a southern outlet, since the system as it then stood was little more than a collecting ground for other companies. He bemoaned that the MS & LR got perhaps 5s (25p), whilst other people got 15s (75p) out of a sovereign (£1). 'We are the jackal or lions provider—the other companies are the lions and we are the jackals. We take the traffic and give in some cases the bulk of it to other companies'. He also thought the Extension brought up a national question of whether expansion of existing lines, 'plastering the old railways' as he called it, was preferable to new construction. On his calculation, 1,500 more miles of main line than actually existed could have been built if companies had constructed new railways instead of laying further tracks on existing lines.

Allied to this, he alluded to a 'revival of trade' in about 1890, when 'it was perfectly clear to anybody who observed it that even that little spurt of trade taxed and overtaxed almost the carrying powers of the railway system'. His proposals would be of 'enormous' benefit to London, as it would give a new supply of milk, food, coal and many other wants. Indeed, he believed that there were two or three coalfields south of Nottingham lying absolutely idle, because of the lack of rail facilities. Further benefits would be extended to the agricultural part of the country and the Grimsby fishing trade.

To impress the Select Committee with the strength of the MS & LR case, a procession of notables, including the Mayors of Sheffield, Chesterfield and Nottingham and the Master Cutler, appeared before it to emphasise the especial benefits they and their communities would obtain from the proposed railway. One witness, Baron Ferdinand de Rothschild, MP for Mid Bucks, thought the line would improve local communications, an opinion that was confirmed by Viscount Curzon, MP for South Bucks, who considered that Buckinghamshire had suffered from a lack of good railway communication for a very long time. From Braunston came Colonel John Henry Lowndes, who thought that a direct line to Leicester would aid development of the local shoe industry and that it could open-up milk traffic to Leicester and the carriage of stock to London and the north. However, the population of Braunston was something under a thousand and had fallen by nearly a hundred since the last census. The opposing counsel claimed tellingly that the fox cover was the village's present chief claim to fame. Lastly, Colin Taylor, a corn and coal merchant, thought the line would improve the transit of wheat from Quainton Road to Leicester, where merchants were driven out of a good market for want of railway facilities.

By contrast, other railway companies remained unimpressed with the MS & LR case. Three companies, the London & North Western, the Midland and the Great Northern, already carried traffic from the North to London. The entry of the MS & LR into their ranks was bound to spread the traffic more thinly and as the three were well established, the inaugural years were bound to be hard for the MS & LR. At the opening of the line the tenuous hope was held out that the growth in population and trade that had followed the Midland's extension to London in the 1860s would be repeated, so as to bring success to the MS & LR. Alas, the great future never materialised and the MS & LR had to carry on as best it might, initially handicapped by its hitherto erratic and flighty nature, which meant that the other companies were not disposed to look favourably upon it.

Public opinion about the line is more difficult to assess. Watkin referred to the support, with hardly a dissident, that the project received in the countryside it was to traverse, although he could hardly do otherwise. By 1890 railway construction was not a new phenomenon so it would not arouse undue interest. However, this was a considerable project and it was realised at the time that the construction of a new trunk route was unlikely to be undertaken again. Traders supported the new line, since at best it represented new facilities they could use, at worst a stick with which to beat the other companies. From rural Buckinghamshire petitions in favour of the line were presented by Baron de Rothschild but urban London was not so enthusiastic. The artists of St Johns Wood objected to the disturbance to their tranquility and concern was felt for those who would be rendered homeless by the construction of the Marylebone terminus. So the public reaction would seem to have been mixed, a state of affairs which spilt over into the legislature, as the first application to Parliament failed to obtain an Act and the second modified attempt was successful. Objections mainly centred on the London terminus, particularly the demolition of property, and eventually the company had to construct homes for those it would displace.

But perhaps one of the keenest measures of whether the Extension was necessary is the financial. The MS & LR was never well-off, and the jibe was that its initials stood for 'Money Sunk & Lost' only to become 'Gone Completely' when it changed its name to the Great Central Railway in 1897. The dividend on the ordinary stock was poor; it reached its peak, during Watkin's reign, of $2\frac{7}{8}$ per cent in 1877, a year in which the Midland paid $5\frac{3}{8}$ per cent. In 1891 it was pointed out to ordinary shareholders that the company was paying a relatively high rate of interest on debenture and preference capital, thus reducing the amount that was available for their dividends. Some indication of this higher rate of interest can be seen from the average rate on MS & LR stocks of 4·71 per cent in 1890, when the general expectation was no more than 4 per cent. This preponderance of fixed interest stock was probably necessary in order to induce people to purchase it, but preference shares are best issued by stable businesses, hardly likely in a company controlled by Edward Watkin.

Charles Liddell, engineer of the line, estimated its cost to be £3,625,174 in 1890, which included both land and buildings. When contracts came to be let, they amounted to £3,182,155 but the cost of the rails, rolling stock and signalling for the extension meant that the total cost was much greater. To meet this expenditure, £6,200,000 of new stock was authorised by the Act, together with power to borrow £2,066,666 by mortgage of the undertaking. The first £4,200,000 of this stock was issued in June 1894 and it was decided to issue the remaining £2 million in January 1896. Of this £2 million, £1 million was issued in February 1896, when three times the amount available was applied for, and the issue of the remaining £1 million in May was even more heavily oversubscribed. Obviously confidence was felt in the extension but the capital had become too large to service and by 1901 the company had not paid its last four dividends on the Ordinary Stock and began to pass Preference dividends. In fact, the Ordinary Stock of the Great Central, amounting to £9,668,600 in 1901, never received a dividend.

Perhaps some of the reason for this poor financial performance can be attributed to the traffic desert that the line passed through between Rugby and Aylesbury. The engineer was virtually forced to adopt this route as all other approaches to London were used and he had to join the Metropolitan at Quainton Road. So the line had to run across the grain of the country, reaching a summit at Charwelton and necessitating heavy works in parts. Nor was the engineer helped by the insistence on a maximum gradient of 1 in 176 on this section and a minimum radius for curves of one mile, eased only in one case to sixty chains. This was specified so that the company could have a line on which high speeds could be attained. Though the result was a railway that appeared to stride across the landscape, it must have appreciably increased the cost.

It thus represents the ultimate development of railway construction, a fine mastery of technique and part of the final filling-in of the railway map. But to return to the original question; as a trunk route, was it necessary? Given that it existed, it provided a valuable relief to Paddington and King's Cross and was an important freight route from Manchester to Woodford. If, one asks whether it should have been constructed, the answer must surely be no. Its financial results were poor and the only real places of note it served were Rugby, Leicester and Nottingham, all of which were amply served by other companies. It came on to the scene too late to make any appreciable impact, particularly as Watkin's departure removed the close connection with the Metropolitan and South Eastern systems, so the grand design was never consummated. Instead it became merely another line from the north to London, initially handicapped by its erstwhile ally the Metropolitan. Despite gallant attempts by Sir Sam Fay, a later General Manager, to capitalise on its connections to nearly all the main railway companies by the introduction of through trains, it still remained a mute reminder of Sir Edward Watkin's grandiose dreams.

Impact

To facilitate construction of the new Extension to London, it was divided into three sections. The Northern Division ran from Annesley to Rugby, the Southern Division from Rugby to Quainton Road and the Metropolitan Division covered the portion from Canfield Place into Marylebone. Of these three, the Southern Division comes within the concern of this book.

This 40 mile long division was itself sub-divided into four contracts and employed 5,000 men, 150 horses, 50 locomotives and 1,700 wagons and trucks amongst other resources in its construction. Building the line must have been a fairly formidable task, as it passed through a series of ridges running roughly east to west. As the railway ran north to south, considerable work was involved in cutting through the ridges and embanking the valleys, with the added difficulties caused by the necessity for a high-speed line. To reach the highest point on the section, at Charwelton, 503ft above sea level, the line had to start to climb from Quainton Road and this produced a whale-backed gradient profile.

Starting at Quainton Road, the Great Central curved away westwards from the Aylesbury & Buckingham line of the Metropolitan Railway. The Metropolitan provided a new signalbox to control this junction and the box was the scene of an acrimonious dispute between the Metropolitan and the Great Central. Since Watkin's retirement, the close connection between the two companies had disappeared, and, by the opening of the Extension had been replaced by a spirit of animosity. Eventually an *entente* was reached but not before the Great Central had formed an alliance with the Great Western to build an alternative route into London. At the outset, Quainton Road remained a Metropolitan Railway enclave, and the only services provided by the Great Central in 1904 were for passengers and horseboxes. By 1956 Metropolitan services had been cut back to Aylesbury and the station was exclusively under the aegis of British Railways. In the interregnum, too, a Ministry of Agriculture Food Buffer Depot had been erected, served by its own private siding.

Before the line reached Calvert, the connection to the Great Western & Great Central Joint route came in at Grendon Underwood Junction. This railway developed out of the quarrel with the Metropolitan, which owned a line measuring up in no way to the Great Central's absence of sharp curves or steep gradients, and which seemed to take a great delight in obstructing Great Central trains. Consequently the Great Central joined the Great Western, which wanted a more direct route between London and Birmingham, in the construction of this project, which the Great Central met at Ashendon Junction. By a mixture of new construction and improvement of existing lines, a new route via High Wycombe and Ruislip to Neasden, enabled the greater part of the Metropolitan route to be by-passed. Stations were opened on the Grendon Underwood to Ashendon Junction section at Wotton and Akeman Street. These did not see much traffic and were closed to passengers comparatively early but part of this line still remains to serve Westcott Depot.

Since there was no village in the vicinity, Calvert station was named after a local landowner. It typified the style of stations on the Extension, which all followed a similar pattern. The platform was of the island type, as it was considered that these would enable the stations to be worked with the smallest possible staff, would economise on the use of land and would also make future widening to four tracks as easy as possible! Access to the platform was obtained by a staircase from the centre of the road overbridge. All station overbridges were built with sufficient room for four tracks and the centre piers were left hollow to provide lamp rooms. Calvert marks the end of the only track remaining on this portion of the GC extension line today, a track which extends from Aylesbury to Claydon (LNE) Junction on the Bletchley to Oxford line; the private siding of the London Brick Company provides the bulk of the traffic. Beyond Calvert all the tracks have been removed.

Finmere exemplified the alternative type of station, where access was obtained by a flight of steps from the centre of the road underbridge, each track having a separate bridge span. As at other places, a house was provided for the stationmaster, and here provision was made in drawings for the site of future cottages. The Great Central described the station as 'Finmere for Buckingham' but as that town is five miles from the station and was served by the LNWR, it must be very doubtful if many passengers for Buckingham alighted at Finmere. However, for those few, a slip coach was attached to the 18.20 from Marylebone and slipped here at 19.28.

Some evidence of the cutting across ridges and valleys could be seen around Finmere. South of Finmere the railway crossed an embankment of nearly 200,000 cubic yards, whilst to the north a cutting of 180,000 cubic yards had to be excavated. A determined effort was made to eliminate level crossings on the Extension, sources of considerable danger, inconvenience and cost, as the Directors realised. However, the abolition of crossings was bound to mean more bridge works for roads both great and small, even in the cutting north of Finmere a timber overbridge for the convenience of the Hunt.

Going northward the line crossed the LNWR Banbury branch, whose construction gave valuable warning of the difficult character of the clay in the Ouse valley. Building the GC viaduct across the valley was accordingly difficult. The line passed on through a limestone cutting, which yielded material for use in the concrete foundations of Brackley viaduct, and reached the viaduct itself. Approached by embankments, it was 320ft long and crossed a large area of flood land at a maximum height of 62ft. The twenty 34ft 3in span brick arches and two 35ft steel spans made an impressive sight from the Brackley to Buckingham road.

Brackley, together with Woodford and Rugby, was considered a station of importance. Although the town boasted a Mayor and Corporation, as a reminder of its more prosperous days, it had a population of less than 3,000 in 1900. It enjoyed seven trains a day from Marylebone, including an express which took eighty-four minutes for the journey, as against a two to two and three quarter hour journey from Euston via Bletchley. To cater for the expected traffic, the GC built a station to the north of the town, where the Brackley to Towcester road crossed the railway. Instead of the customary approach from the centre of the road overbridge, a side access from a new road was insisted on by the Corporation, as they feared the station traffic would block the main road. The station and yard lay partially in a cutting of 336,000 cubic yards and provision was made for the later addition of a third platform. To add a final touch, the plans specified that 'Walls of Urinals to be faced with Warrington's "Granite" Glazed Bricks'! Despite the better service given by the Great Central, the LNWR was probably content to let such a small prize go to its rival.

The River Tove was crossed by another impressive viaduct of nine arches at Helmdon, similar to those at Brackley and Catesby. Along the river valley and through one of the arches of the viaduct ran the Northampton & Banbury Junction Railway. This provided a convenient way to bring in materials, and so the contractors set up another work camp to the north of the viaduct. However, to provide some of the bricks, a brickmaking plant was erected in Great Covert Wood nearby, which produced 12 million bricks in three years.

Over the 486,000 cubic yard embankment close to Sulgrave, the line reached Culworth station. Since the road had to be raised 17ft above the rails, an extensive diversion of the road was necessary. Between 1913 and 1956 Eydon Road Halt was nearer to Culworth village than was Culworth station. This halt and Chalcombe Road Halt were situated on the Banbury branch of the Great Central, which left the main line at Culworth Junction, a little to the north of the station. This branch dated from the time of the alliance with the Great Western, whose Birmingham line it joined, and was authorised in 1897. The junction with the Great Western at Banbury was to be constructed to enable exchange sidings to be laid out and power was given to the Great Western to construct the branch in certain events. Eventually the Great Western financed the branch, which opened in 1900, an occasion which led one observer to remark that it would make as great a change in the railway geography as the Severn Tunnel and the Forth Bridge, and would bring Leicester as close to Oxford as Wellington in New Zealand would be brought to London, if a ship canal were opened through the middle of the earth. Culworth Junction signalbox belied its importance for it stood on an embankment looking towards Eydon, on its hill, surrounded by upland country, deafeningly quiet except when the birds' song was broken by the sound of a train.

Onwards through Woodford, whose story forms a separate section, the line reached its summit and the water troughs at Charwelton. By the authorising Act the Great Central was required to 'construct a goods and passenger station at . . . Charwelton' and 'shall upon the opening of that railway and for ever thereafter maintain and use the said station for passenger and goods traffic'. North of the station was Catesby Tunnel, a source of difficulty to the engineers.

Here the railway had to cross one of the series of ridges, this time of unusual height, and a 3,000yd tunnel was needed. However, the owner of Catesby House objected to the intrusion of his privacy. To protect him the Act provided that the centre line of the railway should be more than 100yd from the residential part of Catesby House and that the northern end of the tunnel should not be nearer than 133yd. Furthermore, should the water supply to the house be interfered with, the Great Central had to supply an equally good source and was also responsible for any structural injury their works might cause to Catesby House. As no ventilation shafts were allowed in the grounds of the House, none were sunk within 500yd of the north end of the tunnel, meaning that the most difficult part had to be constructed in awkward conditions. Ventilation was provided by five shafts, four of 10ft diameter and one of 15ft. Because of this restriction, the 15ft shaft was situated ¾ mile from the north end of the tunnel, where it had to perform extra duty. Between 18 February 1895 and 22 May 1897, 290,000 cubic yards of spoil were removed and replaced by a lining of thirty million bricks. The tunnel was completed at quite a rapid pace, an average of 110yd per month and throughout fell on a gradient of 1 in 176 towards the north.

Once through the tunnel, trains passed under a bridge built in stone instead of the usual blue brick, again as a condition imposed by the owner of Catesby House, and then crossed the twelve arches of Catesby Viaduct spanning the River Leam. Beginning the descent from the summit, trains had by now regained some of the speed that they had lost and expresses would pass through Braunston & Willoughby station, at the foot of the bank, travelling at about eighty mph. After crossing Rains Brook on the 357ft long Staverton Viaduct, the largest cutting on the Extension was entered, extending for 1¾ miles and containing 1,400,000 cubic yards of material. The steam navvies could not get to work here until the wet earth had been considerably drained. Towards its northern end was Rugby Central.

'Central' was a misnomer in Rugby but the policy on the Extension was to add Central to the name of the GC station where other companies had stations. However, Charles Liddell consoled himself with the thought that, 'although it is some distance from the centre of the town, it is as convenient a station as can be obtained and is quite as near as the present London & North Western station'. Although Rugby was described as a Second Class station, the Great Central provided full facilities and even constructed up and down 'lay-by' sidings of 500ft each to enable slow trains to be cleared from the main line. A signal box, Rugby Cattle Sidings, controlled facilities which were used fairly extensively for market day cattle traffic. But Rugby was already centred on the LNWR and no great expansion was ever needed at Rugby Central. Although of the standard island platform design, the booking office was situated at road level instead of on the 500ft platform as was usual.

Between the station and the viaduct over the LNWR, known to railwaymen as the 'Birdcage', the cutting continued through what was at the time of its construction a new building area. Consequently Chester Street, Rokeby Street and Clifton Road had to be diverted. The viaduct spanned fourteen lines of the LNWR and space was left for sidings to be extended. Since the LNWR considered that the viaduct would obstruct sighting of their signals, a massive gantry had to be erected on the LNWR, which had to be paid for by the Great Central.

Originally, it was intended to link the two railways by means of a spur from the GC to the LNWR Peterborough branch, but this authorised link was never constructed. Finally, the GC crossed the Oxford Canal. This viaduct was another considerable engineering feat, as the canal was not to be obstructed during its construction. The viaduct marked the end of the Southern Division and the Northern Division took over for the 51 miles 69 chains to Annesley Junction.

Construction of the Southern Division was shared among four contracts. The first originally ran from Rugby to Charwelton but was subsequently amended to terminate at Woodford Halse. This 15 miles 69 chains, including Catesby Tunnel, was entrusted to T. Oliver & Sons of Horsham at a cost of £513,308. The second contract onwards to Brackley, 12 miles 39 chains, and the third to the junction at Quainton Road, 12 miles 61 chains, were undertaken by Walter Scott & Co of London and Newcastle-on-Tyne for a total cost of £470,000. The fourth contract, 8 miles 40 chains of the Banbury branch were also undertaken by Walter Scott. The average cost of the three contracts of the main line was £23,980 as against an average of £33,500 per mile for the whole extension. This reflects the lower cost of the Southern Division as against the Northern and Metropolitan Divisions, borne out by the 43 per cent of the total mileage that the Southern Division represented accounting for only 31 per cent of the total cost. The expense of cutting through Nottingham, Leicester and London would no doubt account for the greater cost of the other sections. In addition the cost of land would increase the expense of the Metropolitan Division.

The railway ran through a mainly thinly-populated agricultural area. The only places of note on the line were Rugby and Brackley, with Banbury on the branch. Although alternative railway facilities did exist in the area of the line, they were mainly aligned on an east-to-west axis, rather than the north-to-south route of the Great Central. The only stations which did not have convenient alternatives were Charwelton, Finmere, Eydon Road Halt and Chalcombe Road Halt. To stimulate patronage of the local train service, the Great Central offered market tickets to Rugby and Brackley on Saturdays, and to Banbury on Thursdays. Parcels agents such as Mr W. Cave in Banbury, Mrs Kate Hailey of the 'Crown Hotel' in Brackley, Mr S. Hearn in Helmdon, Mr J. W. Berry in Braunston and Messrs H. Cheney & Co of Bicycle Warehouse, High Street, Rugby, amongst others, were appointed to solicit for Great Central traffic.

During the twentieth century the rural population declined generally and in Northamptonshire the fall was from 100,365 in 1901 to 84,410 in 1951. The Extension did not arrest this decline, except perhaps in Woodford Halse: no new industries or areas developed, the area did not become more nationally important and the pattern of activity was not greatly changed. The line, as it were, ran through the area but was not part of it. Great efforts were made, especially in the time of Sir Sam Fay, to encourage use of the line, particularly for through services such as Oxford to Leicester and York to Southampton. But never were the hopes realised that were expressed at the opening and, as *The Economist* laconically reported, 'Probably too much was expected of the first return of the Great Central, comprising the full receipts of the London extension. The stocks have declined substantially'.

Yet to run these services, locomotives and therefore depots to house them were required. Similarly marshalling sidings were necessary to sort wagons destined to and from the London Extension. Both were to be found at Woodford Halse.

Woodford Halse

The parish of Woodford-cum-Membris lies in the south-western part of Northamptonshire, about twelve miles from Northampton. Within the parish there are three villages Woodford Halse, Hinton and West Farndon, the last two being separated from Woodford Halse by the River Cherwell. The area lies at a height of four to five hundred feet in undulating, mainly agricultural country. In the sixteenth century it had been champaign country, dotted with numerous parks and variegated by unevenly distributed woodland. Writing in 1791, John Bridges, the historian of Northamptonshire, had described Woodford as a place of sixty one houses, with two watermills situated on the Cherwell. Hinton he described as a hamlet of thirty-four houses and West Farndon had sixteen houses. Interestingly enough at that time the Lord of the Manor at Woodford was the Duke of Bridgewater, the Canal Duke.

By the time of the census of 1851, the population was 455 and amongst the occupations were limeburner, agricultural labourer, cattle dealer, shopkeeper, wheelwright, lacemaker, innkeeper, carpenter, baker and butcher. Amongst the farmers included in the census, one farmed 266 acres with the help of nine labourers, whilst another cultivated 230 acres and employed six labourers. Although no detailed analysis of birthplaces has been attempted, inspection of the manuscript census returns suggested that the majority of the inhabitants were born locally. In the next forty years the population increased to 527, but the general air of the village would not be greatly different in 1891 from that of 1851. By contrast, the census of 1901 showed a population of 1,220, 230 per cent above what it had been just ten years earlier, explained by the footnote, 'The increase of population in Woodford-cum-Membris Civil Parish is mainly attributed to the opening of a station on the Great Central Railway and the establishment of an engine depot'. Of course, the Great Central was not the first railway in the Woodford area since the East & West Junction had been opened in 1873, but the nearest station on that line to Woodford was Byfield,

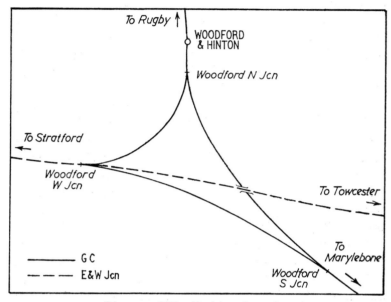

Diagram of Woodford junctions 1899

an intermediate station on a cross-country line, whereas the new station of Woodford & Hinton was on a main line.

That the village appreciated the coming of the Great Central is shown by the address of congratulation that was presented to the company by the Parish. It read:

> My Lords and Gentlemen,—It is with the greatest pleasure that we, the undersigned, the Chairman and members of the Parish Council of Woodford-cum-Membris, do hereby tender our hearty congratulations to you, on the completion and opening of the Great Central Railway, which will confer a great benefit on the districts through which it passes, and will also further be a connecting link between the great industries of the North and the bustle and life of the Metropolis.

Similarly in its report of the opening, the *Northamptonshire*

Herald said, 'To Woodford, the new railway has indeed proved a God-send, and the good people of that neighbourhood have not failed to appreciate to the fullest extent the enormous benefit that has been conferred upon them'.

The layout at Woodford is illustrated in the track diagram on page 201. The Great Central main line ran north to south through the area and was crossed by the single-track East & West Junction. A south-to-west double-track spur ran from the Great Central to the East & West. Opened on 9 March 1899, it carried passenger services only for the month of August 1899, and only one train, the 17.20 from Marylebone, which terminated at Byfield at 19.36, with a connection to Stratford. This spur ceased to operate as a through line on 22 October 1900 and was used for many years as a siding. Tradition associates this spur with the Great Central's attempt to gain entry to the Birmingham area; certainly the spur would fit in with these plans, as it gave a direct link for expresses to and from London.

A further spur ran from Woodford West Junction on the East & West northwards to the Great Central and it was to this link that the 17.20 train was diverted, Saturdays excepted, in September 1899, being cut back to Woodford in the following month. Through coaches were still worked, one or more daily, until the withdrawal of the slip coach off the 18.20 from Marylebone on 1 February 1936. This spur was really more important for freight, as it was here that wagons were exchanged with the Great Central. Indeed, Woodford West Junction signalbox was of Great Central design.

Wagons for exchange were worked up to the siding by the Great Central and then collected by the SMJ. In later years, use was made of this junction to carry freight from the Woodford Marshalling Yards. Thus in 1952 four trains a day each way from Woodford to Cardiff traversed the connection, together with a daily Woodford to Stoke Gifford freight each way.

To the north of the station, which was constructed on the usual island pattern, marshalling yards flanked each side of the line. These yards occupied thirty-five acres of embankment, formed principally from spoil taken from Catesby Tunnel.

Further to the north, on the east of the line, a depot was constructed capable of holding thirty locomotives, a snowplough and a 15 ton steam crane and was supplied with a 54ft turntable. Nearby were wagon and sheet repairing shops to complete the railway facilities. To provide housing for the staff that would be needed, 136 houses were built principally in Sidney, Percy, and Castle Roads. Expansion was much in the air and rumours circulated that the carriage works for the new line, as at Wolverton, were to be built here. Furthermore, in the triangle formed by the junctions to the south of the station, 14½ acres were acquired, 'admirably suited for workmen's cottages, workshops, etc, when the increasing importance of the junctions renders this necessary'.

The ceremonial opening day of the line was a great occasion and 'Thursday, March 9th, [1899] will [be] sure to linger in the memory of Woodford people, and especially the youngsters, as hitherto by far the most eventful day in the whole history of the village'. About 130 schoolchildren had been given a half-holiday in honour of the occasion and were taken to the station by the schoolmaster, Mr S. Stubbs. There they joined 'a crowd of some Hundreds', which had assembled on the station platform, adorned with flags by the 'genial Station Master', Mr. Stanton. They had all come to see the three special trains from Manchester, Sheffield and Nottingham, which took the guests to the opening ceremony at Marylebone, and expected an exciting hour from 11.00 to 12.00 when the special trains were due to pass. The first was due at 11.25 and a hearty cheer went up as it passed through, accompanied by a salvo of fog signals. The four-coach train was in fact running late, as some of the axle boxes had run hot on the new coaches. A similar fate befell the second train, which was held at Rugby to allow the third to pass it. In fact this delayed arrival at Marylebone meant that luncheon was taken before the official opening ceremony instead of after it, as was originally intended. But those onlookers in Northamptonshire were not to know that and despite the crowd on the platform and the prevailing excitement, 'everything passed off well and without mishap'.

When the specials returned in the evening, the station was closed to the public, although it was illuminated with lamps, as the electric supply had not been fully installed. It had been intended to present the address of congratulation to the directors, but as there were no principal officers on the train which stopped at Woodford, it was resolved to dispatch it by post to Manchester, where the General Manager would bring it before the directors. But no matter, it had been quite a day.

Inevitably the fever pitch of excitement died away but steady expansion saw the population increase to 1,520 in 1911, when footnotes to the census tables explained again 'The large increase in the population of Woodford-cum-Membris Civil Parish is attributed mainly to the extension of the railway works'. Expansion of traffic, particularly the opening of the Banbury branch, increased Woodford's importance and thus the facilities that had to be provided. In turn the staff to work the yards and depot came from all over the country and it was a very mixed company that settled down together. Amongst the leisure time activities were a choral society, an orchestra, two bands, a male voice choir which won many awards, and an annual flower show. Eventually the village boasted a cinema and a railway social club. Village life was geared to the railway since, apart from a few men who worked at the AEI works in Rugby, this was the only major source of employment. It was an example of the one-industry town dependent for its existence on the railway. It was this that imparted an air of unreality to the place; one expected a sleepy village, not a transplanted industrial suburb. Woodford owed nothing to Northamptonshire and everything to the Great Central Railway. So long as the railway was prosperous, so was Woodford. Changes seemed minor, like the change of name of the station from Woodford & Hinton to Woodford Halse. So confident was the community that as late as 1950 a new estate was started. Growing affluence meant that fewer people wanted lodgers and railwaymen began to find it difficult to obtain housing. So in a time of shortage, a special building allocation was given to Woodford to ease the problem.

Yet this confidence can be understood. Although the line lost a great deal of importance for passenger traffic, after it had been absorbed into the London & North Eastern Railway in 1923, this did not concern Woodford unduly with its concentration on freight services. New yards were opened under the pressure of wartime traffic in 1941. Situated on either side of the main lines, north of the existing yards, they brought the total capacity to 3,500 trucks. Woodford men were proud of their yard and could cite the 'windcutters', the Annesley to Woodford 'out-and-home scheme' as proof of their competence. Men from Annesley could work a train into Woodford Yard and in an average of an hour be on their way back again, a return trip of 136 miles within the confines of an eight-hour shift. To do this, prompt departures, a minimum turnround interval and prompt relief of the crews were necessary. One set of men would take the incoming locomotives to the shed, coal and water them and return, sometimes reducing the turnround to thirty-four minutes.

The station and yards at Woodford witnessed a great variety of motive power during the course of their life. After his appointment as Locomotive Engineer in 1894, Harry Pollitt had been building locomotives with an eye to the needs of the new extension but his successor of 1900, J. G. Robinson, designed classes which were to become familiar on Marylebone expresses. His first design was Class 9J 0–6–0 for goods traffic, closely followed by Class 11B 4–4–0 for express passenger trains. But the Class 11E 4–4–0s of 1913, better known as the Directors, were probably his *pièce de résistance*. At the head of a London express they epitomised power and grace and continued on into LNER days, when indeed more were built. Robinson symmetry was followed by Gresley syncopation after the introduction in 1936 of Class V2 2–6–2s. Class K3 2–6–0s and Class K2 2–6–0s were also to be found and the Gresley look was completed by Class A3 4–6–2s, which began to take over principal trains after World War II. Edward Thompson's ubiquitous Class B1 4–6–0s were used on mixed duties after their introduction in 1942, while the LMS Stanier Class 5 4–6–0s, similar general purpose locomotives, were drafted to the line in its declining years. Among the locomotive miscellany of those latter days were Jubilee 4–6–0s, Royal Scot 4–6–0s, BR Britannia 4–6–2s and GT3, a 2,750hp 4–6–0 gas turbine locomotive. Experimentally produced by English Electric in 1961, this strange visitor was based on a steam locomotive frame and was coupled to an adapted BR standard tender.

By 1960 the pattern of traffic had settled down primarily to freight from Yorkshire and the North East to Banbury, with a particular emphasis on coal from the East Midlands to the Western Region, with a return flow of empties. Four boxes controlled the yards and connections at Woodford, where there were thirty-three sidings for northbound traffic, eleven for Banbury departures and ten for other destinations to the south. The yard dealt with forty-four northbound arrivals and forty three northbound departures on weekdays; southbound arrivals totalled forty-two and departures forty-seven. Eventually the yards, carriage and wagon repair depot, station and locomotive depot with sixty allocated locomotives meant employment for 650 men.

Storm clouds had by then begun to gather over the future of the Great Central, and with it that of Woodford Halse. Questions about the necessity for the line were raised, against the deteriorating financial position of British Railways. Aware of this, the Woodford Halse branch of ASLEF held a special meeting on 26 August 1962 and adopted this resolution:

> That this meeting of railwaymen and the public of Woodford Halse and district strongly protest to the Minister of Transport [Ernest Marples] concerning the proposed withdrawal of passenger trains from the ex-Great Central Railway and ask him to refute to the press their publications of the complete closure of the railway from Marylebone to Sheffield.

Four days later a by-election candidate alleged that the government was deliberately killing the efficiency of the Great Central to provide an excuse for closing it down. The Beeching Report gave further cause for concern, as it proposed the closure of Woodford Halse station, but left open the question of the future of the yards and shed. Protests such as 'they think we are just a place on a map, not people' were to no avail against the anticipated savings of over £1 million a year. The arithmetic was unanswerable, but by contrast to Brackley where no great hardship was expected, Woodford was fighting for its life.

The 1961 population was 1,775, only thirty-seven above the 1931 population, indicating a levelling-off in the growth of the community. About 450 were expected to be made redundant by the railway closure. In the hope of a last-minute reprieve, the representatives of the men sent a letter to the Prime Minister which ended 'We trust, sir, that you will see fit to allow our line to remain open to give a service to all for the future greatness of our beloved Britain'. But it was to no avail for 'In the light of . . . the very high cost of retaining the existing services the Minister [Mrs Barbara Castle] has decided to give her consent to the closure . . .' The last passenger train ran on Saturday 3 September 1966 but the yards had closed to regular traffic on 1 March 1965. As the only factory in the village employed female labour, the men had to go outside for employment, mainly to engineering works at Banbury, Daventry and Rugby. Fears were expressed that the village would become predominantly inhabited by older people and headlines ran 'Town sentenced to death'. Times were difficult but gradually Woodford picked up again and designation as a key centre for rural expansion by Northamptonshire County Council in December 1968 gave cause for hope.

The remaining twenty-five railway workers looked out in 1968 over crumbling platforms and overgrown yards. Despite reports that Rover Cars or York Trailers were interested in taking over the railway premises, nothing had happened. Similarly the sale of the Manor House and its three acres of land, owned by the railway, came to naught, as the bidding failed to reach the reserve price and it was withdrawn. The railway seemed indestructible. Even the stores withstood four attempts by the Royal Marines armed with explosives to demolish it. Not so lightly was the railway to be abandoned. Watkin would have been pleased.

Gazetteer

The gazetteer has a twofold purpose. First, it aims to provide essential background information including the opening dates, major changes of ownership (where applicable) and the closure sequence for each of the railways mentioned in the text; secondly, it attempts to establish a record of the more interesting physical remains, the present use made of the track alignment and the outstanding scenic sections of every line so described.

Only those relics whose continued existence seems reasonably assured have been entered. Buildings, structures and earthworks which merit inclusion but are likely to have disappeared by the time this register appears in print have been excluded. Nevertheless, seemingly permanent features may suddenly be destroyed whereas certain derelict buildings can be rescued and renovated. Though this has been taken into account as far as possible, discrepancies are quite likely to occur.

To explore the region by rail is difficult today as so many lines have been closed and as a consequence the best way to trace the lines is by bus or car. Certain particularly attractive stretches of track or areas nearby which are considered worthwhile examining by foot, or are suitable picnic spots, have been mentioned in the gazetteer under 'setting'.

The location of all sites is given by an appropriate six-figure grid reference for the relevant Ordnance Survey map. The 1:50,000 First Series sheets covering the area are as follows: 140, 141, 142, 150, 151, 152, 153, 163, 164, 165, 166, 176.

In some cases former railway property has been converted into private residences and readers are asked to bear this in mind.

LONDON: NORTHERN HEIGHTS AND GREEN BELT

FINSBURY PARK–ALEXANDRA PALACE, EDGWARE AND
BUSHEY HEATH   10½ miles

Edgware, Highgate & London Railway
Muswell Hill Railway
London Passenger Transport Board

Acts:

3 June 1862; 13 May 1864; 30 July 1866; 20 July 1937

Opened:

22 August 1867 (Finsbury Park–Edgware); 24 May 1873 (Highgate–Alexandra Palace)

Running Powers:

Granted to South Eastern Railway, and London, Chatham & Dover Railway (Alexandra Palace branch); North London Railway (Finchley–Edgware—never exercised)

Track Layout:

Originally single from the west end of west tunnel, Highgate (later Park Junction) to Edgware, later doubled to Finchley. High Barnet and Alexandra Palace branches were double from opening.

Miles	Station	Grid ref	Note	Opened to Passengers	Closed Passengers	Closed Goods
—	Seven Sisters Road	313868	1	1 Jul 1861	—	—
¾	Stroud Green	308877	2	11 Apr 1881	5 Jul 1954	—
1¼	Crouch End	299878	2	22 Aug 1867	5 Jul 1954	—
2¼	Highgate	286882	2	22 Aug 1867	5 Jul 1954	1 Oct 1962
3	Cranley Gardens	284891	2	2 Aug 1902	5 Jul 1954	18 May 1957
3¾	Muswell Hill	289896	3	24 May 1873	5 Jul 1954	14 Jun 1956
4¼	Alexandra Palace	295901	4	24 May 1873	5 Jul 1954	—
3¼	East End, Finchley	272892	5	22 Aug 1867	—	1 Oct 1962
4¾	Finchley & Hendon	253907	6	22 Aug 1867	—	1 Oct 1962
5¾	Mill Hill	240915	7	22 Aug 1867	—	1 Oct 1962
7½	The Hale (for Mill Hill)	213918	8	11 Jun 1906	11 Sept 1939	29 Feb 1964
8¾	Edgware	194918	—	22 Aug 1867	11 Sept 1939	1 Jun 1964

Notes

(1) Renamed *Finsbury Park* 1 January 1870.

(2) Closed 29 October 1951 due to coal shortage: re-opened 7 January 1952.

(3) Closed August 1873–May 1875 and as (2) above.

(4) Closed and re-opened eight times between 1873 and 1898 and closed as (2) above.

(5) Renamed *East Finchley* 1 February 1887.

(6) Renamed *Finchley* 1 February 1872; *Finchley Church End* 1 February 1894 and *Finchley Central* 1 April 1940.

(7) Renamed *Mill Hill East* 1 March 1928.

(8) Renamed *Mill Hill (For The Hale)* 1 March 1928.

Remains:

Crouch End: station frontage and platforms (299878); *Highgate*: High level station (rebuilt by LPTB for electrification) (286882); tunnels (284883/287881); *Muswell Hill*: viaduct (288894); *Mill Hill (Page Street)*: substation (223912); In use by LTE (eg *Dollis Valley*: viaduct (245912); *Park Junction*: sidings (281885) etc); *Aldenham Works* (170948).

Uses:

Predominant part of trackbed still traceable, particularly from Finsbury Park to Highgate. Most bridges are still in situ. Parts of the trackbed are used for residential/commercial purposes between Park Junction and Alexandra Palace, although the London Borough of Haringey has proposals for a parkland walk over this section. Various parts of the trackbed west of Mill Hill East station are now used eg motorway works, although the London Borough of Barnet has also proposed to use part of the route as a footpath. Land for the Aldenham Extension in the Edgware area has been built over, but the remainder has been predominantly absorbed back into farmland.

WATFORD–RICKMANSWORTH AND UXBRIDGE   4½ miles
Watford & Rickmansworth Railway

Acts:

3 July 1860; 28 June 1861; 11 August 1881; 21 May 1896.

Opened:

1 October 1862.

Running Powers:

Granted to London Electric Railway (LTE) over section from Watford High Street to Watford Junction.

Working Agreement:

Worked from outset by LNWR; absorbed by LNWR under Act

of 27 June 1881 which allowed one month for completion of conveyance.

Track Layout:
Originally single converted to double from Croxley Green Junction to Watford Junction.

Miles	Station	Grid ref	Note	Opened to Passengers	Closed Passengers	Goods
—	Watford Junction	111973	1	1 Oct 1862	—	—
1	Watford High Street	113961	2	1 Oct 1862	—	—
4½	Rickmansworth	063942	3	1 Oct 1862	3 Mar 1952	2 Jan 1967

Notes
(1) Rickmansworth branch services only; as in (2) below.
(2) Still served by BR and LTE services.
(3) Renamed *Rickmansworth (Church Street)* 25 September 1950.

Remains:
Moor Park: mansion, former home of Lord Ebury (075933); original bridges and structures are mostly still in existence; there are no traces existing of the proposed Uxbridge extension.

Uses:
The trackbed is almost totally complete and unaltered. Track is still laid and in occasional use between Croxley Mill (084953) and Croxley Green Junction (107953). There are proposals to convert part of the trackbed across Croxley Moor into a public footpath. The site of the former Rickmansworth Church Street station and coal yard site is being developed.

Setting:
Moor Park; Rickmansworth Lido; Croxley Moor; Grand Union Canal; Cassiobury Park.

THE CHILTERN FOOTHILLS

BOURNE END–HIGH WYCOMBE   5½ miles
Wycombe Railway

Act:
27 July 1846.

Opened:
1 August 1854.

Working Agreement:
Worked from outset by GWR; absorbed into GWR 1 February 1867.

Track Layout:
Originally single broad gauge converted to standard gauge 1
September 1870.

Miles	Station	Grid ref	Note	Opened to Passengers	Closed Passengers	Goods
—	High Wycombe	869931	–	1 Aug 1854	—	—
2¾	Loudwater	901903	1	1 Aug 1854	4 May 1970	18 Jul 1966
4¼	Woburn Green	912885	2	1 Aug 1854	4 May 1970	11 Sept 1967
5½	Marlow Road	894872	3	1 Aug 1854	—	11 Sept 1967

Notes
(1) Site of goods passing loop.
(2) Renamed *Wooburn Green* in October 1872.
(3) Renamed *Bourne End* 1 January 1874, also served by Great Marlow trains
from 28 June 1873.

Remains:
Bourne End: station still open (894872); *Wooburn Green*: station
platform and buildings (912885); *Loudwater*: station platform and
buildings (901903).

Uses:
At the time of writing track had only recently been lifted and
therefore track bed and facilities still largely in situ.

Setting:
The Thames Valley around Marlow, Bourne End, Cookham and
Maidenhead; around Wooburn Common.

HEMEL HEMPSTEAD–HARPENDEN   8¾ miles
Hemel Hempstead Railway

Acts:
13 July 1863; 16 July 1866; 18 July 1872.

Opened:
16 July 1877.

Working Agreement:
Worked from outset by Midland Railway until absorbed on 25
June 1886.

Track Layout:
Single.

Miles	Station	Grid ref	Note	Opened to Passengers	Closed Passengers	Goods
—	Harpenden	137142	1	13 Jul 1868	—	5 Oct 1964
1½	Roundwood Halt	125147	–	8 Aug 1927	16 Jun 1947	—
3½	Redbourn	111121	–	16 Jul 1877	16 Jun 1947	6 Jul 1964
4¼	Beaumont's Halt	099114	2	9 Aug 1905	16 Jun 1947	—
6¾	Godwin's Halt	068088	2	9 Aug 1905	16 Jun 1947	2 Mar 1964
8	Hemel Hempstead	059074	–	16 Jul 1877	16 Jun 1947	1 Jul 1963
8¾	Heath Park Halt	054062	3	9 Aug 1905	16 Jun 1947	31 Aug 1959

Notes

(1) Trains not operated to Harpenden until July 1888, when new south-facing curve opened at Harpenden Junction.

(2) Opened in connection with the Midland Railway's motor-train service introduced on 9 August 1905.

(3) As in (2) above. Line continued for further half mile from Heath Park across Boxmoor to the gasworks at the entrance to the LNWR goods yard. Access also at this point to Cotterell's goods depot (054065). Line west of Heath Park closed officially on 19 September 1959. The connection to the Boxmoor gasworks from the LNWR line was abandoned officially on 1 April 1960.

Remains:

Harpenden: traces of original cutting to north facing junction (134153); *Roundwood*: halt platform (125147); *Redbourn*: station approaches, goods yard and platform (111121); *Hemel Hempstead*: Claydale's sidings (075093): track in private ownership to this point, fragments of trackbed including impressive overbridge (063078), sections of track into former LNWR goods yard at Hemel Hempstead & Boxmoor Station (050057), remains of embankment on Boxmoor (053057); several distant signals still standing on operational part of track.

Uses:

About two-thirds of the line now in private operation. Trackbed in the Hemel Hempstead area largely absorbed into the New Town development, with part used as footpath (066085). Route of the line over Boxmoor has reverted to pastoral use.

Setting:

Harpenden Common (138135); around Redbourn; along the valley of the River Gade and the Grand Union Canal; Boxmoor; Chipperfield Common (045013).

HATFIELD–ST ALBANS ABBEY   6½ miles
Hatfield & St Albans Railway

Act:

30 June 1862.

Opened:

16 October 1865.

Running Powers:

Granted over the LNWR into St Albans Abbey station; over the GNR into Hatfield station.

Working Agreement:
Worked from the outset by the GNR until absorbed on 1 November 1883.

Track Layout:
Single.

Miles	Station	Grid ref	Note	Opened to Passengers	Closed Passengers	Closed Goods
—	Hatfield	232087	–	7 Aug 1850	—	—
1	Lemsford Road Halt	222087	–	1 Aug 1942	1 Oct 1951	—
2	Nast Hyde Halt	209078	–	1 Feb 1910	1 Oct 1951	—
2¾	Springfield	197073	1	1866	1 Oct 1951	1 Jan 1969
4¼	Hill End	177070	–	1 Aug 1899	1 Oct 1951	5 Oct 1964
5¼	Salvation Army Halt	163071	2	1899	1 Oct 1951	7 Dec 1964
5¾	St Albans (London Road)	155064	–	16 Oct 1865	1 Oct 1951	5 Oct 1964
6½	St Albans Abbey	145064	3	5 May 1858	—	5 Oct 1964

Notes
(1) Renamed *Smallford* 1 October 1879—precise opening date not known.
(2) Precise opening date not known.
(3) GNR passenger trains terminated in bay platform, probably from October or November 1866.

Remains:
Hatfield: Lemsford Road halt platform (222087), Fiddle Bridge Sidings site (219087); *Nast Hyde*: old level crossing and platform (210078); *Smallford*: station platform and buildings (197073); *Hill End*: Coalyard site (177070); *St Albans*: overbridge (156066), London Road Station platform and buildings (155064), site of junction with LNWR at Abbey Station (147063), traces of the alignment at the western end of the contractor's railway between Park Street and Napsbury (148037).

Uses:
The trackbed is traceable throughout the entire length of the route. Stations at Smallford and St Albans (London Road) are owned by scrap metal merchants who use the buildings and yards for business purposes.

Setting:
Hatfield House and Park (236084); around Smallford and Nast Hyde; the park at St Albans Abbey (146071).

HATFIELD–LUTON AND DUNSTABLE   20¼ miles
Hertford, Luton & Dunstable Railway

Acts:
  16 July 1855; 28 June 1858.

Opened:
  5 April 1858—goods; 3 May 1858—passengers (Luton–Dunstable); 1 September 1860 (Luton–Hatfield).

Running Powers:
  Granted to LNWR between Dunstable North and Luton Bute Street; granted to GNR into Dunstable North station.

Working Agreements:
  The LNWR provided the service between Dunstable and Luton from 5 April 1858 until 31 August 1860. The GNR began working the branch from Welwyn Junction to Dunstable from 1 September 1860 until finally absorbing the company from 12 June 1861.

Track Layout:
  Single with passing loops at Ayot, Harpenden East, and Bute Street.

Miles	Station	Grid ref	Note	Opened to Passengers	Closed Passengers	Goods
—	Hatfield	232087	–	7 Aug 1850	—	—
2¾	Welwyn Garden City	239129	1	16 Aug 1920	20 Sept 1926	—
4¼	Ayott St Peters	222144	2	2 Jul 1877	26 Sept 1949	1 May 1963
7½	Wheathampstead	177143	–	1 Sept 1860	26 Apr 1965	26 Jul 1965
9½	Harpenden	143151	3	1 Sept 1860	26 Apr 1965	25 Nov 1963
12	New Mill End	120179	4	1 Sept 1860	26 Apr 1965	25 Nov 1963
15	Luton	093215	5	3 May 1858	26 Apr 1965	26 Jun 1967
19¼	Dunstable Church Street	026219	6	1 Oct 1860	26 Apr 1965	7 Dec 1964
20¼	Dunstable	012227	7	1 Jun 1848	26 Apr 1965	9 Oct 1967

Notes

(1) Welwyn Junction station closed 1 September 1860; Dunstable trains never terminated at Welwyn Junction but ran through to Hatfield, at first on the main line; separate single lines were brought into use: Dunstable line—December 1868; Hertford line—3 July 1876; points were removed at Welwyn Junction: Dunstable line—January 1869; Hertford line—October 1876, when Welwyn Junction closed entirely; Welwyn Garden City station opened 200yd south on the main line on 20 September 1926.

(2) Renamed *Ayot* in April 1878 and burnt down on 26 July 1948.

(3) Renamed *Harpenden East* 25 September 1950.

(4) Renamed *Luton Hoo* 1 December 1891.

(5) Renamed *Luton Bute Street* 25 September 1950.

(6) Renamed *Dunstable Town* 1 January 1927.

(7) Renamed *Dunstable North* 25 September 1950; the new LNWR station was opened in January 1866—in the intervening time GNR trains had to reverse into the old station.

Remains:

> *Wheathampstead*: station platform (177143); *Leasey Bridge*: level crossing (162144); *Harpenden*: part of former station platforms (143151); *Chiltern Green*: bridge under former Midland main line (127172); *Luton Hoo*: station buildings and platform (120179); *Luton*: façade of GNR goods depot (092216), many bridges along the route still remain.

Uses:

> Part of trackbed near Ayot used for motorway works (224143); site of former Harpenden East station used for residential purposes, obliterating most of the remains of the station; track alignment from Luton Ground Frame to London Road, Dunstable still in situ and in use for goods traffic purposes—the local authority has long-term objectives for acquiring this land for road improvement purposes.

Setting:

> Hatfield House and Park (236084); around Lemsford, Ayot and Wheathampstead; Luton Hoo (104186) and surrounding area.

LEIGHTON BUZZARD–DUNSTABLE   7 miles
The Dunstable Railway

Act:

30 June 1845.

Opened:

29 May 1848—goods; 1 June 1848—passengers.

Working Agreements:
Worked from outset by LNWR.

Track Layout:
Double.

Miles	Station	Grid ref	Note	Opened to Passengers	Closed Passengers	Goods
—	Leighton	911250	1	9 Apr 1838	—	6 Feb 1967
2¾	Stanbridgeford	970230	2	1849	2 Jul 1962	1 Jun 1964
7	Dunstable	012227	3	1 June 1848	26 Apr 1965	9 Oct 1967

Notes

(1) Present station opened 14 February 1859 replacing original station which was a little to the north; renamed *Leighton Buzzard* 1 July 1911.

(2) Precise opening date not known; probably in use from late 1849—shown in LNWR timetables about October 1860 when platforms were built.

(3) Renamed *Dunstable North* 25 September 1950.

Remains:

> *Dunstable*: Dunstable North station platform and site of goods

yard on which the original station was built (012227); *Stan-bridgeford*: station building and part of platforms (970230); *Leighton Buzzard*: part of original platforms (911250); earthworks over majority of route still complete.

Setting:
Dunstable Downs (005195); around Totternhoe (983217); Leighton Buzzard Narrow Gauge Railway.

Uses:
Predominant part of trackbed traceable and has largely become derelict, with little use.

THE VALE OF AYLESBURY

AYLESBURY–CHEDDINGTON   7 miles
Aylesbury Railway

Act:
19 May 1836.
Opened:
10 June 1839.
Track Layout:
Single.

Miles	Station	Grid ref	Note	Opened to Passengers	Closed Passengers	Goods
—	Cheddington	922186	1	10 Jun 1839	2 Feb 1953	2 Dec 1963
4¼	Marston Gate	886167	2	(see note)	2 Feb 1953	—
7	Aylesbury	823137	3	10 Jun 1839	2 Feb 1953	2 Dec 1963

Notes
(1) Aylesbury branch facilities only.
(2) First shown in *Bradshaw* in 1860, but probably in use earlier.
(3) Original terminus in coal yard (822138): new station opened 16 June 1889.

Remains:
Cheddington: Aylesbury branch platform (922186); *Marston Gate*: station buildings, platform and traces of level crossing (886167); *Broughton*: traces of crossing and original gatekeeper's house (840146); *Aylesbury*: traces of station and goods yard (823137).

Uses:
The sites of station and goods yard at Aylesbury are being developed. Parts of the alignment have been taken for road improvements in the Aylesbury area eg Park Street crossing

(825140). The predominant part of trackbed still traceable but parts have reverted to agricultural use.

Setting:

Hulcott Village (853167).

AYLESBURY–VERNEY JUNCTION   12¼ miles
Aylesbury & Buckingham Railway

Act:

6 August 1860.

Opened:

23 September 1868.

Running Powers:

Granted to GCR between Quainton Road and Aylesbury.

Working Agreements:

Worked initially by GWR and later by LNWR before being absorbed by the Metropolitan Railway from 1 July 1891.

Track Layout:

Originally single; doubled throughout by Metropolitan Railway; later singled in two stages—stage 1 between Verney Junction and Quainton Road and stage 2 between Quainton Road and Aylesbury (associated with closure of former GCR main line).

		Grid		Opened to	Closed	
Miles	*Station*	*ref*	*Note*	*Passengers*	*Passengers*	*Goods*
—	Aylesbury	817135	1	1 Oct 1863	—	—
4¾	Waddesdon Manor	757179	2	1 Jan 1897	6 Jul 1936	—
6	Quainton Road	738189	3	23 Sept 1868	4 Mar 1963	4 Jul 1966
9¾	Grandborough Road	746243	4	23 Sept 1868	6 Jul 1936	6 Jul 1936
11	Winslow Road	750260	–	23 Sept 1868	6 Jul 1936	6 Jul 1936
12¼	Verney Junction	736274	5	23 Sept 1868	1 Jan 1968	6 Jan 1964

Notes

(1) Joint station opened by Metropolitan and GWR on 1 Jan 1894; in 1908, track layout to south of station modified and down main line platform widened and made into island; GWR trains used outer face by locomotive depot; bay added at south end of up platform in 1926.

(2) Renamed *Waddesdon* 1 October 1922.

(3) Metropolitan trains withdrawn from 6 July 1936, although some extended again from Aylesbury in 1943 until withdrawn finally from 31 May 1948.

(4) Renamed *Granborough Road* 6 October 1920.

(5) Metropolitan trains withdrawn from 6 July 1936; no regular passenger train services ever ran direct between Aylesbury and Buckingham as suggested by the title of the authorising Act; Metropolitan trains terminated at the south face of an island platform shared with west-bound LNWR trains.

Remains:

Quainton Road: station and buildings (738189), site of junction with GCR (733193); *Winslow Road*: platforms (750260); *Granborough Road*: platforms (746243); *Verney Junction*: site of junction with LNWR (742275), platforms (736274), site of former transfer sidings (738275).

Uses:
Single track alignment between Aylesbury and Quainton Road still in occasional use for BR freight. Trackbed north of Quainton Road remains fairly well defined, although some sections have reverted to agricultural use. Cutting (739225) largely filled by refuse tip.

Setting:
Waddesdon Manor (734165); Claydon House (720253); around Quainton and East Claydon.

QUAINTON ROAD–BRILL   6¼ miles
Duke of Buckingham and Chandos

Opened:
1 April 1871 (Quainton Road–Wotton); November 1871 (Wotton –brick and tile works, near Brill); Summer 1872 (brick and tile works–Brill); passenger service commenced about January 1872.

Working Agreements:
Worked initially privately by Wotton Tramway until 1894; Oxford & Aylesbury Tramroad Company from 15 October 1894;

Metropolitan Railway from 1 December 1899; Metropolitan & Great Central Joint Committee from 2 April 1906.

Track Layout:
Single.

Miles	Station	Grid ref	Note	Opened to Passengers	Closed Passengers	Closed Goods
—	Quainton Road	738189	1	23 Sept 1868	4 Mar 1963	4 Jul 1966
1¼	Waddesdon Road	726176	–	c. Jan 1872	2 Dec 1935	2 Dec 1935
1¾	Westcott	721168	2	c. Jan 1872	2 Dec 1935	2 Dec 1935
3¾	Wotton	695154	–	c. Jan 1872	2 Dec 1935	2 Dec 1935
5	Wood Siding	673154	3	Nov 1871	2 Dec 1935	2 Dec 1935
6¼	Brill	657154	–	Summer 1872	2 Dec 1935	2 Dec 1935

Notes
(1) Station resited in 1896 and bay platform provided for Brill branch trains.
(2) Named *Wescott* in some early timetables.
(3) Station advertised at Church Siding (691157), junction with Kingswood Lane branch, in some timetables.

Remains:
Quainton Road: branch yard (738189)—used by preservation society; *Westcott*: station buildings and original booking hall—

now garden shed (721168); *Wotton*: station buildings and old railway shed (695154); *Church Siding*: site of branch to Kingswood Lane and well where water tower was sited (690157); *Brill*: bridge over former EWR, site of Wood Siding platform (673154); works at site of brick and tile works (665153), station buildings with GPO box named *Brill Station* (657154).

Uses:

Trackbed well defined throughout length, although section between Westcott and Wotton blocked by Ministry of Defence land; site of Waddesdon Road station used for road improvement; Waddesdon Road to Westcott section now footpath over farmland.

Setting:

Waddesdon Manor (734165); around Westcott, Wotton Underwood and Brill—particularly good line to walk.

VERNEY JUNCTION–BANBURY (MERTON STREET)   21¼ miles
Buckinghamshire Railway

Acts:

26 June 1846; 27 July 1846; 22 July 1847.

Opened:

1 May 1850.

Running Powers:

Granted to Stratford-upon-Avon & Midland Junction Railway from Cockley Brake Junction to Banbury (Merton Street).

Working Agreement:

Worked from outset by LNWR until absorbed by LNWR in 1879.

Track Layout:

Single, with passing places.

Miles	Station	Grid ref	Note	Opened to Passengers	Closed Passengers	Goods
—	Verney Junction	736274	1	23 Sept 1868	1 Jan 1968	6 Jan 1964
2¼	Padbury	713305	–	1 Mar 1878	7 Sept 1964	6 Jan 1964
4¼	Buckingham	695333	2	1 May 1850	7 Sept 1964	5 Dec 1966
5¾	Radclive Halt	677342	–	13 Aug 1956	2 Jan 1961	—
7¼	Water Stratford Halt	653342	–	13 Aug 1956	2 Jan 1961	—
8¾	Westbury Crossing	627347	3	1 Aug 1879	2 Jan 1961	2 Dec 1963
11¾	Brackley	585365	–	1 May 1850	2 Jan 1961	2 Dec 1963
17½	Farthinghoe	523404	4	1 May 1850	3 Nov 1952	2 Dec 1963
21¼	Banbury (Merton Street)	463406	4	1 May 1850	2 Jan 1961	6 Jun 1966

Notes

(1) Station originally opened to serve Aylesbury & Buckingham trains, but provided interchange with all services of the Buckinghamshire Railway.

(2) A temporary structure only on the Lenborough Road side of the line; permanent station opened by early 1861.

(3) Renamed *Fulwell & Westbury* 1 October 1880.

(4) Also served by SMJR trains from Blisworth and Towcester from 1 June 1872 until 2 July 1951.

Remains:

Verney Junction: platforms and some station buildings (736274); *Padbury:* platform and station approach (713305); *Buckingham:* station platforms (695333); *Radclive:* level crossing keeper's house at site of halt platform (677342), site of former siding and keeper's house at Bacon's Crossing (646343); *Fulwell & Westbury:* station platforms and keeper's house (627347); *Brackley:* station platforms, buildings, approach and goods yard (585365); *Cockley Brake:* site of junction with SMJ (546414); various bridges and viaducts along route eg at Buckingham (692335).

Uses:

Line is traceable throughout and long stretches can be walked. Some small sections have reverted to agricultural use, and demolition of some bridges along the route make parts difficult to follow. The site of Padbury station is to be used for a small residential development. Much of Brackley goods yard is being converted to warehousing. The site of Banbury (Merton Street) station is now a BRS and National Carriers Depot. No trace remains of the timber Radclive or Water Stratford Halts, while there is little evidence of Farthinghoe.

Setting:

Around Verney Junction; Stowe School and Park (675375); around Radclive, Finmere and Water Stratford Villages.

THE OUSE BASIN

BEDFORD–HITCHIN   16¼ miles
Midland Railway

Act:

4 August 1853.

Opened:

15 April 1857—minerals; 4 May 1857—goods; 8 May 1857—passengers.

Running Powers:

Granted to LNWR from Bedford Junction to Howard's Works.

Track Layout:
Originally double, converted to single except between Southill and Shefford, from 1 May 1911.

Miles	Station	Grid ref	Note	Opened to Passengers	Closed Passengers	Goods
—	Bedford	042496	1	1 Feb 1859	—	30 Aug 1971
3	Cardington	085474	–	8 May 1857	1 Jan 1962	1 Jan 1962
7¼	Southill	130424	–	8 May 1857	1 Jan 1962	1 Jan 1962
9½	Shefford	142390	–	8 May 1857	1 Jan 1962	28 Dec 1964
12	Henlow	166358	2	8 May 1857	1 Jan 1962	2 Dec 1963
16¼	Hitchin	195296	3	7 Aug 1850	—	1 Jan 1964

Notes
(1) Renamed *Bedford (Midland Road)* 2 June 1924.
(2) Renamed *Henlow Camp* 1 March 1933.
(3) Although the Midland used the GNR station, it had its own goods depot.

Remains:
Shefford: Viaduct (142390); *Old Warden:* tunnel (111448); *Southill:* station (130424); *Ireland:* monument to W. H. Whitbread in Keepers Warren (133419).

Uses:
Henlow Camp Station site has been used for new development. The cutting south of Shefford is used as a tip.

Setting:
Around Southill and Old Warden.

BEDFORD–SANDY   8½ miles
Bedford & Cambridge Railway

Act:
6 August 1860.

Opened:
7 July 1862—passengers; 1 August 1862—goods.

Working Agreements:
Worked by LNWR from opening until absorbed on 5 July 1865.

Track Layout:
Single track with passing loops at Goldington, Willington and Blunham.

Miles	Station	Grid ref	Note	Opened to Passengers	Closed Passengers	Goods
—	Bedford	052489	1, 2, 3, 4	18 Nov 1846	—	10 Aug 1970
4	Willington	112503	–	1 May 1903	1 Jan 1968	13 Jul 1964
6¼	Blunham	148506	–	7 Jul 1862	1 Jan 1968	13 Jul 1964
7	Girtford Halt & Siding	165504	–	1 Jan 1938	17 Nov 1940	1 Nov 1951
8½	Sandy	178488	5	7 Jul 1862	1 Jan 1968	4 Feb 1963

Notes
(1) Renamed *Bedford (St Johns)* 2 June 1924.
(2) Bedford & Cambridge trains used the LNWR station.
(3) Staff withdrawn 15 July 1968.
(4) Re-opened to goods 4 December 1972.
(5) Former GNR section of station remains open.

Remains:
Blunham: station (148506); *Sandy*: viaduct over GNR (176495),
Captain Peel's Monument in Sandy Parish Church (174491).

Uses:
A single track remains from Bedford to serve Goldington Power
Station. Housing and industrial development have removed part
of the trackbed at Sandy.

Setting:
Around Great Barford and Blunham.

KETTERING JUNCTION–THRAPSTON   7½ miles
Kettering & Thrapstone Railway

Act:
29 July 1862.

THRAPSTON–HUNTINGDON   18¼ miles
Kettering, Thrapstone & Huntingdon Railway

Act:
28 July 1863.

Opened:
21 February 1866—goods; 1 March 1866—passengers.

Running Powers:
None on this section of line, although the Midland did exercise
such powers to reach Cambridge from Huntingdon.

Working Agreements:
Worked by Midland from opening until absorbed on 1 July 1897.

Track Layout:
Single track with passing loops at Butlin's Siding, Thrapston and
Kimbolton.

Miles	Station	Grid ref	Note	Opened to Passengers	Closed Passengers	Goods
—	Kettering	864780	–	8 May 1857	—	—
4¾	Cranford	925768	–	1 Mar 1866	2 Apr 1956	6 Nov 1961
7	Twywell	958780	–	1 Mar 1866	30 Jul 1951	30 Jul 1951
9¼	Thrapston	995779	1	1 Mar 1866	15 Jun 1959	28 Oct 1963
12½	Raunds	020737	–	1 Mar 1866	15 Jun 1959	28 Oct 1963
17½	Kimbolton	088711	–	1 Mar 1866	15 Jun 1959	28 Oct 1963
19	Longstow	109703	2	—	—	1 Jun 1953
22¼	Grafham	161694	–	1 Mar 1866	15 Jun 1959	15 Jun 1959
24¾	Brampton	204690	3	1 Mar 1866	15 Jun 1959	15 Jun 1959
27½	Huntingdon	233715	4, 5	1 May 1883	18 Sept 1959	—

Notes
(1) Renamed *Thrapston (Midland Road)* 14 July 1924.
(2) Goods only.
(3) Renamed *Buckden* 1 February 1868.
(4) Renamed *Huntingdon East* 1 July 1923.
(5) Passenger services only

Remains:
   Thrapston: viaduct (992780); *Buckden*: station (204690).
Uses:
   A single track remains from Kettering Junction to Twywell to serve the ironstone industry. Thrapston station and yard are used as a storage depot, garage and offices. The course of the line is used as a slip road for the A1 at Buckden.
Setting:
   Around Thrapston and Kimbolton.

IRCHESTER JUNCTION–HIGHAM FERRERS 3½ miles
Midland Railway

Act:
   25 July 1890.
Opened:
   1 September 1893—goods; 1 May 1894—passengers.
Track Layout:
   Single track.

Miles	Station	Grid ref	Note	Opened to Passengers	Closed Passengers	Goods
—	Wellingborough	904681	1	8 May 1857	—	—
3¾	Rushden	956672	–	1 May 1894	15 Jun 1959	1 Sept 1969
4¾	Higham Ferrers	963685	2	1 May 1894	15 Jun 1959	3 Feb 1969

Notes
(1) Renamed *Wellingborough (Midland Road)* 14 July 1924.
(2) Renamed *Higham Ferrers & Irthlingboro'* 1 July 1902: reverted to original name 1 October 1910.

Remains:
> *Irchester*: site of junction (922673); *Rushden*: station and yard (956672); *Higham Ferrers*: station and yard (963685).

Uses:
> The yard at Rushden is in use as a lorry park, and the station buildings house a tailor and outfitter.

Setting:
> Around Higham Ferrers.

THE NORTHAMPTON UPLANDS

BLISWORTH–COCKLEY BRAKE JUNCTION   15¼ miles
Northampton & Banbury Junction Railway

Act:
> 28 July 1863.

Opened:
> 1 May 1866 (Blisworth to Towcester): August 1871—goods (Towcester to Helmdon); 1 June 1872 (Towcester to Banbury).

Running Powers:
> The East & West Junction Railway exercised running powers between Greens Norton Junction and Blisworth and the N & BJ utilised powers over the Buckinghamshire Railway from Cockley Brake to Banbury.

Working Agreements:
> Worked by LNWR from 1 October 1866 to 1872 and from 1 November 1876 to 30 June 1910.

Track Layout:
> Single track with passing place at Towcester.

GREENS NORTON JUNCTION–STRATFORD-UPON-AVON   33¼ miles
East & West Junction Railway

Act:
> 23 June 1864.

Opened:
> 1 June 1871 (Fenny Compton to Kineton); 1 July 1873 (Greens Norton Junction to Fenny Compton and Kineton to Stratford-upon-Avon).

Running Powers:
These were exercised over the Northampton & Banbury Junction between Greens Norton Junction and Blisworth.

Track Layout:
Single track with passing places at Blakesley, Moreton Pinkney, Byfield, Fenny Compton, Kineton, Ettington and Stratford-upon-Avon.

TOWCESTER–RAVENSTONE WOOD JUNCTION   10½ miles
Easton Neston Mineral & Towcester, Roade & Olney Junction Railway

Act:
15 August 1879.

Opened:
13 April 1891—goods; 1 December 1892—passengers.

Running Powers:
The Midland granted running powers from Ravenstone Wood to Olney.

Junctions:
With LNWR at Roade.

Track Layout:
Single track.

STRATFORD-UPON-AVON–BROOM JUNCTION   7½ miles
Evesham, Redditch & Stratford-upon-Avon Junction Railway

Act:
5 August 1873.

Opened:
2 June 1879.

Running Powers:
Although these were granted over the Midland between Evesham and Redditch, only the five chains into Broom station were used.

Working Agreements:
Worked by the East & West Junction from opening until absorbed into the Stratford-upon-Avon & Midland Junction Railway on 1 January 1909.

Track Layout:
Single track.

Miles		Station	Grid ref	Note	Opened to Passengers	Closed Passengers	Closed Goods
—		Blisworth	721546	1	1 May 1866	7 Apr 1952	6 Jul 1964
1½		Tiffield	—	2	Oct 1869	Mar 1871	—
—	—	Olney	893520	3	—	5 Mar 1962	6 Jan 1964
—	5½	Salcey Forest	814537	-	1 Dec 1892	31 Mar 1893	1 Jul 1908
—	10¾	Stoke Bruern	736505	-	1 Dec 1892	31 Mar 1893	2 Jun 1952
4¼	14	Towcester	689494	-	1 May 1866	7 Apr 1952	3 Feb 1964
8¼		Wappenham	635464	-	1 Jun 1872	2 Jul 1951	29 Oct 1951
11¾		Helmdon	588439	4	1 Jun 1872	2 Jul 1951	29 Oct 1951
8½		Blakesley	625498	5	1 Jul 1873	7 Apr 1952	3 Feb 1962
11½		Morton Pinkney	575499	5	1 Jul 1873	7 Apr 1952	7 Apr 1952
15¾		Byfield	519528	5	1 Jul 1873	7 Apr 1952	4 May 1964
18		Aston-le-Walls Siding	494512	6	—	—	5 Jan 1953
22½		Fenny Compton West	428528	5	1 Jun 1871	7 Apr 1952	4 May 1964
29		Kineton	330511	5	1 Jun 1871	7 Apr 1952	11 Nov 1963
33		Ettington	269502	5	1 July 1873	7 Apr 1952	11 Nov 1963
37½		Clifford Siding	204537	6	—	—	4 Nov 1963
38		Stratford-upon-Avon	199541	5, 7	June 1876	7 Apr 1952	11 Nov 1963
42		Binton	144532	8	2 Jun 1879	23 May 1949	7 Mar 1960
44½		Bidford	099529	8, 9	2 Jun 1879	23 May 1949	7 Mar 1960
45¾		Broom Junction	085534	10	1 Nov 1880	1 Oct 1962	1 Oct 1962

Notes
(1) N & BJ station as distinct from LNWR station.
(2) This station appeared in timetables between October 1869 and February 1871.
(3) This station was situated on the Bedford & Northampton Railway and was reached by running powers.
(4) Renamed *Helmdon Village* 1 July 1950.
(5) Previously closed to passengers 1 August 1877 and re-opened 22 February 1885.
(6) Goods only.
(7) Renamed *Stratford-upon-Avon Old Town* 7 April 1952.
(8) Temporarily closed to passengers from 16 June 1947, permanently closed from 23 May 1949.
(9) Renamed *Bidford-on-Avon* 1 July 1909.
(10) This was an unadvertised changing place from July 1879 to October 1880.

Remains:

Blisworth: SMJR Company Houses (718547); *Stoke Bruern*: station buildings (736505); *Kineton*: station buildings and goods shed (330511); *Stratford*: viaduct over River Avon (200540); site of Old Town station and junctions with GWR (198541).

Uses:

The only portion still used as a railway is an army private siding from Fenny Compton to Central Ammunition Depot, Kineton.

Towcester station area is used as a yard for an adjoining factory, Helmdon station site is used for a coach depot and Wappenham as a cow byre.

Setting:

The whole length of the line is attractive but Morton Pinkney, near the Washington's ancestral home at Sulgrave, and Stratford-upon-Avon are particularly worth visiting.

KINGHAM–CHIPPING NORTON   4½ miles
Oxford, Worcester & Wolverhampton Railway

Act:

31 July 1854.

Opened:

10 August 1855.

CHIPPING NORTON–KINGS SUTTON   15¾ miles
Banbury & Cheltenham Direct Railway

Act:

21 July 1873.

Opened:

6 April 1887.

Working Agreements:

Worked by GWR from opening until absorbed from 1 July 1897.

Track Layout:

Single track with passing places at Chipping Norton, Hook Norton and Bloxham; double track from Adderbury to Kings Sutton.

Miles	Station	Grid ref	Note	Opened to Passengers	Closed Passengers	Goods
—	Chipping Norton Junction	256227	1	10 Aug 1855	—	7 Sept 1964
1¾	Sarsden Halt & Siding	276247	–	2 Jul 1906	3 Dec 1962	3 Dec 1962
4½	Chipping Norton	307270	2	6 Apr 1887	3 Dec 1962	7 Sept 1964
7½	Rollright Halt	324302	–	12 Dec 1906	4 Jun 1951	—
11	Hook Norton	363336	–	6 Apr 1887	4 Jun 1951	4 Nov 1963
15¼	Bloxham	426354	–	6 Apr 1887	4 Jun 1951	4 Nov 1963
17	Milton Halt	453353	–	1 Jan 1908	4 Jun 1951	—
18½	Adderbury	474349	–	6 Apr 1887	4 Jun 1951	4 Dec 1967
20¼	Kings Sutton	495360	3	1 Dec 1873	—	4 May 1964

Notes
(1) Renamed *Kingham* 1 May 1909.
(2) Replaced the first station on the opening of the Banbury & Cheltenham Direct.
(3) Staff withdrawn 2 November 1964; renamed *Kings Sutton Halt* 6 May 1968.

Remains:
> *Chipping Norton*: tunnel (306272); *Hook Norton*: viaduct piers (361327); *Adderbury*: station buildings (474349).

Uses:
> Part of the avoiding loop at Kingham is being removed and a housing estate has been built partially on the course of the railway at Bloxham.

Setting:
> Around Kingham, Rollright and Hook Norton.

THE VALE OF EVESHAM

REDDITCH–ASHCHURCH   28 miles
Evesham & Redditch Railway
Midland Railway

Acts:
> 7 June 1861; 13 July 1863.

Opened:
> 1 October 1864 (Ashchurch–Evesham); 16 June 1866—goods; 17 September 1866—passengers (Evesham–Alcester); 4 May 1868 (Alcester–Redditch).

Running Powers:
> Granted to GWR into Alcester station, and to the Evesham, Redditch & Stratford-upon-Avon Junction Railway (later SMJR) between Redditch and Evesham.

Working Agreement:
> The Evesham & Redditch Railway worked from outset by the Midland Railway.

Track Layout:
> Single with passing loops between Redditch and Evesham; double Evesham–Ashchurch.

Miles	Station	Grid ref	Note	Opened to Passengers	Closed Passengers	Goods
—	Redditch (1st station)	041683	1	19 Sept 1859	3 May 1868	—
—	Redditch (2nd station)	038675	2	4 May 1868	—	8 Sept 1969
3¼	Studley & Astwood Bank	059636	–	4 May 1868	1 Oct 1962	6 Jul 1964
5½	Coughton	074607	–	4 May 1868	30 Jun 1952	30 Jun 1952
7¼	Alcester	085577	–	17 Sept 1866	1 Oct 1962	6 Jul 1964
9¼	Wixford	086546	–	17 Sept 1866	2 Jan 1950	2 Jan 1950
10¼	Broom Junction	085534	–	2 Jun 1879	1 Oct 1962	1 Oct 1962
11½	Salford Priors	080513	–	17 Sept 1866	1 Oct 1962	1 Oct 1962
13¼	Harvington	061488	–	17 Sept 1866	1 Oct 1962	1 Oct 1962
17	Evesham	037444	–	1 Oct 1864	17 Jun 1963	—
18¾	Bengeworth	027431	–	1 Oct 1864	8 Jun 1953	8 Jun 1953
20¼	Hinton	019406	–	1 Oct 1864	17 Jun 1963	1 Jul 1963
22	Ashton-Under-Hill	005377	–	1 Oct 1864	17 Jun 1963	17 Jun 1963
24	Beckford	981356	–	1 Oct 1864	17 Jun 1963	1 Jul 1963
28	Ashchurch	927334	3	24 Jun 1840	15 Nov 1971	1 Jun 1964

Notes

(1) Opened by the Redditch Railway.
(2) Now replaced by new station to the north (038676).
(3) Opened by Birmingham & Gloucester Railway; Evesham branch platform
    opened 1 October 1864.

Remains:

Redditch: cutting and tunnel south of former station (039672);
Studley & Astwood Bank: station buildings (059636); *Coughton*:
station buildings and platform (074607); *Alcester*: station buildings, platforms and site of junction and goods yard (085577);
Wixford: station platform (086546); *Broom*: station buildings and
platform (085534), site of triangle junction and south junction
signal box (081525); *Salford Priors*: station buildings and platform
(080513); *Harvington*: station buildings and platform (061488);
Evesham: part of original Midland station buildings and platforms
037444); *Bengeworth*: station platform (027431); *Hinton*: station
platform (019406); *Ashton-Under-Hill*: station buildings and platforms (005377); *Beckford*: station buildings and platforms
(981356); *Ashchurch*: long siding and station platforms (927334).

Uses:

The site of the Evesham & Redditch Railway station at Redditch
is now used for the bus station as part of the New Town development. Station buildings along the route of the line have largely
been sold for residential purposes. The station at Broom is used as a
depot, while Evesham Midland station (apart from railway use
of the buildings) is used for garage and warehousing. Bengeworth

has been partly absorbed by residential development, and Hinton as a depot. The route of the line is well defined and long stretches are easily walkable. Some bridges, however, have been demolished, including those over the River Avon at Evesham and the River Arrow at Wixford, which make walking of the whole length difficult.

Setting:

Ragley Hall (073555); around Broom, Evesham, Ashton and Beckford.

ALCESTER–BEARLEY   6½ miles
Alcester Railway

Act:

6 August 1872.

Opened:

4 September 1876.

Running Powers:

Granted into Alcester and Bearley stations.

Working Agreement:

Worked from outset by GWR.

Track Layout:

Single.

Miles	Station	Grid ref	Note	Opened to Passengers	Closed Passengers	Goods
—	Alcester	085577	–	17 Sept 1866	1 Oct 1962	6 Jul 1964
2¼	Great Alne	116592	1	4 Sept 1876	25 Sept 1939	25 Sept 1939
4	Aston Cantlow Halt	143608	–	18 Dec 1922	25 Sept 1939	—
6½	Bearley	172608	2	10 Oct 1860	—	20 May 1963

Notes

(1) Unadvertised workmen's trains ran from Coventry to Great Alne until 3 July 1944 to serve the works of the Maudslay Motor Co.

(2) Opened by Stratford-upon-Avon Railway which ran from Hatton to Stratford-upon-Avon. Renamed *Bearley Halt* 6 May 1968.

Remains:

Alcester: site of former junction with Midland Railway and GWR locomotive shed (084580); bridge over River Alne (085583); *Great Alne*: station platform and buildings (116592); *Edstone*: aquaduct and site of later junction with GWR Stratford line (163608).

Uses:

Most of the former alignment is traceable and can be easily

walked. A few short sections have reverted to agricultural use. Great Alne station has been converted to residential use.

Setting:

Around Alcester; the mill and weir, Great Alne (123588); around Aston Cantlow; along the Stratford-upon-Avon Canal.

THE NENE AND WELLAND VALLEYS

BLISWORTH–PETERBOROUGH   47½ miles
London & Birmingham Railway

Act:

4 July 1843.

Opened:

13 May 1845—passengers (Blisworth to Northampton); 2 June 1845—passengers (Northampton to Peterborough); 15 December 1845—goods (Blisworth to Peterborough).

Running Powers:

The GNR passenger service from Peterborough to Leicester (Belgrave Road) used this line between Longville Junction and Yarwell Junction and the GNR, as lessor of the Stamford & Essendine, exercised running powers into Wansford Station from Wansford Junction.

The Midland possessed running powers from Wellingborough Junction to Islip Furnaces at Thrapston and also to Northampton Junction.

The LNWR had running powers over the Midland from Wellingborough Junction into Wellingborough Station, over the GNR from Wansford to Stamford and from Longville Junction to Crescent Junction and over the GER from Peterborough Junction to Peterborough Station (ie East). In addition the LNWR had powers over the one chain to GE & Midland Junction and from there to GN & LNW (Agreed) Junction.

Track Layout:

Double track, originally single from Northampton to Peterborough, conversion completed in September 1846.

Miles	Station	Grid ref	Note	Opened to Passengers	Closed Passengers	Goods
—	Blisworth	721546	1	—	4 Jan 1960	6 Jul 1964
4¼	Northampton (Bridge Street)	754594	–	13 May 1845	4 May 1964	—
8¼	Billing Road	816607	2	Dec 1845	6 Oct 1952	1 Jun 1964
11¾	Castle Ashby (White Mill)	860618	3	2 Jun 1845	4 May 1964	1 Feb 1965

Miles	Station	Grid ref	Note	Opened to Passengers	Closed Passengers	Closed Goods
15¾	Wellingborough	902664	4	2 Jun 1845	4 May 1964	7 Nov 1966
18	Ditchford	930684	–	2 Jun 1845	1 Nov 1924	15 May 1950
20	Higham Ferrers	958705	5	2 Jun 1845	4 May 1964	6 Jun 1966
22¾	Ringstead	970743	6	2 Jun 1845	4 May 1964	2 Mar 1964
26	Thrapston	992788	7	2 Jun 1845	4 May 1964	7 Jun 1965
28½	Thorpe	024813	–	2 Jun 1845	4 May 1964	4 May 1964
31¾	Barnwell	046850	–	2 Jun 1845	4 May 1964	4 May 1964
34¼	Oundle	048890	–	2 Jun 1845	4 May 1964	6 Nov 1972
38¼	Elton	079948	–	Jan 1847	7 Dec 1953	7 Dec 1953
40¾	Wansford	092980	–	2 Jun 1845	1 Jul 1957	13 Jul 1964
42	Castor	113978	–	1847	1 Jul 1957	28 Dec 1964
44½	Overton	151970	8	2 Jun 1845	5 Oct 1942	28 Dec 1964
47½	Peterborough (GE)	194980	9, 10	2 Jun 1845	6 Jun 1966	17 Apr 1966

Notes
(1) This was the second station and replaced the original, ½ mile to the south pre-1853.
(2) Renamed *Billing* 1 April 1883.
(3) Renamed *Castle Ashby & Earls Barton* May 1869.
(4) Renamed *Wellingborough (London Road)* 14 July 1924.
(5) Renamed *Higham Ferrers & Irthlingborough* 28 April 1885, *Irthlingborough* 1 October 1910.
(6) Renamed *Ringstead & Addington* 1 April 1898.
(7) Renamed *Thrapston (Bridge Street)* 14 July 1924.
(8) Renamed *Orton Waterville* 1 August 1913.
(9) Renamed *Peterborough East* 1 July 1923.
(10) Retained as a parcels concentration depot after withdrawal of goods services.

Remains:
   Northampton (Bridge Street): goods shed and signalbox (754594); *Wellingborough (London Road)*: station platforms and signalbox (902664); *Irthlingborough*: goods shed and level crossing gates (958705); *Oundle*: station building (048890); *Wansford*: station buildings, signalbox, level crossing gates, some signals and tunnel (092980).

Uses:
   A single track remains through Northampton (Bridge Street) to serve Far Cotton goods depot and Hardingstone Power Station. The single line, formerly used as far as Oundle, is in part proposed as a steam railway as part of the Nene Valley Park. Thrapston station site is used as a joinery works, part of the trackbed is a stacking ground at Castle Ashby, the trackbed is used as a road near Ditchford, and at Ringstead and Castor the station yards are used as carparks for the River Nene nearby.

Setting:
   Around Blisworth, Irthlingborough, Oundle and Wansford.

RUGBY–LUFFENHAM JUNCTION
London & Birmingham Railway   35 miles

Act:

18 June 1846.

Opened:

1 May 1850 (Rugby to Market Harborough); 1 June 1850
(Market Harborough to Rockingham); 2 June 1851 (Rockingham to Luffenham).

Running Powers:

The GNR passenger service between Peterborough and Leicester
(Belgrave Road) used this line from Seaton to Drayton Junction
but it did not exercise its powers from Drayton Junction to
Northampton.

The LNWR exercised running powers over the Midland to
reach Stamford.

Track Layout:

Double track; the section from Rugby to Market Harborough
was opened as a single line and doubled from 22 July 1878. The
section from Seaton to Luffenham Junction was reduced to single
track during June and July 1880.

Miles	Station	Grid ref	Note	Opened to Passengers	Closed Passengers	Goods
—	Rugby	512759	1	10 Apr 1886	—	—
1	Clifton Mill	524763	–	1 May 1850	6 Apr 1953	6 Apr 1953
3½	Lilbourne	562778	2	1 May 1850	6 Jun 1966	—
5¼	Stanford Hall	589784	3	1 May 1850	6 Jun 1966	6 Jul 1964
9¼	Welford	624836	4	1 May 1850	6 Jun 1966	6 Jul 1964
12½	Theddingworth	665861	–	1 May 1850	6 Jun 1966	6 Apr 1964
14¾	Lubenham	700870	–	1 May 1850	6 Jun 1966	6 Apr 1964
17½	Market Harborough (LNW plats)	742875	5	28 Jun 1885	6 Jun 1966	—
22½	Medbourne Bridge	793917	6	1 Jun 1850	18 Jun 1951	18 Mar 1963
27½	Rockingham	866932	–	1 Jun 1850	6 Jun 1966	6 Apr 1964
31½	Seaton & Uppingham	909979	7	2 Jun 1851	6 Jun 1966	6 Apr 1964
33½	Morcott	929008	–	1 Dec 1898	6 Jun 1966	4 May 1964

Notes

(1) This is the third station on the LNWR main line and was brought into use in
two stages. The down side was opened on 5 July 1885 and the up side on
10 April 1886. The work was finally completed in June 1886.

(2) Partially unstaffed 16 January 1965.

(3) Renamed *Yelvertoft* 1 June 1870, *Yelvertoft & Stanford Hall* December 1880,
Yelvertoft & Stanford Park 1 February 1881. Partially unstaffed 16 January
1965.

(4) Renamed *Welford, Kilworth* May 1853, *Welford & Kilworth* April 1855, *Welford
& Lutterworth* 1 May 1897, *Welford & Kilworth* 13 January 1913.

(5) The original LNWR station was replaced by a LNW & Midland Joint Station on 28 June 1885.
(6) Renamed *Ashley & Weston* 1 March 1878 but shown in official records as 1 January 1880.
(7) Renamed *Seaton* 1 October 1894.

Remains:

    Rugby: Clifton Mill Junction (520755); *Yelvertoft*: platform buildings and canopies (589784): *Theddingworth*: signal box and platform shelter (665861); *Market Harborough*: one LNWR platform and a signalbox (742875); *Seaton*: station buildings, bridge and platform shelter (909979); *Morcott*: tunnel (925004).

Uses:

    The part of the line from the junction with the Northampton branch into Market Harborough still remains. The station houses are occupied at Lilbourne, Yelvertoft, Theddingworth, Ashley & Weston, Rockingham and Seaton. The site of Morcott station is used by a sawmill.

Setting:

    Around Stanford-on-Avon, Husbands Bosworth and Caldecott.

SEATON–YARWELL JUNCTION   11¼ miles
London & North Western Railway

Act:

    21 July 1873.

Opened:

    21 July 1879—goods; 1 November 1879—passengers.

Running Powers:

    The GNR passenger service from Peterborough to Leicester (Belgrave Road) used this line. It commenced on 2 July 1883 and was withdrawn from 1 April 1916.

Track Layout:

    Double track.

Miles	Station	Grid ref	Note	Opened to Passengers	Closed Passengers	Goods
—	Seaton & Uppingham	909979	1	2 Jun 1851	6 Jun 1966	6 Apr 1964
3	Wakerley & Barrowden	956997	–	1 Nov 1879	6 Jun 1966	28 Dec 1964
7¼	Kingscliffe	009978	–	1 Nov 1879	6 Jun 1966	3 Jun 1968
11½	Nassington	068968	–	1 Nov 1879	1 Jul 1957	3 Aug 1957
13	Wansford	092980	–	2 Jun 1845	1 Jul 1957	13 Jul 1964

Note

(1) Renamed *Seaton* 1 October 1894.

Remains:
> *Wakerley & Barrowden*: station buildings (956997); *Kingscliffe*: stationmaster's house (009977).

Uses:
> A single track, disused, remains as far as Kingscliffe.

Setting:
> Around Kingscliffe.

SEATON–UPPINGHAM   3¼ miles
London & North Western Railway

Act:
> 4 August 1890.

Opened:
> 17 September 1894—goods; 1 October 1894—passengers.

Running Powers:
> The GNR possessed running powers into Uppingham but they were not exercised.

Track Layout:
> Single track with a run around loop at Uppingham.

Miles	Station	Grid ref	Note	Opened to Passengers	Closed Passengers	Goods
—	Seaton &					
	Uppingham	909979	1	2 Jun 1851	6 Jun 1966	6 Apr 1964
3¼	Uppingham	870995	2	1 Oct 1894	13 Jun 1960	1 Jun 1964

Notes
(1) Renamed *Seaton* 1 October 1894.
(2) Special trains for the school continued to run after the withdrawal of the passenger service.

Remains:
> *Seaton*: site of junction with Stamford line (916989); *Bisbrooke*: road overbridge (879992); *Uppingham*: stationmaster's house, goods shed and part of the platform (870995).

Uses:
> Seaton station yard is used for scrapping cars. A factory stands on the site of Uppingham station.

Setting:
> Around Seaton, Harringworth and Uppingham.

THE GREAT CENTRAL RAILWAY

RUGBY–QUAINTON ROAD JUNCTION   39¼ miles
Manchester, Sheffield & Lincolnshire Railway

Act:
28 March 1893.

Opened:
25 July 1898—coal; 15 March 1899—passengers; 11 April 1899
—goods.

Running Powers:
None on this section of line. Originally the GCR exercised powers
over the Metropolitan to Canfield Place Junction but from 1906
these arrangements were altered, when the Met & GC Joint Committee was established.

Junctions:
With branch at Calvert North to Claydon LNE Junction on
Bletchley–Oxford line (opened 14 September 1940).

Track Layout:
Double track.

Miles	Station	Grid ref	Note	Opened to Passengers	Closed Passengers	Goods
—	Rugby Central	514746	1	15 Mar 1899	5 May 1969	14 Jun 1965
4¾	Willoughby	524670	2	15 Mar 1899	1 Apr 1957	1 Apr 1957
11¾	Charwelton	536562	–	15 Mar 1899	4 Mar 1963	4 Mar 1963
14¼	Woodford & Hinton	540524	3	15 Mar 1899	5 Sept 1966	5 Apr 1965
17¼	Culworth	564484	4	15 Mar 1899	29 Sept 1958	4 Jun 1962
20¾	Helmdon	586431	–	15 Mar 1899	4 Mar 1963	2 Nov 1964
24	Brackley Central	590380	–	15 Mar 1899	5 Sept 1966	14 Jun 1965
28¾	Finmere	629313	–	15 Mar 1899	4 Mar 1963	5 Oct 1964
34½	Calvert	689247	–	15 Mar 1899	4 Mar 1963	4 May 1964
39¼	Quainton Road	738189	5	23 Sept 1868	4 Mar 1963	4 Jul 1966

Notes
(1) Staff withdrawn 5 September 1966.
(2) Renamed *Braunston & Willoughby* 1 January 1904.
(3) Renamed *Woodford Halse* 1 November 1948.
(4) Coal depot only closed 29 September 1958.
(5) Original Metropolitan Railway station replaced in 1896 by a new station to
    the south, served by Metropolitan trains prior to the opening of the GCR.

Remains:
Calvert: platform (689247); *Brackley*: station buildings (590380),
viaduct (595374); *Helmdon*: viaduct (583437); *Charwelton*: station
master's house (535562); *Catesby*: tunnel (533570); *Rugby*: viaduct
(518758).

Uses:

A single line remains from Quainton Road to Calvert and Claydon LNE Junction. Brackley yard is used for car storage. Rugby goods shed and yard is occupied by a timber merchant.

Setting:

Pleasant countryside flanks the entire line but it is perhaps as well to avoid the brickworks at Calvert.

WOODFORD & HINTON–WOODFORD WEST JUNCTION (a) $\frac{3}{8}$ mile
WOODFORD SOUTH JUNCTION–WOODFORD WEST JUNCTION (b)
$\frac{5}{8}$ mile

Manchester, Sheffield & Lincolnshire Railway

Act:

28 March 1893.

Opened:

(a) 15 March 1899; (b) 9 March 1899.

Running Powers:

Stratford-upon-Avon & Midland Junction Railway had running powers into Woodford (coaching only).

Track Layout:

(a) and (b) double track.

Closed:

(a) 9 November 1965 (passenger service withdrawn 31 May 1948); (b) 22 October 1900.

Remains:

The site of these junctions remain and it is possible to follow them.

Uses:

None, they lie derelict as do the station and yards.

Setting:

Anywhere around Woodford, particularly towards Eydon.

CULWORTH JUNCTION–BANBURY JUNCTION $8\frac{1}{4}$ miles
Manchester, Sheffield & Lincolnshire Railway

Act:

3 June 1897.

Opened:

1 June 1900—goods; 13 August 1900—passengers.

Track Layout:

Double track.

Miles	Station	Grid ref	Note	Opened to Passengers	Closed Passengers	Goods
—	Culworth Junction	555500	–	—	—	—
2¼	Eydon Road Halt	537472	1	1 Oct 1913	2 Apr 1956	—
6	Chalcombe Road Halt	490443	1	17 Apr 1911	6 Feb 1956	—
8¼	Banbury Junction	463424	–	—	—	—

Note
(1) Passenger station only.

Remains:
Eydon Road: road underbridge and gate (537472); *Chalcombe Road*: gradient post (491443).

Uses:
None.

Setting:
Around Eydon and Culworth.

GRENDON UNDERWOOD JUNCTION–ASHENDON JUNCTION
Great Western & Great Central Joint Committee   6 miles

Act:
1 August 1899.

Opened:
20 November 1905—goods; 2 April 1906—passengers.

Track Layout:
Double track, quadruple at stations.

Miles	Station	Grid ref	Note	Opened to Passengers	Closed Passengers	Goods
—	Grendon Underwood Junction	710219	–	—	—	—
2½	Akeman Street	705182	–	2 Apr 1906	7 Jul 1930	6 Jan 1964
4½	Wotton	695152	–	2 Apr 1906	7 Dec 1953	7 Dec 1953
6	Ashendon Junction	693134	–	—	—	—

Remains:
Akeman Street: station buildings (705182); *Wotton*: station buildings (695152).

Uses:
A single line remains from Grendon Underwood to serve Westcott Depot, transferred to the Ministry of Technology 1 January 1968.

Setting:
Around Wotton.

Bibliography

Each chapter section and gazetteer entry is intended to be only an introduction to each line included. As a result, for those wishing to read further, the bibliography has been built up on a chapter and line basis.

Chapter 1   London: Northern Heights and Green Belt

Finsbury Park—Alexandra Palace, Edgware and Bushey Heath
Barker, T. C. and Robbins, R. M. *A History of London Transport Vol 1* (1963)
Bennett, A. E. and Borley, H. V. *London Transport Railways: A List of Opening, Closing and Renaming dates of Lines and Stations* (1963)
Day, J. *The Story of London's Underground*
Grinling, C. H. *History of the Great Northern Railway 1845–1922* (reprinted 1966)
Jackson, A. A. and Croome, D. F. *Rails through the Clay* (1962)
Kellett, J. R. *The Impact of Railways on Victorian Cities* (1969)
Perkin, H. *The Age of the Railway* (1970)
Wilmot, G. F. A. *The Railway in Finchley* (reprinted 1973—Barnet Borough Libraries)

'Improving London's Transport' (1946) *Railway Gazette* (Supplement to)

'GNR Promotional Map', *Railway Magazine* (May 1906)

Barrie, D. S. M. 'The Northern Heights Branches of the LNER', *Railway Magazine* (August 1939)

Bayes, G. 'The GN Suburban Electrification Plan of 1903', *Railway World* (April 1964)

Hopwood, H. L. 'The Edgware, Highgate & London Railway', *Railway Magazine* (July 1919)

Jackson, A. A. 'Almost a Tube', *Railway Magazine* (May/June 1973)

Lawrence, A. M. 'The First Railway to Edgware', *Railway World* (September/December 1967)

Lawrence, A. M. 'The Railway Battle of Barnet,' *Railway World* (May 1972)

Young, J. N. 'Centenary of the "Ally Pally" branch', *Railway World* (May 1973)

Watford–Rickmansworth and Uxbridge

Armitage, H. *A History of Moor Park* (1964)

Atkinson, F. G. and Adams, B. W. *London's North Western Electric* (1962)

Bayne, R. *Moor Park* (1871)

Cornwall, G. *History of the Watford & Rickmansworth Railway* (1972)

Edwards, W. E. 'The Watford & Rickmansworth Railway', *Railway Magazine* (October 1921)

Lewis, H. L. 'The Uxbridge & Rickmansworth Railway', *Railway Magazine* (January/February 1945)

Riley, C. J. 'A Walk with a Railway', *Rickmansworth Historian* (Autumn 1966)

Chapter 2   The Chiltern Foothills

Bourne End–High Wycombe

Mowat, C. L. 'The Wycombe Railway', *Railway Magazine* (September/October 1933)

'How Bucks got its First Railway Line', *Bucks Interest* (September/November 1955)

Marlow/Maidenhead, Railway Passengers Association. '100 Years of the Marlow Donkey' (1973)

Hemel Hempstead–Harpenden

Barrie, D. S. M. 'The Hemel Hempstead and Harpenden Railway', *Railway Magazine* (March/April 1945)

Crook, W. E. S. 'Puffing Annie in Retrospect', *Hertfordshire Countryside* (Spring 1958)

Lea, V. 'The Road-Railer of the Nicky Line', *Hertfordshire Countryside* (Autumn 1958)

Williams, E. M. 'The "Nicky" Railway', *Hertfordshire Countryside* (January 1967)

'Railways and More London Planning', *Railway Magazine* (March/April 1945)

Hatfield–St Albans Abbey

Workers' Educational Association (Hatfield Branch). *Hatfield and its People Part 5* (1960)

Edwards, W. E. 'The St. Albans Branch of the London and North Western Railway', *Railway Magazine* (September 1922)

Goodman, F. 'The Hatfield Branches of the Great Northern Railway', *Railway Magazine* (October/November 1908)

Norris, P. J. 'The Watford–St. Albans Branch', *Railway Magazine* (April 1957)

Hatfield–Luton and Dunstable

Cockman, F. G. *The Railway Age in Bedfordshire* (Unpublished—County Record Office in Bedford)

Workers' Educational Association (Hatfield Branch). *Hatfield and its People Part 5* (1960)

Body, G. and Eastleigh, R. L. 'The Hatfield–Dunstable Line', *Bedfordshire Magazine*, Vol 10 (1966)

Gilks, J. Spencer. 'The Hertford, Luton & Dunstable Railway', *Railway World* (January 1961)

Goodman, F. 'The Hatfield Branches of the Great Northern Railway', *Railway Magazine* (October/November 1908)

Summerson, S. 'The Welwyn–Dunstable Branch', *Trains Illustrated* (November 1953)

Webb, Geoffrey. 'Luton's First Railway', *Bedfordshire Magazine*, Vol 6 (1958)

Webb, Geoffrey. 'Luton and the Great Northern Railway', *Bedfordshire Magazine* (1960)

Leighton Buzzard–Dunstable
Summerson, S. 'The Leighton Buzzard–Dunstable Branch', *Trains Illustrated* (1951)

Chapter 3   The Vale of Aylesbury

Aylesbury–Cheddington
Cockman, F. G. *The Railway Era in Buckinghamshire*, Records of Bucks, Vol 19, Part 2 (1972)

Fowler, J. K. *Echoes of Old Country Life* (1892)

Gadsden, E. J. S. *The Aylesbury Railway* (1962)

Machell, G. 'Railway Development at Aylesbury', *Railway Magazine* (November 1955)

Aylesbury–Verney Junction
Eland, G. *The Chilterns and the Vale* (1911)

Fowler, J. K. *Records of Old Times* (1898)

Gadsden, E. J. S. *Duke of Buckingham's Railways* (1962)

Edwards, W. E. 'The Aylesbury & Buckingham Railway', *Railway Magazine* (1908)

Quainton Road–Brill
Lee, C. E. 'The Duke of Buckingham's Railways', *Railway Magazine* (October 1935)

Verney Junction–Banbury (Merton Street)
Whitehall, C. *The Buckinghamshire Railway* (1849)

Hampson, R. S. 'Buckingham and the Railway', *Records of Bucks*, Vol 18

Richards, P. S. 'Bletchley: The Influence of Railways on Town Growth', *Records of Bucks*, Vol 17

Chapter 4   The Ouse Basin

Bedford to Hitchin

Barnes, E. G. *The Rise of the Midland Railway 1844–1874* (1966)

Williams, Frederick S. *Williams's Midland Railway* (1876, reprinted Newton Abbot 1968)

Barnes, E. G. 'The Midland Drive for London —I', *Railway World* (September 1962)

Norris, P. J. 'Centenary of Bedford—Hitchin Line', *Railway World* (November 1957)

Tripp, G. W. 'How the Midland Railway Reached London', *Railway Magazine* (August and September 1903)

Bedford to Sandy

Goodman, F. 'How the Railways Deal with Special Classes of Traffic—No. 8 Bedfordshire Market-Garden Traffic', *Railway Magazine* (February 1901)

Hull, Peter. 'Captain William Peel, V.C., and the Sandy–Potton Railway', *Bedfordshire Magazine* (Autumn 1955)

Webb, Geoffrey. 'The Bedford and Cambridge Railway', *Bedfordshire Magazine* (Winter 1962/3)

'London Bypass Route for Freight Traffic', *Railway Magazine*, (February 1958)

Kettering to Huntingdon

Lloyd, R. *The Fascination of Railways* (1951)

Marlow, N. *Footplate and Signal Cabin* (1956)

Tonks, E. S. *The Ironstone Railways and Tramways of the Midlands* (1959)

Norris, P. J. 'The Higham Ferrers Branch', *Branch Line News* (June 1957)

Webster, V. R. 'To Cambridge by the Midland Railway', *Trains Illustrated* (March 1957)

'Notes and News—Passenger Trains at Higham Ferrers' *Railway Magazine* (November 1964)

Chapter 5   The Northampton Uplands

Stratford-upon-Avon & Midland Junction Railway

Dunn, J. M. *The Stratford-upon-Avon & Midland Junction Railway* (South Godstone 1952)

Robbins, Michael. *Points and Signals* (1967)

Barrie, D. S. 'The Stratford-upon-Avon and Midland Junction Railway, L. M. S. R.', *Railway Magazine* (April 1933)

Beacock, D. A. 'On the S. M. J. by Freight Train', *Railway Magazine* (April 1956)

Simpson, C. R. H. 'The Northampton & Banbury Junction Railway', *The Locomotive* (15 November 1946)

'Illustrated Interview—Mr Russell Willmott', *Railway Magazine* (April 1910)

'Pertinent Paragraphs—Exploring New Ground', *Railway Magazine* (August 1927)

Kingham to Kings Sutton

Macdermot, E. T. *History of the Great Western Railway Volume II 1863–1921* (1927, revised by C. R. Clinker, 1964)

Gilks, J. Spencer. 'The Banbury & Cheltenham Direct Railway', *Railway Magazine* (August 1955)

Husband, J. F. 'The Banbury and Cheltenham Railway', *Railway Magazine* (November 1926)

Chapter 6   The Vale of Evesham

Redditch–Ashchurch

Dunn, J. M. *The Stratford-upon-Avon & Midland Junction Railway* (1952)

Tolson, J. M. 'Birmingham & Gloucester Loop', *Railway Magazine* (November/December 1964)

Alcester–Bearley
Tolson, J. M. 'Birmingham & Gloucester Loop', *Railway Magazine* (November/December 1964)

Chapter 7   *The Nene and Welland Valleys*

Blisworth to Peterborough
Franks, D. L. *The Stamford & Essendine Railway* (Leeds, 1971)
Gordon, D. I. *A Regional History of the Railways of Great Britain Volume V The Eastern Counties* (Newton Abbot, 1968)
Clinker, C. R. 'The Southern Division of the LNWR in the 1870's—2', *Railway Magazine* (February 1960)
Clinker, C. R. and Dane, R. A. 'The Railways of Peterborough', *Railway Magazine* (April 1959)
Sekon, G. A. 'Roundabout Railway Routes', *Railway Magazine* (December 1923)

Rugby to Stamford and Peterborough
Simmons, Jack. *Rugby Junction*, Dugdale Society Occasional Papers No 19 (Oxford, 1969)
Victoria County History. *Leicestershire Volume III* (1955)
Clinker, C. R. 'The Southern Division of the LNWR in the 1870's—2', *Railway Magazine* (February 1960)
Dickens, Charles. 'Mugby Junction', *All the Year Round* (Christmas 1866)
Lawrence, J. T. 'Notable Railway Stations No 44 Rugby', *Railway Magazine* (January 1909)
Lodge, H. 'A Short History of the LNWR at Rugby', *Rugby Advertiser* (26 December 1908)

Seaton to Uppingham
Fenman. *Images of Steam* (1968)
'Prototype Station Plan—Seaton, Rutland', *Railway Modeller* (October 1963)
'Seaton (Rutland) Signalling', *Railway Modeller* (December 1963)
Railway News (6 October 1894)

Chapter 8   The Great Central Railway

Clapham, Sir John. *An Economic History of Modern Britain—Volume III Machines and National Rivalries* (Cambridge, 1938)

Dow, George. *Great Central Volumes I, II and III* (1959, 1962 and 1965)

Dow, George. *Great Central Album* (1969)

Macdermot, E. T. *History of the Great Western Railway Volume II 1863–1921* (1927, revised by C. R. Clinker, 1964)

Tuplin, W. A. *Great Central Steam* (1967)

Rolt, L. T. C. *The Making of a Railway* (1971)

Fox, Francis Douglas. 'The Great Central Railway Extension; Southern Division', The Institution of Civil Engineers, Paper No 3209, *Minutes of Proceedings* (1899–90)

Gadsden, E. J. S. 'Last Rites on the GC', *Railway World* (November 1966)

Pollins, Harold. 'The Last Main Railway Line to London', *Journal of Transport History*, Vol 4, No 2 (1959)

Scott, W. J. 'The New Competitor', *Railway Magazine* (October 1900)

Acknowledgements

The preparation of this book has brought the authors into contact with a considerable number of people and organisations. As a consequence, it would be quite impossible to mention personally all those who have so generously assisted us with personal knowledge, documents, photographs and advice. Some in addition have gone through our drafts and suggested many valuable improvements and have highlighted errors and ambiguities. We are indebted to them all and offer our sincere thanks.

Considerable effort has been made to ensure that all inaccuracies have been eliminated but if any remain we are of course fully responsible.

During the course of research we have met particular kindness from the staff of the House of Lords Record Office; Public Record Office; County Record Offices at Aylesbury, Bedford, Huntingdon, Leicester, Northampton, Oxford and Warwick; Public Libraries and local newspapers.

In addition, the main organisations who have helped us are the Chipping Norton Local History Society; the Institution of Civil Engineers; the LCGB (St Albans Branch); the London

Underground Railway Society; the Office of Population Census and Surveys; the Omnibus Society, Public Relations Officers of BR (Eastern, London Midland and Western Regions) and LTE; the Rickmansworth Historical Society and RAF Henlow. Those who wish to find more information about lines covered by the book should contact the appropriate body.

From the many who have helped us, it has been extremely difficult to select just a few people for a special mention. Nevertheless we are particularly grateful to G. J. Aston, P. S. Brown, W. F. Cameron, F. G. Cockman, G. Cornwall, T. Daw, A. A. Jackson, R. Lewis, R. N. Mann, A. N. Marlow, S. Summerson, J. M. Tolson, M. F. Woodward and Ian L. Wright.

Finally our research has been considerably lightened by Clinker's Register.

Index

Adderbury, 146
Alcester, 149–52, 155–8, 161
Aldenham, 23
Alexandra Palace, 20–1, 26–30
Annesley, 187, 192, 205
Ashchurch, 149, 150, 153–5
Ashendon, 89, 94, 193
Ashton-under-Hill, 153
Aston Cantlow, 156–8
Aylesbury, 77–86, 89–91, 94, 96, 98, 102–3, 108
Aynho, 94–5
Ayot, 65

Baker Street, 86
Banbury, 102–4, 107–8, 131, 135, 136, 195, 196, 199
Barnt Green, 149, 151
Bearley, 149, 153, 156–8
Beaumont's Halt, 53
Beckford, 153
Bedford, 109, 111, 114, 115, 119
Bengeworth, 153
Benskin & Co, 40
Bidder, George, 165
Blakesley Hall Railway, 136
Bletchley, 89, 100, 102–4, 107, 168
Bliss, William, 145
Blisworth, 135, 165, 168, 173

Bloxham, 146, 147
Blunham, 118–20
Board of Trade Inspection, Rugby & Stamford Railway, 172
Bourne End, 43–6
Bourton-on-the-Water, 143
Bouverie, Edward, 166
Boxmoor, 31, 48–50, 54
Brackley, 102, 195, 199
Braunston, 188–9, 197
Brill, 82, 91–3, 95
Bristol, 14, 100, 149, 154, 156
Broad gauge, 43, 84, 101
Broad Street, 27, 38
Broom, 138, 153
Brunel, I. K., 45
Buckingham, 78, 81, 83, 103–4, 107–8, 194
Bushey & Oxhey, 31, 37
Bus services, 11, 17, 24, 26, 39, 40, 48, 154
Byfield, 201–2

Calvert, 82, 89, 193–4
Calvert, Frederick, 83
Cambridge, 103
Captain Mark Huish, 100
Captain William Peel, *VC*, 117
Cardington, 113

Catesby House, 196, 197
Central Ammunition Depot, Kineton, 137
Chalfont Road (Chalfont & Latimer), 85
Channel Tunnel, 85, 187
Charwelton, 192, 196
Chaul End Halt, 67
Cheddington, 78–9, 84
Chesham, 85, 90
Chess Valley, 38
Chipping Norton, 143–5
Claydon, 83–4, 102
Colne Valley, 37
Colne Valley Water Co, 40
Comte de Paris, 107
CONSTRUCTION:
    Ashchurch–Redditch, 152
    Bedford–Hitchin, 111
    Buckinghamshire Railway, 102
    GCR, 190–1, 198–9
    Watford & Rickmansworth Railway, 36
Cotterell's Depot, 49, 50
Coughton, 154
Coventry, 157
Cranley Gardens, 28
Croxley Green, 39
Croxley Mills, 40
Croxley Moor, 31
Culworth, 195

Dean & Chapter of Peterborough, 165
De Havilland, 59
Delapré Abbey, 166
Denbigh Hall, 100
Dickens, Charles, 171
Dividends (GC stock), 190, 191
DOUBLING:
    Aylesbury & Buckingham Railway, 86
    Bedford & Cambridge Railway, 118
    Blisworth & Peterborough Railway, 168
    EH & L, 21
    Watford & Rickmansworth Railway, 37
Duke of Buckingham (Second), 102
Duke of Buckingham and Chandos (Third), 83, 91, 93, 95–7, 107

DUNSTABLE:
    North, 67, 73, 75, 76
    Town, 67

Earl Fitzwilliam, 164, 166
Earl Temple, 97
Eastbury Pumping Station, 40
East Finchley, 18, 21, 23, 24, 27, 28, 30
East-to-west trunk railway, 129
Edgware, 20–5, 29
Edstone Aqueduct, 158
ELECTRIFICATION:
    Northern Heights branches, 18, 23–6
    Watford–Rickmansworth, 37–8
Euston, 31, 37, 38, 47, 48, 111, 169
Evesham, 149, 151–5
Evesham Road Crossing, 137
EXPERIMENTS:
    Diesel railcar, 25, 104, 115
    Road-rail bus, 53, 131
    Sentinel-Cammell steam railcar, 22

Farthinghoe, 104
Fenny Compton, 101, 137
Finchley Central, 18, 21, 28
Finmere, 194
FIRST TRAIN:
    Banbury & Cheltenham Direct Railway, 147
    East & West Junction Railway, 139
    Uppingham branch, 180
FORMAL OPENING:
    Blisworth–Peterborough, 167
    GCR, 203
Freight routes, 35, 53, 103
FREIGHT SERVICES:
    Blisworth–Peterborough, 169–70
    Dunstable branch (GNR), 68, 71
    Dunstable branch (LNWR), 73
    GCR, 206
    Hitchin–Bedford, 112
    Kettering–Huntingdon, 127–8
    Metropolitan Railway, 89
    Northern Heights branches, 27–8
    Redditch–Ashchurch, 153
    SMJR, 140
    Verney Junction–Banbury, 104
    Watford–Rickmansworth, 40, 42
Fulwell & Westbury, 104

Gauge Commission, 101
Girtford, 119–20
Gloucester, 149, 150
Godwin's Halt, 53
Goldington, 120
GRADIENTS:
  Ayot, 65
  Dunstable, 73
  Great Central, 191
  Harpenden, 50
  Highgate, 28, 31
  Kinwarton, 158
  Kettering, Thrapstone & Huntingdon, 125–6
  Leighton Buzzard, 73
  Lickey Incline, 150
  Northampton & Peterborough, 165
  Rugby & Stamford, 171
Grandborough Road, 84
Grand Union Canal, 31, 35, 42, 81, 103
Great Alne, 153, 156–8
Great Western & Great Central Joint Committee, 14, 44, 89, 193
Green Belt, 17–19, 25
Grendon Underwood, 89, 193
Grimsby, 188
Grosvenor, Robert, 31, 35

Harpenden, 48–50, 53, 54, 61, 65
Harrow, 102
Hatfield, 55–9, 61–5, 112
Hatfield House, 55, 58
Heath Park Halt, 49, 50, 54
Hemel Hempstead, 48–50, 53, 54
Hemel Hempstead Lightweight Concrete Co, 54, 55
Henlow, 113, 114
Hertford, 35, 57, 63, 64
Higham Ferrers, 126, 127
High Barnet, 18, 20–2, 24, 27–30
Highgate (LNER/LPTB), 20–4, 26–8, 30
Highgate (Archway), 23, 26
High Wycombe, 43–6
Hill End, 60
Hinton, 153
Hitchin, 110–16
Hook Norton, 145–7
Hudson, George, 167
Human geography, 15

Huntingdon, 122, 125–8

Irchester & Raunds branch, 126–7
Ireland, 116
Ironstone, 125, 127, 131, 144, 146, 181
Islip, 102

JUNCTIONS:
  Ashendon, 89, 94, 193
  Aynho, 94, 95
  Bearley, 157
  Broom, 138, 153
  Canfield Place, 186, 192
  Chipping Norton, 143
  Claydon, 194
  Clifton Mill, 175
  Cockley Brake, 103, 104, 131, 136
  Colne, 37
  Croxley Green, 37, 40
  Culworth, 195–6
  Greens Norton, 133, 135
  Grendon Underwood, 193
  Harpenden, 50, 54
  Harrow South, 89
  Hatton, 157
  Kettering, 128
  Park, 21, 24, 28–30
  Ravenstone Wood, 135
  Uppingham, 182
  Verney, 84, 86, 89–91, 102–4, 108
  Watford, 37
  Watford High Street, 31, 37, 40
  Welwyn, 65
  Woodford West, 202
John Dickinson & Co Ltd, 40

Karrier Motor Co, 53, 131
King George VI, 107
Kingham, 143–4
Kingscliffe, 173
King's Cross, 24, 111, 191
King's Sutton, 144, 146

Land use, 15
LAST TRAIN:
  Aylesbury Branch (LNWR), 81
  Bedford–Hitchin, 116
  Brill Branch, 98
  Kingham–Banbury, 147–8
  Leighton Buzzard–Dunstable, 76

LAST TRAIN—*continued*
Northampton–Peterborough, 170
Leicester, 173, 191
Leicester & Hitchin Extension, 110, 112
Leighton Buzzard, 73
Lemsford Road Halt, 59
Level crossings, 162–4, 194
Lewis, Frederick, 40
Liddell, Charles, 171, 190, 197
LOCOMOTIVES:
BR, 177, 181
Edge Hill Light Railway, 137
GCR, 205
GNR, 28–9, 59, 71–3, 176, 181
GWR, 46, 90, 161
Hook Norton, 146
LMSR, 126, 177, 181
LNWR, 76, 81, 170, 176
Metropolitan, 90–1, 97–8
Midland, 54–5, 126, 155
Shannon, 117–18
SMJR, 138–9
Uppingham Quarry, 150
London Extension (MS & LR), 186
London General Omnibus Co, 39
London Transport, 19, 23, 26–7, 30, 53, 89, 97
Lord Ebury, 35–9, 42, 58
Lord Norton, 179
Loudwater, 45–6
Luffenham, 172
Luton, 66
Luton Hoo, 66
Luton Town Football Club, 75

Manchester, 191
Manning, George, 147
Market Harborough, 173–4
Market Tickets (GCR), 199
Marquis of Chandos, 83
Marquis of Salisbury, 55
Marston Gate, 79
Marylebone, 45, 89, 190, 192
Maudslay Motor Co, 156–7
Metroland, 22
Metropolitan & Great Central Joint Committee, 89, 97
Mill Hill East, 21, 23–5, 27–8, 30
Mill Hill (The Hale), 25, 28
Moor Park Golf Club, 35
Moor Park Mansion, 35, 39

MOTIVE POWER DEPOTS:
Alcester, 158
Aylesbury (LNWR), 81
Blisworth, 139
Brill, 95
Cheltenham, 155
Cricklewood, 48
Hatfield, 59, 72–3
Kentish Town, 48
Kingham, 144
Leighton Buzzard, 76
Peterborough (MR), 170
Peterborough (LNWR), 170
Seaton, 181
Stratford (SMJR), 139
Towcester, 139
Woodford, 200, 203
Mugby Junction, 170
Muswell Hill, 20–1, 28

Nast Hyde Halt, 59
National Omnibus & Transport Co, 39
Nene Valley Park, 170
New Barnet, 27
NICKNAMES:
'Alcester Coffee Pot', 161
'Chippy Dick', 147
'Contys', 175
'Hooky Flyer', 147–8
'Marlow Donkey', 45
'Puffing Annie of the Nicky Railway', 48
'The Last Dasher', 76
'The Skimpot', 76
'Watercress trains', 38
Northampton, 107, 164, 167–9
Northampton & Peterborough Railway, 163, 165
Northern Heights, 18, 21–3, 32
Nottingham, 188, 191

Olney, 134
Opening Dinner (Uppingham branch), 180
Oxford, 44, 77, 94, 96, 98, 100, 102

Padbury, 107
Paddington, 45, 89, 100, 191
Pain, James, 181
Parkland walks, 30, 54

Passenger services (Northampton–Peterborough), 169–70
Peterborough, 164–5, 170
Peterborough & Wellingborough Turnpike, 163
Peto, Samuel, 145
Physical geography, 12–13
Pitchcott Gap, 83
Population, 15
Ports to Ports Express, 144
Potts, William, 103
PRESERVATION:
 Nene Valley, 170
 Quainton Road, 98
 Sandy–Potton (proposed), 121
Princes Risborough, 44, 85, 89
Pullman cars, 50, 90
Push-and-pull trains, 147, 177, 181

Quainton Road, 82, 84, 86, 89–90, 94, 96, 98, 186, 189, 192, 193
Queen's Park, 38

Radclive Halt, 104
RAF camps, 113
Railbuses, 104, 115
RAILWAY COMPANIES:
 Aylesbury & Thame Junction Railway, 80
 Bedford & Cambridge Railway, 118–21
 Birmingham & Gloucester Railway, 150–1
 Birmingham & Oxford Junction Railway, 101
 Bristol & Gloucester Railway, 150
 Buckingham & Brackley Junction Railway, 101–2
 Cambridge & Oxford Railway, 80
 Easton Neston Mineral & Towcester, Roade & Olney Junction Railway, 133
 Edge Hill Light Railway, 137
 Evesham, Redditch & Stratford-upon-Avon Junction Railway, 132–3, 137
 Hertford & Welwyn Junction Railway, 64
 Kettering & Thrapstone Railway, 121

Kettering, Thrapstone & Huntingdon Railway, 122
London, Worcester & South Staffordshire Railway, 80 100–1
Luton, Dunstable & Welwyn Junction Railway, 64, 67
Midland Counties & South Wales Railway, 132
Muswell Hill Railway, 21–2
Northampton & Banbury Junction Railway, 103–4, 130–4, 138–9, 195
Northern & Eastern Railway, 165
North London Railway, 20, 27, 37
North London, Highgate & Alexander Park Railway, 20
Oxford & Aylesbury Tramroad Co, 97
Oxford, Aylesbury & Metropolitan Junction Railway, 96
Oxford & Bletchley Junction Railway, 101–2
Oxford & Rugby Railway, 100–1
Oxford, Worcester & Wolverhampton Railway, 14, 90, 100–1, 143, 151
Stratford-upon-Avon, Towcester & Midland Junction Railway, 133
Warwickshire & London Railway, 101
Watford & Edgware Junction Railway, 20, 23
Watford & Rickmansworth Railway, 31, 36–8
Raunds, 126, 127
Redbourn, 39, 53, 54
Redditch, 149, 151–3, 155
Refreshment room (Mugby Junction), 171
Rickmansworth, 31, 35, 36, 38, 39, 40, 42
Rickmansworth & District Omnibus Co, 39
Roade, 134
Rockingham, 172
ROLLING STOCK:
 Aylesbury & Buckingham Railway, 90
 Joint LNWR/LER Electric Tube Stock, 38

ROLLING STOCK—*continued*
  Sandy & Potton Railway, 117
  SMJR, 139
Rollright, 145
Roundwood Halt, 53, 54
Royal Train, 24, 107
RUGBY:
  Central Station, 197, 198
  Generally, 172, 175, 176, 186, 191,
    192, 198, 199, 207
  LNWR Midland stations, 170,
    171, 174
Rugby & Stamford Railway, 162,
    171, 173
Rushden, 126, 127

St Albans, 56–8, 60–2
St Pancras, 47, 48, 111, 114, 135, 138
Salcey Forest, 133
Salford Priors, 154
Salvation Army Halt, 60
Sandy, 117–19, 120, 121
Sandy & Potton Railway, 117, 118,
    121
Sarsden Halt, 144
Seaton, 162, 177, 179–82
Seaton & Wansford Railway, 173
Shakespeare Route, 131, 135
Shefford, 111–13, 115
SIDINGS:
  Benskin's, 40
  Blackbridge, 68, 71
  Church, 94, 95
  Claydale's 54
  Croxley Mill, 40
  Fiddle Bridge, 59
  Fleetville, 60, 61
  Hill End Hospital, 60, 61
  Plowman's, 113
  Watford Electricity Generating
    Plant, 40
  Wellington, 24, 29
  Wood, 93, 95
Signalling, 182
Sir Edward Watkin, 85, 96, 184–92
Sir Harry Verney, 78, 83, 84, 96, 102
Sir Sam Fay, 192, 199
Smallford, 60
Southill, 112, 113
South Midland Railway, 109
South Midlands, 12
Special trains, 46, 75, 104, 107, 108,
    114, 127, 128, 135, 153, 157,

    167, 177, 180–3, 203, 204
Stamford, 165, 172, 175, 177
Stanbridgeford, 75, 79
Stephenson, George, 78
Stephenson, Robert, 31, 74, 78,
    164, 165
Stoke Bruern, 133
Stowe, 107, 108
Stratford-upon-Avon, 131, 132, 135,
    137–40, 149, 158
Stratford-upon-Avon Canal, 158
Straw hat industry, 50, 68
Syston & Peterborough Railway,
    165, 172

Tewkesbury, 149, 153
Thame, 43
Thrapston, 125, 128, 167
Thring, Edward, 178
Tindal, Acton, 83
Totteridge & Whetstone, 28
Towcester, 103, 133, 135, 139, 140
Tring, 77, 100
TUNNELS:
  Archway–East Finchley, 24
  Catesby, 196, 197
  Chipping Norton, 145
  Highgate, 20, 21
  Hook Norton, 145
  Redditch, 152
  Warden, 152, 153
Tyseley, 158

Uppingham, 177–82
Uppingham School, 177, 178, 180–2
Urban Development, 22
Uxbridge, 35

Vauxhall Motors, 66, 68
VIADUCTS:
  Brackley, 194, 195
  Brockley Hill, 23
  Catesby, 195, 197
  Dollis, 20
  Helmdon, 195
  Hemel Hempstead, 54
  Watford, 31

Waddesdon Manor, 84
Waddesdon Road, 94
Wansford, 166, 169
Warwick, 149
Water Stratford Halt, 104

Watford, 31, 35–40, 42
Watford Electric Suburban Trains, 31, 37, 38, 42
Watford Football Club, 39
Weight restrictions, 50, 126
Welford & Kilworth, 175
Wellingborough, 169
Welwyn Garden City, 65
Westcott, 94, 193
Wheathampstead, 65
Whitbreads, 112
Whitbread, William, 110, 112
Wigsthorpe, 166
Willington, 120

Willmott, Russell, 134
Winslow Road, 84, 91
Wixford, 154
Wooburn Green, 46
Woodford, 136, 186, 191, 195, 196, 199–207
Woodside Park, 28
World War I, 67, 90, 104, 120, 156, 157
World War II, 19, 23, 24, 39, 48, 59, 89, 104, 120, 138, 156
Wotton, 83, 93, 107
Wotton Tramway, 94
Wroxton, 107